Fighting for US

Scot Brown

Fighting for US

Maulana Karenga, the US Organization, and
Black Cultural Nationalism

Foreword by Clayborne Carson

New York University Press • New York and London

NEW YORK UNIVERSITY PRESS
New York and London
www.nyupress.org

First published in paperback in 2005

Library of Congress Cataloging-in-Publication Data
Brown, Scot, 1966–
Fighting for US : Maulana Karenga, the US organization, and black cultural nationalism / Scot Brown.
p.   cm.
Includes bibliographical references and index.
ISBN 0-8147-9877-2 (cloth : alk. paper)
ISBN 0-8147-9878-0 (pbk : alk. paper)
1. US (Organization)—History. 2. Black nationalism—United States—History—20th century. 3. Black power—United States—History—20th century. 4. Karenga, Maulana. 5. African American political activists—Biography. 6. African Americans—Race identity. 7. African Americans—Intellectual life—20th century. 8. African Americans—Politics and government—20th century. 9. United States—Race relations.   I. Title.
E185.5.B95 2003
305.896'073'0092—dc21   2003004811

Contents

All illustrations appear as a group following p. 134.

Foreword

I first talked with Maulana Karenga in 1966, when I conducted a long interview with him for a *Los Angeles Free Press* article. He was already widely known in the Los Angeles area as an influential young Black nationalist. At UCLA, where he was a graduate student in African linguistics and I was an undergraduate history major, his powerful orations, peppered with sardonic humor, always drew crowds. He had created a tightly organized and loyal group of followers called US—"Anywhere we are, US is." I had been suspicious of those Black nationalists who stood on the sidelines of the southern freedom struggle during the first half of the 1960s, but I was impressed that Karenga had emerged as an effective leader in post-Watts rebellion Los Angeles. At a time of uncertainty and disorganization in the African-American freedom struggle, Karenga's US exhibited confidence and discipline.

Karenga impressed me with his ability to bring new vitality to traditional Black nationalism. He adapted ideas drawn from African cultures and political movements, but his public statements conveyed an appealing originality and exceptional intelligence I looked forward to meeting him when I arrived for the interview at the office of a group called Self-Leadership for ALL Nationalities Today or SLANT, headed by Karenga's friend Tommy Jacquette. There was an élan associated with US that was immediately apparent. Members wore African-style green bubas and used Kiswahili terms. In a way similar to Nation of Islam members, they took pride in their appearance and often prefaced their remarks by deferring to the words of Maulana, their Master Teacher. The indications that US had formed a leadership cult worried me, but Karenga himself was reassuringly modest, eager to express his admiration for other leaders, such as Malcolm X, and for organizations such as the Student Nonviolent Coordinating Committee (SNCC). I learned that he had tried without success to establish ties with SNCC. During the interview, he described the seven principles that would later be celebrated during Kwanzaa, the African-American holiday he invented. I could see even then that Karenga would become a major force in the African-American freedom struggle. I was not surprised when he played major roles in the national Black Power conferences of the next few years.

We maintained occasional contact during the tumultuous years that followed my initial interview. In 1968, when I returned to UCLA after graduation and a period of draft-avoidance in Europe, the US organization had consolidated its influence in the Black Congress, the umbrella group which included most of the groups that were then active in south-central Los Angeles. In the meantime, the Black Panther Party had also become an important and competitive political force. I supported the Black Panthers, because they had the same kind of brash militancy that I had admired in SNCC, but I regretted that the two groups were fighting with one another. I believed that there was no necessary conflict between the so-called 'revolutionary nationalism' of the Black Panthers and the 'cultural nationalism' of US. I knew from my conversations with Karenga that he had wanted to become the cultural arm of SNCC and the Black Panthers. He had tried to forge a working relationship with the latter group early in 1968, during the 'Free Huey' campaign to save the Black Panther defense minister from being executed for allegedly murdering an Oakland policeman. Karenga's group had even provided security for the Newton support rally held in February 1968 at the Los Angeles sports area.

As relations between US and the Black Panthers deteriorated during 1968, I saw terrible consequences of the abrasive way in which some Panther leaders—especially Eldridge Cleaver—provoked conflicts through their attacks against cultural nationalism. I understood that the Black Panthers saw themselves as revolutionaries facing brutal repression and thus were impatient with any group that did adopt their confrontation political style. But I also appreciated the dedication of US members and the widespread popular support for cultural nationalism in Black communities throughout the nation. By this time, Karenga's close relationship with Amiri Baraka had broadened his influence on the East coast. Yet, as the Black Panthers began to worry legitimately about police agents in their own ranks, they also began to ridicule Karenga and his followers. They referred to them as "pork-chop nationalists," implying that Karenga collaborated with the Los Angeles police chief and California governor Ronald Reagan. Karenga, like previous Black nationalists, including Elijah Muhammad, Marcus Garvey, and Martin Delany, had left himself open to this charge by insisting that all white people were the same and that therefore negotiating with powerful white conservatives made as much sense as the Black Panthers' willingness to collaborate with less powerful white leftists. The FBI predictably exploited the US/Panther conflict, to the detriment of both groups.

In January 1969, I attended a meeting at UCLA's Campbell Hall of the Black Student Union where Black Panthers and US members stood glaring at each other from opposite sides of a classroom in which intimidated students discussed how to establish a Black studies program at UCLA. Karenga pushed his candidate to head the planned Black studies program on the campus, arguing that US, not the Panthers, could mobilize the Los Angeles Black community on behalf of the program. I was not completely surprised when the escalating intergroup tensions exploded two days after the meeting into a deadly clash that left two Black Panthers dead. Subsequent police raids severely damaged both groups and ultimately contributed to the decline of the entire African-American freedom struggle. The subsequent allegation that the killings had been a planned execution rather than a shoot out also severely damaged the reputation of Karenga and his organization.

I have since concluded that that the US/Panther conflict represented a lost opportunity for merging the two major elements of African-American resistance to racial oppression. The Black Panther Party made an important contribution to the African-American tradition of militant political struggle, while US made a similarly important contribution to the tradition of psychological and cultural struggle. Both traditions were necessary components of our liberation, but they have unfortunately often been competing traditions. Like the verbal sparing that marred relations between Malcolm and King, the US/Panther conflict weakened the modern African-American struggle and spawned divisive ideological conflicts that continue until this day.

Although there are still too few serious scholarly studies of the Black Panther Party, there are even fewer studies of US and other major Black nationalist organizations of the late 1960s and 1970s. The few references to US in the historical literature mostly reflect the Black Panther perspective, viewing it as a reactionary group of police collaborators responsible for the murder of two Black revolutionaries. The true story is more complex and enlightening, for cultural nationalism became the most enduring element of the Black Power movement. The holiday Karenga invented, Kwanzaa, continues to be celebrated, even by people who are unaware of its inventor. Karenga also remains an important influence in the Afrocentric movement, which is itself one of the most popular forms of African-American cultural resistance.

Scot Brown's study of Karenga and US is a major contribution to the historical literature of modern Black nationalism. He has written one of the few scholarly studies that takes seriously the innovative Black nationalist thought of the late 1960s and the only study that draws adequate attention to Karenga's singular contributions to African-American cultural thought. He has written a sympathetic but also judicious account that draws attention to the roles played by activists other than Karenga in the building of US. He sheds useful light on the relationship between Karenga and Baraka and between US and the Black Panther Party, offering the best balanced account of the UCLA killings that has yet to appear. Finally, Brown provides an insightful assessment of the lasting impact of Karenga and US. I am confident that *Fighting for US* will be seen as a pioneering contribution to an emerging literature regarding African-American militancy during the period after the major civil rights reforms of the 1960s. This thoroughly-researched study represents engaged scholarship at its best.

Clayborne Carson
Professor of History, Stanford University
Director, Martin Luther King Jr. Papers Project

Acknowledgments

I must begin by giving thanks to my beloved and ever-supportive family: my loving and brilliant parents, James Brown and Maxine Childress Brown; two ingenious sisters, Nikki and Kimberly Brown; my cousins and dear brothers Deon (special thanks) and Reginald Johnson; my grandfather Ernest "Papa" Brown (may your spirit continue to guide us); my grandmothers, Anne Brown and Thomasina Childress; my aunts, Beverly Brown, Shirley Childress Saxton, Carol Brown, and Khaula Murdtaha; my cousins Abdul Khaliq, Adam, Abdul Haleem, Ahmed, Yusuf, Usama, and Thomasina; and my uncle, Billy Brown. Also thanks to extended family members Ayodele Ngozi, Jesse, Joann, and Heshima James, and Pascale and Arno Boli.

The idea of conducting a historical study of US came from my contact with Gerald Chaka and Terry Chaka, owners of the Kitabu Kingdom bookstore in Rochester, New York. In early 1991, Gerald Chaka, a former member of US's San Diego chapter, inspired my interest in the organization's story with intriguing tales of his 1960s life as a cultural nationalist revolutionary. In December of that year, I met Maulana Karenga for the first time in Buffalo, at a *Kwanzaa* lecture. He and his wife, Tiamoyo, invited me to attend the organization's summer institute at its headquarters in Los Angeles.

Karenga's lectures at the institute provided a stimulating and fresh interpretation of Afrocentricity, nationalism, the still-smoldering 1992 uprising in Los Angeles, and other political events of the day. Those encounters with the 1990s version of US provoked my further interest and immersion in the group's cultural-nationalist philosophy called *Kawaida,* and its Black Power–era legacy. I began doing research on US as a dissertation topic in 1994. Though Karenga and I have come to disagree in our respective views on key issues and events in US's history, this study could not have occurred without his generous provision of access to US's papers and contacts with former US members.

Over the years, many people and institutions have contributed to the evolution of this story. Crucial support from the outset came from faculty and comrades at the Africana Studies and Research Center and history department at Cornell University: especially James Turner, Ken McClane, Robert Harris, Gary Okihiro, Daisy Rowe, Thomas Weissinger, Anne Adams, Herbert Finch, Abdul Nanji, Joel Silbey, Salah Hassan, Ndri Assie-Lumumba, Don Ohadike, Micere Mugo, Ali Mazuri, Beverly Blacksher, Margaret Washington, Michael Kammen, Biodun Jeyifu, Benedict Anderson, Bruce Lewenstein, Sandra Greene, Tim Bor-stelmann, Gerald Jackson, Ayele Berkerie, Winston and Lisa Grady-Willis, Kevin Jackson, Stanford Lewis, Maceo Cleaver, Ken Glover, Henri Boyi, Laurie Atkins, Cliff Albright, Jan Jasper, Baye Wilson, Rhea Combs, Diedra Hill, Shani Carter, Rosetta Haynes, Lori Atkins, Claudia Boykins, Margo Perkins, Eldred Harris, Bill Barrett, Christine Barksdale, Joe Palermo, Kevin Days, Brian Sales (main man), Ibe Ibeike-Jonah, David Reed, Fouad Makki, Sherrie Randal, Rosa Clemente, Agyei Tyehimba, Rona Frederick, Kendall Segars, Verdene Lee, Leslie Alexander, Elizabeth Pryor, Denise Rice, Tsekani Browne, Michelle Scott, Rachael Zellers, Michelle Thomas.

Longtime friends, from, or passing through, Rochester (the Rock), have remained steadfastly supportive throughout many of my "life changes" that accompanied the decade-long association with cultural nationalism and this project. Thanks go to Alton Maneiro, Lori Piotter, Ricardo Vazquez, Eric Cliette, Rosemarie Chen, Michael Moore and family, Ronnie Miller, Valentina and Bestman, Clayton Waller, Rick Kittles, Bakari Kitwana, Gium Yobue, Tracy Sharpley-Whiting, Thabiti Lewis, Hashim Shomari, "Laddie" Fitzgerald, Ruth Forman, and Sheena Hoffman.

Former US advocates and those close to aspects of the group's history were indispensable to this study. My gratitude for their collective willingness to share oral histories and personal paper collections cannot be overstated. Thank you all, one thousand times: Randy Abunuwas-Stripling, Ngoma Ali, Aminifu, Arnetta Church Atkins, Amiri Baraka, Ayuko Babu, Thomas "Nrefu" Belton (cuz), Kokayi Bendele, Terry Carr-Damu, James Doss-Tayari, John Floyd, Bobette Azizi Glover, C. R. D. Halisi, Albert Heath, Staajabu Heshimu, Gail Idili-Davis, Ramon "Ray" Tyson-Imara, Tommy Jacquette, Charles Johnson-Sitawisha, Wesely Kabaila, Maulana Karenga, Karl Key-Hekima, Alfred Moore, Charles Massengale-Sigidi, Oliver Massengale-Heshimu, Letta Mbulu, Jean Morris, Ken Msemaji, James Mtume, Kamili Mtume, Joann Richardson-Kicheko, Caiphus Semanya, Alva Stevenson, George Subira, Vernon Sukumu, Amina Thomas, Kwame Toure (may his spirit live on), Daryl Tukufu, and Kalamu ya Salaam.

I am also indebted to the Emory University graduate school staff members Carla Moreland and Kharen Fulton, and Leroy Davis of the history department. Other Atlanta-area scholars, activists, and students were extremely helpful during my stay there in 1997: Akinyele Umoja, Charles Jones, Jakini Auset, Ari, Bobby Donaldson, Angela Brown, Denise Paultre, Derrick Welshe, and Tanisa Foxworth. Colleagues at San Francisco State University were extraordinarily collegial and insightful during my stay there in 1999–2000. Special thanks go to Johnetta Richards, Rickey Vincent, Bill Issel, Oba T'Shaka, Barbara Loomis, Paul Longmore, Wade Nobles, Steve Leiken, Madeline Hsu, Benito "Sonny" Vergara, Jerald Combs, Jule Tygiel, and Frank Kidner.

Several fellowships and other forms of assistance from research institutions have been critical to the completion of this study. My sincere gratitude goes to the Huntington Library Predoctoral Fellowship, UCLA University Archives, Moorland Spingarn Research Center at Howard University (special thanks to Joellen El Bashir), Cornell University Anonymous Donor Fellowship, Mellon Foundation, UCLA Oral History Program, Charles H. Chipman Cultural Center Archives (special thanks to Lisa Atkins and family), and Pacifica Radio Archive. The UCLA Department of History and the Center for African American Studies generously supported a first-year leave, which allowed me to participate in the Visiting Scholar's Initiative at the University of Houston during the 2001–2 academic year and effectively finish the manuscript.

Faculty, staff, and students at the African American Studies program at the University of Houston were especially generous, kind, and supportive throughout a most critical year in the development of this book. Special thanks go to Linda Reed, Jelani Williams (may your spirit continue to guide us), Angela Williams, Phyllis Bearden, Patricia Smith Prather, Chariesse Simpson, Rhea McAllister, Tracy Howard, and Janice Hutchinson. Also thanks to Curtis Flowers, Leslie Lake, Fumilayo, Condi, Nzingah Zamani, Tamika Hebert, and LaQuinta.

Feedback from a range of scholars and friends has been essential to the completion of this project. Thanks go to Fanon Wilkins; Robyn Spencer; Jeff Ogbonna; Peniel Joseph; Lisa Wynters; Yohuru Williams; Keith and Rose Mayes; Nikki Taylor; Clayborne Carson; Ernie Allen Jr.; Komozi Woodard; William Van Deburg; Floyd Hayes III; Sundiata Cha-Jua; James Conyers; Daryl Scott; Karin Klieman; Pascale Boli; Abe and Denise Lee; Bobby Donaldson; James Wesely Johnson; Charles Jones; Leslie Caldwell; Kent Kirkton; and participants and facilitators in the 2002 University of Houston Black History Workshop, Sterling Stuckey, Richard Blackett, Linda Reed, Luis Alvarez, Ruth Doughty, Andrew Kaye, Fionnghula Sweeney, Camille Forbes, Karen Sotiropoulos, Nicole Rustin, and Sylvain Pooson.

I am ever grateful for critical support from my colleagues at the University of California at Los Angeles and friends and associates in Los Angeles. Both the UCLA Department of History and

Ralph J. Bunche Center for African American Studies were most generous in supporting research for this project. I am especially indebted to Brenda Stevenson, Franklin Gilliam, Rene Dennis, Teofilo Ruiz, Henry Yu, Darnell Hunt, Kenny Burrell, Walter Allen, Alex Tucker, Jan Freeman, Ellen Du Bois, Itabari Zulu, Robert Hill, Richard Weiss, Lisbeth Gant-Britton, and Brandy Worrall. The year I spent writing as a visiting scholar in Houston would not have worked as smoothly as it did without assistance from key staff members of the UCLA History Department, Nancy Dennis, Shizuka Suzuki, Cindy Herrier, Sue Jensen, and Doris Dworschak. Thanks also go to A-1 Record Finders, Rosalind Goddard, Alva Moore Stevenson, Kent Kirkton, Eric and Peg Jager, Doris Sosa, Erin Dewitt, and Simon Elliot.

1. Introduction

The history of the cultural nationalist organization called "US," founded by Maulana Karenga and a handful of others in 1965, is, for most students of Black nationalism, an untold story. The Southern California–based organization experienced a high point in its activism during a great resurgence in African American nationalism, popularly known as the Black Power movement, roughly from the mid-1960s to the early 1970s. During these years, US, a relatively small group, established an impressive network of alliances in the Midwest, in the South, and on the East Coast. As a result, US's brand of cultural nationalism influenced a diverse body of activists, artists, and organizations throughout the United States. As the 1960s unfolded, many California-based radical organizations asserted themselves, in an unprecedented manner, in national politics and American cultural life in the form of the Black Panther Party, Students for a Democratic Society, the Peace and Freedom Party, and a host of others. US, in keeping with this trend, rapidly developed a national audience and constituency.

US's story, mirroring the wider Black Power movement, traveled a course shaped by an array of historical factors, including the anticolonial struggles in Africa, Asia, and Latin America, the Vietnam War, and state repression via Federal Bureau of

Investigation counterintelligence operations. Internal organizational matters, such as the cult of personality, authoritarianism, alternative lifestyles, gender stratification, and vanguard self-perceptions were also driving forces in the organization's plight. Other contextual factors contributing to the makeup of US appear in Karenga's own cultural nationalist theories, inspired by Negritude, African nationalism, the Third World neutralism (or what would become the "non-aligned" movement), and African Studies as an academic discipline in the United States.

The rhetorical stress on racial solidarity, popularized during the era of Black Power, masked underlying tensions and intergroup rivalries that persisted throughout the late 1960s. An intense and bitter feud between US and the Black Panther Party degenerated into violent warfare in Southern California from the beginning of 1969 through 1970. Indeed, this sectarian struggle made lasting impressions on historical commentary and autobiographies written by veteran Black Panther activists. The repeated usage of the term "united slaves," as a reference for the US Organization, is perhaps the best example of the lasting consequences of the US/Panther conflict.[1] The name "US" actually stands for Black people: the pronoun "US" as opposed to "them," the White oppressors. As an article in the journal *Black Dialogue* in 1966 stated, "US means exactly that—all of US (black folks)."[2] During the late 1960s, some of US's rivals and opponents used the term "united slaves" to ridicule the group. This slur has been given, unwittingly, scholarly credence in several works on the Black Power movement, in spite of the fact that there are no documents or recorded speeches in which Karenga or any US members refer to their organization as such.

A series of other writings that mention US have restated, uncritically, the Black Panther Party's allegations, made during the heat of battle, that the US Organization was a collaborator with the United States government for the purpose of bringing about the Black Panther Party's demise.[3] US leaders also accused the Black Panther Party of working with the Los Angeles Police Department in a strategy to neutralize their organization. US's perspective, in any case, did not have a comparable impact on scholarly or anecdotal interpretations of the Black Panther Party's historical legacy. Chapter 5 of this study, examining the nuances of the ideological and "turf" struggle between US and the Panthers, attempts to move the discussion past the limitations of simple accusation and vilification by focusing on the dynamic and complex relationship between these groups.

This book is part of a growing historical literature on the Black Power movement and its activist organizations.[4] The coming dialogue and debate about US's story, and other Black radical formations of the 1960s and 1970s, should inform a wider synthesis and understanding of the Black Power movement's place in African American history. Komozi Woodard's *A Nation within a Nation: Amiri Baraka (LeRoi Jones) & Black Power Politics* maintains that independent politics and the goal of nationality formation were key developments in Black Power–era cultural nationalism. A centerpiece in this process was the launching, in Woodard's term, of the Modern Black Convention Movement—the 1966, 1967, and 1968 Black Power conferences, the 1970 and 1972 Congress of African People conventions, the 1972 National Black Political Convention in Gary, Indiana, and a series of other major Black political gatherings. Woodard sheds important light on the period from 1969 through 1974 in which Amiri Baraka, the Committee for a Unified Newark (CFUN), and the Congress of African People (CAP) peaked in the leadership of Black cultural nationalist politics. CAP and CFUN applied US's blueprint for political power and succeeded in bringing about bold new levels of mass participation in electoral politics and grassroots community organizing. From 1966 through 1968, US led the initiating phase of the Modern Convention Movement, playing a leadership role, along with Newark's Rev. Nathan Wright Jr. and others, in the planning of the 1967 and 1968 Black Power conferences. Baraka, a close ally of Karenga in the late 1960s and early 1970s, found the tools for building a mass movement in US's organizational structure and ideology. Baraka and affiliated cultural nationalists peaked during a time when US's activism was thwarted, from 1969 to the mid-1970s, by conflict with the Black Panther Party and internal divisions.

How US, a relatively small, disciplined, self-declared vanguard group based on the West Coast, became the central force behind an expansive cultural nationalist movement is the story of a single organization's dynamic relationship to wider networks of groups that comprised a social movement. The relationship between group size and overall influence is especially important for the era of Black Power, given its occurrence at a time when radical organizations had gained increased access to American mass media. These developments in the 1960s made it possible for small locally based, largely unknown groups like US and the Black Panther Party to acquire a swift entrée to national audiences and constituency. In the case of US, the group's extensive impact was dramatically disproportionate to its size—at its height US probably did not exceed five hundred to six hundred members. US sought to induce other formations to accept its ideology —a technique Karenga called "programmatic influence"—while maintaining a small membership. Awareness of these organizing techniques empowers us with a clearer understanding of how small organizations in this period were often at the core of highly visible mass movements.

This history of US is told as a topical and linear narrative. Specific areas of focus, such as US's political legacy and influence on the arts, are explored independently, yet other events herein are contained as part of the story of US's rise and decline in the era of Black Power. Chapter 2 opens with a brief discussion of cultural nationalism as one among many types of Black nationalist trends in American history. An overview that introduces the US Organization follows, focusing on its genesis and ideology. The rest of the chapter sheds light on the historical context and intellectual currents that shaped Maulana Karenga's conception of the US Organization, its philosophy, and its program. Chapter 3 presents a broad sketch of the alternative lifestyle that membership in US required. The organization's own division of labor and gender and its internal hierarchy are explored for the purpose of describing the varied and complex responsibilities, roles, and experiences of rank-and-file members and leaders.

Chapter 4 begins with a discussion of US's organizational and political strategies, highlighting the group's activism in electoral politics, anti-Vietnam protest, and underground violent resistance. Chapter 5 analyzes the discourse of the US/Panther conflict and the impact of the sectarian feud and government repression, and their combined impact on the day-to-day functioning of US. Chapter 6 looks at US's outreach to larger Black audiences through African dance, jazz, and literature. Finally, the concluding chapter on Afrocentricity and Kwanzaa briefly reviews the organization's activities since 1975.

2. From Ron Everett to Maulana Karenga

The Intellectual and Political Bases for the US Organization

Black nationalist ideologies have historically maintained that people of African descent share a common history and life chances in a White or European-dominated political, economic, and social order. Studies of Black nationalism have made use of varied typologies and categories to distinguish the disparate, and sometimes competing, tendencies within nationalism. In broad terms, different Black nationalisms have been defined by a relationship to a dominant or notable area of emphasis: politics, economics, culture, and religion—to name a few.[1]

Black cultural nationalism has been broadly defined as the view that African Americans possess a distinct aesthetic, sense of values, and communal ethos emerging from either, or both, their contemporary folkways and continental African heritage. This collective identity informs, from a cultural nationalist perspective, African Americans' historical and prospective mission and unique contributions to humanity.[2] Typologies of nationalism provide significant insights into specific dimensions of Black political thought but tend to fall short of capturing the ideological complexity of a given activist or organization. Historians have situated the literary works of nineteenth-century nationalist Martin Delaney, for instance, in the cultural nationalist tradition, while his pursuit of Black nationhood finds company among those associated with territorial nationalism. The ideas espoused by the US Organization, during the late 1960s and early 1970s, were similarly complex and multifaceted. Karenga is distinct, however, in that he defined himself, and US, as "cultural nationalist," explicitly embracing the term as an identifier of the organization's philosophy. Also, the broad-based 1960s Black cultural nationalist movement was literally comprised of thousands of organizations, artists, and activists. The deliberateness with which Karenga sought to detail the theoretical underpinnings of his self-styled liberation strategy helped thrust his organization to the center of Black cultural nationalist politics and the more expansive Black nationalist resurgence of the period. This chapter explores the intellectual grounds for the US Organization's program and philosophy—canvassing discourses central to the emergence and character of the organization.

From Everett to Karenga: Eastern Shore, LACC, UCLA, and Africa

In December 1998, more than three decades after the first Kwanzaa in 1966, Maulana Karenga came back home to Salisbury, Maryland, the region of his upbringing, as a guest speaker for a pre-Kwanzaa celebration. The event, hosted by Project Sisterhood, a rites-of-passage organization for adolescent girls, attracted families, public officials, community activists, and a large number of Karenga's relatives. The crowd listened attentively as Karenga beckoned them to ponder and celebrate the moral lessons born of their African history and culture. "So we come and we celebrate this ancient history," he declared, ". . . this history that taught us to speak truth and to do justice, to honor our elders and our ancestors, to cherish and challenge our children and care for the vulnerable."[3] These teachings, for Karenga and many in the room, though cited from the philosophers of Black antiquity, were integral to a lived experience as African Americans, raised in modern-day Eastern Shore, Maryland.

Karenga, born Ronald Everett in 1941, was the youngest among fourteen children. Throughout his childhood years, Everett family members labored as farmers in Parsonsburg, a small town just outside of Salisbury. The living and work arrangement was tantamount to sharecropping, with the landowner providing living space and permitting the Everetts to keep 50 percent of the produce they picked. Young Ronnie spent his mornings and afternoons with his siblings, picking potatoes, cucumbers, strawberries, and tomatoes that were eventually "trucked" out for sale at a local market.[4] He may have spent more time in a single day with his sisters than with his parents, who worked incessantly and found means to supplement family earnings through occasional migrant labor and domestic work. Ronnie's initial respite from the land came as he began elementary school in neighboring Salisbury.[5]

His mother and father, Addie and Levi Everett, saw Ronnie as a "special child" because he was their seventh son.[6] Their perspective was informed by a deep Christian faith and spirituality. Levi, a Baptist minister, was undoubtedly familiar with the Old Testament figures David, Eliel, Elioenai, and Enoch, each of whom was the seventh son within his respective familial place in the unfolding of the Hebrew narrative.[7] Many African Americans in Eastern Shore and beyond were familiar with some version of the lore that the seventh child (male or female) was "blessed" with special potentialities. Arnetta Church Atkins, a high school peer of Ronnie's older brother Chestyn, remembered that the seventh child was seen as a "good omen" of sorts.[8]

If Ronnie's success in school occurred as a measure of divine will, it was, indeed, a prophecy fulfilled by others in the family. The Everett children were known throughout the region as exceptionally bright and hard-working students. By the time Ronnie attended high school his siblings and extended family members had earned a solid reputation for academic achievement.[9] The Everetts came to be known by some in Salisbury as those "smart folks" who lived on the outskirts of town.[10]

Scholastic excellence, though, was hardly an exception for students who attended the all-Black Salisbury High School. The school's principal, Charles Chipman, an extraordinary educational leader, had graduated from Howard University and conducted graduate studies at the University of Pennsylvania, the University of Chicago, and the University of Heidelberg in Germany. A specialist in languages, mathematics, and the sciences, Chipman established a curriculum and culture at Salisbury High that fostered a collective sense that education was the key vehicle for a student's contribution to the uplift of the race. Scores of Salisbury graduates went on to attend college at neighboring Morgan and Bowie State universities and colleges elsewhere.[11]

After graduating from high school in 1958, Ronnie then moved to Los Angeles from his rural hometown of Parsonsburg, Maryland, and lived in Los Angeles with Chestyn, who, after graduating from Howard and Johns Hopkins universities, was working as an artist and schoolteacher.[12] There, Ronnie acquired California state residency and attended Los Angeles City College (LACC) and later the University of California at Los Angeles (UCLA).[13] Having internalized Chipman's mandate to excel, his activism and leadership on campus paved the way for a historic victory in the 1961 election for student-body president at LACC —he was the first African American elected to the position.[14]

The young student leader had built a large constituency among international students. This support was reflected in his election platform, calling for "a more extensive international students program."[15] These connections to international students coincided with a blossoming interest in Africa. The climate at

LACC also facilitated encounters with various aspects of African culture. The two-year college introduced an African history course to the curriculum in the spring of 1961. The course's instructor, Joseph Hearn—who had earned a Ph.D. in African studies from UCLA—boasted that LACC was "one of the first two-year colleges to offer such a course."[16]

Everett, who had already demonstrated a facility for foreign languages in high school, found that the Kiswahili course spoke to the identity and cultural questions with which he struggled: "I said to myself, 'I'm African, why don't I know an African language?'"[17] Kiswahili, also called Swahili, had a special appeal to him and eventually to other African American cultural nationalists, as it is spoken by a broad range of ethnicities and regions throughout eastern and central Africa and parts of southern Africa. "Swahili is a pan-African language," the US leader stated in 1966. "We don't know what tribe we came from, so we chose an African language that is non-tribal, which is widely spoken in Africa."[18] In 1964, Everett began teaching Kiswahili to African Americans in an adult education class in Los Angeles.[19] His affinity for Kiswahili was in tandem with arguments presented by continental African supporters of pan-Africanism engaged in a search for an African lingua franca to accommodate strides toward economic and political unification. Position statements made at the Second Congress of African Writers held in Rome in 1966 called for a continentwide adoption of a single African language. Kiswahili came to be seen as the optimum choice by many advocates of pan-Africanism. The movement in support of Kiswahili persisted well into the 1970s and brought together a diverse body of African intellectuals, including Wole Soyinka and Ali Mazuri.[20]

Everett's study of Kiswahili, and the US Organization's eventual encouragement of its widespread usage in the later 1960s, significantly advanced its popularity among African Americans—

particularly among a growing number of students and activists interested in the language as a basis for identifying with an African cultural identity.[21] As this trend persevered, a debate raged over the origins of Kiswahili. Responding to a factional claim that Kiswahili's genealogy had Middle Eastern roots, a core group of linguists vigorously demonstrated its Africanity—by virtue of its syntax, grammatical structure, and grounding in the Bantu class of African languages. The scholarly effort to reclaim the Africanity of the language mirrored in passion and tone the efforts of African Americans to embrace it as a cultural bridge to the land of their historical roots.[22]

After acquiring an Associate's degree at LACC, Everett transferred to UCLA to complete a Bachelor of Arts in political science and a Master's in the same field, with a specialization in African affairs. Throughout the time spent at UCLA he continued his study of Kiswahili and Arabic. Many of the texts on Africa used in classes during this period were anthropological and ethnographic studies. The disciplinary orientation of these works presented a view of culture as a holistic composite of a particular group's thought and practices, rather than simply a people's arts and folkways. Most influential on Everett's thought were studies of African cultural groups and ethnicities that attempted to present an overview of the entire way of life of a given people. Eileen Krige's *The Social System of the Zulus,* for instance, explores Zulu life from "death and burial" practices to systems of "law and justice."[23] Similarly, Jomo Kenyatta's study of the Gikuyu people of Kenya, *Facing Mount Kenya,* profoundly influenced Karenga. The book describes Gikuyu systems of kinship, land tenure, economics, industry, education, sex life, government, marriage, initiation, and religion.[24] Studies like Krige's and Kenyatta's discuss politics and economics as subdivisions or categories within a larger cultural whole, a conception of culture that informed the US Organization's own "Seven Criteria of a Culture": mythology, history, social organization, political organization, economic organization, creative motif, and ethos.[25] Critics of the organization who misunderstand this anthropological view of culture have incorrectly described US's philosophy as nonpolitical and solely dedicated to the arts and aesthetic expression. As far as US was concerned, its perspective was summarized best in *The Quotable Karenga*: "Everything that we do, think, or learn is somehow interpreted as a cultural expression. So when we discuss politics, to US that is a sign of culture. When we discuss economics, to US that is a sign of culture. . . . In other words, we define culture as a complete value system and also means and ways of maintaining that value system."[26]

In addition to its effect on what would become the philosophy of US, *Facing Mount Kenya* had a distinct impact on Everett's personal identity transformation. This treatise introduced him to the term "Kareng'a," a description for the Gikuyu independent schools that Kenyatta described as "entirely free from missionary influence, both in educational and religious matters."[27] The text's glossary defines Kareng'a as "[a] pure-blooded Gikuyu, a nationalist."[28] Everett embraced the nationalistic connotations of the term rather than its ethnic affiliation and later changed his last name to "Karenga"—which he interpreted to mean the "keeper of tradition." By 1963 he was using the name in public forums and gatherings on campus.[29]

Senghor

Kwame Nkrumah, Julius Nyerere, Sekou Toure, and Leopold Senghor, intellectuals who had arisen as heads of state in the blossoming African postcolonial period of the late 1950s and early 1960s, made a great impression on Karenga. Lilyan Kesteloot, in *Intellectual Origins of the African Revolution*, maintained that anticolonial writers and political leaders saw their role as a "duty to lead the way on a new path, to restore order to the chaos of acculturation, and bring their subjugated people back to life."[30] Karenga identified cultural restoration as a political mandate for African American liberation.

Karenga also read works by African and Caribbean francophone writers affiliated with Negritude, a pan-African literary and cultural movement that stressed the value and utility of traditional Black cultures, albeit sometimes through an overly romanticized lens.[31] One of Karenga's mentors at UCLA, anthropologist Councill Taylor, was a Negritude enthusiast and looked to its themes as a source for discussing African American identity and cultural politics. Robert Singleton, Karenga's classmate in the early 1960s, recalled, "I never heard of Frantz Fanon until I took a class with Councill Taylor."[32] Taylor, as Singleton recalled, also had a powerful impression on the would-be US chairman: by 1962 Karenga had planned on "taking some of the teachings of Councill Taylor to the streets."[33]

Negritude poet and theorist Leopold Senghor produced a treatise, *On African Socialism,* that had clear implications for the US Organization's blueprint for social change. Senghor held that African socialism is rooted in traditional communal culture. He contrasted African socialism with communism as practiced by the Soviet Union and Eastern bloc countries. "In the communist countries," Senghor exclaimed, "the 'dictatorship of the proletariat,' contrary to the teachings of Marx, has made the state an omnipotent, soulless monster, stifling the natural freedom of the human being, drying up the sources of art, without which life is not worth living."[34] Senghor also scrutinized Karl Marx's critique of religion, suggesting that its origins sprung from Marx's personal struggles with religious identity.[35] Karenga was also suspicious of the idiosyncratic and cultural foundations of Marx's conclusions. Karenga, therefore, rejected Marx as the ultimate socialist authority and would eventually find him worthy of ridicule, labeling him "a madman who put his doctrine together in a room in England."[36]

Senghor's search for egalitarian alternatives, in traditional African culture, proved even more germane to Karenga's path than the shared irreverence for Marx. "Negro-African society," Senghor wrote, "is collectivist or, more exactly, communal. . . . We had already achieved socialism before the coming of the European."[37] He regarded the task of finding a traditional African model of socialism as part of an Africanization process that would help counter colonialism's negative impact on African society and culture. Senghor declared that "cultural independence, is the necessary prerequisite of other independences: political, economic, and social."[38] Karenga revived this axiom to fit his organization's objectives, situating culture at the base of genuine revolutionary change. Sekou Toure, francophone political theorist and Guinean president, also found postcolonial emancipatory possibilities in African culture. Karenga embraced Toure's concept of "re-Africanization."[39]

Julius Nyerere, Sukarno, and the African-Asian Alliance

The first Tanzanian head of state, Julius Nyerere, attempted to operationalize the idea of African socialism as state policy, naming his government's African socialist program *Ujamaa*, a Kiswahili word that literally means familyhood. As was the case with Senghor, Nyerere saw traditional Africa as a source for organic models for building a modern socialist society.[40] He also considered a people's capacity to practice socialism as a product of its values: "Socialism—like democracy—is an attitude of mind." "In a socialist society," he proclaimed, "it is the socialist attitude of mind and not the rigid adherence to a standard political pattern which is needed to ensure that the people care for each other's welfare."[41]

Karenga adopted Ujamaa as one of the Seven Principles of Blackness (*Nguzo Saba*) that he formulated. His organization came to see it as the authentic socialist proposition for African Americans, rooted in African history and culture.[42] Karenga was also critical of the idea that a "socialist attitude" could come into existence through coercive institutions. In keeping with Nyerere and Senghor, Karenga believed that the will and values of the people were the genuine pillars of socialist transformation. This matter, from Karenga's standpoint, distinguished African models of socialism from European ones. In his political vocabulary, collectivism or communism represented the European model, whereas "communalism" was the term he used for the African one. "To be communalistic," Karenga stated, "is to share willingly, but to be collectivistic is to force to share, which is a European concept."[43]

Before Tanzanian independence, the Indonesian nationalist and head of state, Sukarno, had popularized the process of state restoration of folk communitarian traditions in the postcolonial order. With his nation's independence from Japanese occupation on the horizon in 1945, he introduced the *Pantja Sila*, or five pillars—(1) nationalism, (2) internationalism, (3) democracy, (4) social prosperity, and (5) belief in God—as a core set of principles that he argued captured the essence of Indonesian national identity. J. D. Legge noted that "[t]he principles were devised in a form which would, [Sukarno] hoped, embrace the separate currents of nationalism and make possible the unity he so desired."[44] As Nyerere did later, Sukarno conceptualized these national characteristics in his native language. Sukarno declared that the Indonesian expression *Gotong-rojong,* which he defined as mutual cooperation or reciprocal obligations, best summarized his country's national character.[45]

Notes for a lecture that Karenga gave sometime in the 1960s,

"Indonesia—Sukarno," highlighted Sukarno's bearing on Karenga's own nationalist theory. Karenga linked *Ujima*—collective work and responsibility—the third principle of the Nguzo Saba, as comparable to Sukarno's Gotong-rojong (meaning "let's pull together").[46] Like the Indonesian concept, Ujima emphasized the necessity of mutual cooperation, defined in the Nguzo Saba as an action "[t]o build and maintain our community together and make our brothers' and sisters' problems our problems and to solve them together."[47] Karenga, self-conscious of the commonalities between the two concepts, wrote in his notes that Ujima is the "idea that social survival and existence requires communal integration, action and agreement."[48]

Sukarno selected principles as tools for constructing a common view of the nation or national character. The term *Pantja Sila* (five pillars), both in meaning and sound, is quite similar to Karenga's Nguzo Saba (Seven Principles). However, Sukarno and Nyerere invoked terms to define national principles in the native language of their respective constituencies. The use of non-Western languages, in the course of nation building, spoke directly to a postcolonial need to replace the domination-laden lexicon of the colonial era.[49] US's adoption of Kiswahili served a related purpose as countering the denigration of African culture endemic to American racial discourse.

As president of Indonesia, Sukarno played a leadership role in bringing delegations from twenty-nine Asian and African nations to his country for the April 1955 Bandung conference. The proposition that people of color, worldwide, shared a common anticolonial and anti-imperialist agenda had a special meaning for African American nationalists and radicals.[50] Malcolm X, in the historic 1963 speech "Message to the Grassroots," lauded the event as instructive for African Americans in the pursuit of building unity. "Once you study what happened at the Bandung conference and the results of the Bandung conference," Malcolm X declared, "it actually serves as a model for the same procedure you and I can use to get our problems solved."[51] "At Bandung," he stated, "all the nations came together, the dark nations of Africa and Asia . . . [d]espite their differences they came together."[52] The conference was a platform for key players in the blossoming Third World or Third Force (neither capitalist nor communist) movement—Gamal Nasser of Egypt and Jawaharlal Nehru of India. Sukarno's opening address put forward Indonesia's national motto as a rallying theme, "Unity in Diversity," taken from the phrase "Bhinneka Tunggal Ika."[53] Karenga, also inspired by Bandung, would use the Indonesian motto "Unity in Diversity" to describe his own formula for African American solidarity, which he called "operational unity."

African Culture and Enslavement

Karenga deemed his own restorative task as significantly more challenging than that of the international leaders from whom he found inspiration—he concluded that enslavement was culturally more destructive than colonialism. African and Third World revolutionaries worked to extract oppositional values and ideas from enduring folk traditions, whereas the US Organization conceived of itself as burdened with the responsibility of recovering and reinterpreting lost African customs for a people void of a genuine cultural identity. "The reason why the Black man is such a weak-minded person," Karenga stated in an interview in 1966, "why he is so easily led by the White man is because he has no standards, no culture. He doesn't understand love of Black people because he's a slave-minded person. He can only love his master, and as much attempts as he makes, unless he is imbued with cultural values . . . he will never be able to do that."[54]

Karenga's remarks carried the voice of nineteenth- and early twentieth-century Black nationalists—David Walker, James T. Holly, Edward Wilmot Blyden, Noble Drew Ali, Marcus Garvey, and many others—with the same understanding of enslavement and its consequences. The history of enslavement provided a rationale for bold initiatives to address the purported psychological and cultural deficits suffered by its subjects and their descendants.[55] "It is no wonder that the Negro acts so peculiarly within our present civilization," Marcus Garvey declared, "because he has been trained and taught to accept the thoughts of a race that has made itself by assumption superior." Offering a historical explanation for this condition, Garvey added that "[t]he Negro during the time of slavery accepted his thoughts and opinions from the white race, by so doing he admitted into his system the idea of the superiority of a master in relationship to a slave."[56] Garvey, who was convinced of his organization's (Universal Negro Improvement Association) unique ability to solve this problem, stated that "[i]n one instance he [the Negro] was freed, from chattel slav[e]ry; but up to the time of the Universal Negro Improvement Association, he was not free in mind."[57]

The Nation of Islam (NOI) reiterated assumptions about the impact of enslavement previously expressed by Garvey and others. Minister Malcolm X of the NOI, making the case for the religious nationalist proposition of his leader Elijah Muhammad, maintained that "the poor so-called Negro doesn't have his own name, doesn't have his own language, doesn't have his own culture, doesn't have his own history. He doesn't even have his own mind."[58] As a graduate student, Karenga met frequently with the minister whenever he visited the Los Angeles mosque and worked to bring Malcolm to lecture at UCLA in late 1962.[59] Malcolm X told his audience of six hundred that "the American Negro is a Frankenstein, a monster who has been stripped of his culture and doesn't even know his name."[60]

The NOI, founded in the early 1930s, bridged the gap between nineteenth- and early twentieth-century nationalists and those of the Black Power era. Historian Wilson Moses noted some of the core tenets of Black nationalists of that era: (1) aspirations for a Black nation-state, (2) a sense of divine mission, and (3) an aristocratic or "'high culture' aesthetic" with an incumbent castigation of African culture as uncivilized and primitive.[61] In some respects, the NOI continued the tendency of pre–World War II Black nationalists to regard African culture as backward. On the other hand, its doctrine promoting Arabic as the Black people's authentic language and Islam as their religion valorized a non-Western cultural ideal.

Malcolm couldn't induce the younger graduate student to join the Nation of Islam, though Karenga concurred with its critique of Christianity. According to Karenga, Malcolm X "tried to convert" him to Islam during their initial meeting. Karenga responded by telling him, "I don't really believe in religion."[62] Looking back at his reasoning at the time, Karenga recalled, "I separated myself from the Christian church, and so I didn't see the need for that kind of organized expression of spirituality."[63] Karenga, nevertheless, agreed with the Muslim minister's sharp criticism of Christianity as a doctrine supporting enslavement, colonialism, and imperialism. The NOI's view that Christianity had inextricable connections to an inordinate degree of suffering and oppression for people of color throughout the world spoke to Karenga's earlier studies of works by British philosopher Bertrand Russell.[64] Russell's essay "Why I'm Not a Christian" linked Christianity to a large measure of historical violence, warfare, and general intolerance. These themes would reemerge, Karenga remembered, in a more concrete form throughout his early 1960s contact with the NOI, whereby "Malcolm and the Muslims criticize [Christianity] in even more definitive ways, because they would speak from the Black position."[65]

The NOI also played a key role in Black identity politics, contributing its standpoint to the historic debate over the appropriate name for African Americans.[66] NOI ministers argued against the use of the term "Negro," preferring "Black" as a rightful name for African Americans. "Negro" from this perspective was invalidated by a lack of any relationship to land, language, or situational relevance. "Black," on the other hand, more appropriately illustrated a binary opposition to Whiteness, a pan-European identity formed out of a collective opposition to Africans in America and other people of color in the United States and the diaspora. "No matter how light or dark a white man is," Minister Malcolm X preached, "he's 'white.'" Furthermore, he added, the "[s]ame way with us. No matter how light or dark we are, we call ourselves, 'black,' different shades of black, and we don't feel we have to make apologies about it!"[67]

NOI spokesmen used the phrase "the so-called Negro" as a reference to Black people who had not arrived at a proper identity consciousness. "The so-called Negro" was often derided for backwardness and a pathological attachment to the ways and worldview of the oppressor. Karenga embraced this Negro/Black distinction, and it eventually became a part of US's own doctrine, captured in the organization's song "Mama, Mama," which was taught to children at the organization's School of Afroamerican Culture. The child in the song queries:

> Mama, mama, Negroes are insane
> They straighten their hair and don't know their name.
> They bleach their skin and act so white.
> They don't even have any purpose in life.

The mother then responds, stating,

> You see my child it's a pity and a shame,
> that your sick brother doesn't even know his name.
> It's not his fault, he's not to blame
> The white man robbed him of his Black brain.

This victimized and self-hating Negro was then juxtaposed with the US Organization's definition of Blackness. After the child asks,

Mama, mama, what does it mean to be Black?
Is it like a color so lovely and dark?

the mother states,

To be Black my child is much more than that.
It's the way you think and the way you act.[68]

The NOI also served as an organizational model for what Karenga would develop in 1965. Full membership in both organizations required the complete acceptance of an alternative lifestyle. The dress, mannerisms, and entire social life of a given member of the Nation was extremely different from that of mainstream African American culture. As US would also contend, the NOI regarded its alternative lifestyle as a paradigm for the Black nation. The larger community's lack of acceptance of their way of life was seen by members of both groups as the result of general backwardness plaguing African Americans and, thus, an indication of the emancipatory task before them.

Even though Karenga and his radical contemporaries were ideologically indebted to Malcolm X during his tenure in the NOI, many also felt that the Black Muslims were incapable of meeting the new political demands of that era. In 1966, just one year after US was founded, Karenga asserted that although "[t]he Muslims have made a very positive contribution," in that "[t]hey did a lot of groundwork among the masses in terms of creating consciousness," the demands of the movement required a new generation of leaders.[69] Karenga saw the NOI as a part of an older nationalist trend and considered himself and other

1960s activists as generationally distinct from the Nation, stating that "it is up to us, the younger people, to go on from where they [the NOI] left off."[70]

The contention that the NOI had not kept pace with the demands of a new era was reinforced by the dramatic series of events in 1965. The turbulent year opened with the assassination of Malcolm X in February and moved on to endure a massive Black uprising in the Watts section of Los Angeles in August. Those two developments paved the way for the formation of the US Organization and made a deep imprint on its formative period. Militancy was widespread; a yellow sweatshirt with an imprint of Malcolm X's face and the phrase "St. Malcolm"—worn by various Black activists in Los Angeles, including Karenga, during the revolt's aftermath—came to symbolically represent the intimate connections between the two events.

For many young Black nationalists the advocacy of self-defense and armed resistance became a litmus test for organizational or individual activist legitimacy. Karenga felt that the NOI's focus on religion undermined its capacity to pass this test. When talking about this generational difference, Karenga exclaimed that "we're young and our main attraction is to the people who would make the revolt." "The Muslims," he concluded, ". . . are not a political organization, they are a religious organization."[71] He then distinguished them from his own group: "We [the US Organization] engage in some type of political expression . . . to be an action organization you have to take some stand politically and the Muslims have not done that."[72]

Malcolm X and the OAAU

Just prior to his tragic death, Malcolm X had established himself as a principal supporter of anticolonial and Third World nation-

alist movements abroad. He was also an advocate of revolutionary change in the United States and had founded a coalition of
organizations called the Organization of Afro-American Unity
(OAAU)—modeled after the Organization of African Unity.
Death did not thwart Malcolm's rapid ascendancy as a common
reference point for diverse ideological expressions of Black nationalism and radicalism in the late 1960s and early 1970s. This
phenomenon has been described, figuratively, as the workings of
a "spiritual advisor in absentia," for a generation of "revolutionaries" convinced of their authentic stewardship of Malcolm X's
legacy.[73]

If Malcolm X's religious Black nationalism did not share the
same criteria for nation building that Karenga had in mind in
1962, his brief sojourn into political and secular nationalism
after leaving the NOI not only bridged the gap between the
two positions but quite possibly helped to shape or confirm Karenga's views about cultural revolution. Malcolm X's view of
culture—as expressed in his "Statement of Basic Aims and Objectives of the Organization of Afro-American Unity," presented
in Harlem on June 28, 1964—can be seen as a veritable precur-
sor to Karenga's assertion that "[y]ou must have a cultural revolution before the violent revolution. The cultural revolution
gives identity, purpose and direction."[74] With a similar conception of culture as a foundation for African American collective
consciousness, Malcolm X wrote, "We must recapture our heritage and our identity if we are ever to liberate ourselves from the
bonds of White supremacy. We must launch a cultural revolution
to unbrainwash an entire people."[75]

The OAAU's "Basic Unity Program" indicated Malcolm X's
view that the group had a special purpose, a vanguard sense of
mission akin to that which US embraced seven months later.
After declaring the founding of the OAAU on February 15, 1965,
the document maintained,

Upon this establishment, we Afro-American people will launch a cultural revolution which will provide the means for restoring our identity that we might rejoin our brothers and sisters on the African continent, culturally, psychologically, economically, and share with them the sweet fruits of freedom from oppression and independence of racist governments.[76]

The OAAU's structure as an umbrella formation with diverse Black nationalist groups laid foundations for Karenga's theory of Black unity and the US Organization's leadership role in the establishment of a similar united front in Los Angeles, called the Black Congress. Malcolm X gave a preview of what became the OAAU's position in a famous speech delivered on April 3, 1964, "The Ballot or the Bullet." Interestingly enough, he did not demand that organizations become subordinate to or merge with one particular group. They were only required to adhere to broad principles of Black nationalism and simultaneously remain independent and autonomous. "If the NAACP is preaching and practicing the gospel of black nationalism, join the NAACP," Malcolm X stated. "Join any organization that has a gospel that's for the uplift of the black man."[77] Karenga later called this same approach "operational unity" and used it as a theory that informed the functioning of several umbrella organizations and coalitions that he worked to build.[78]

The Nation of Islam, as an organization, linked the 1960s to an earlier era of Black nationalism. Yet it was Malcolm X, as an eventual dissenter of the NOI's hesitancy to fully engage the popular political demands of the time, who narrowed the gap between the NOI's conservativism and the radical aspirations of a younger group of nationalist activists. Karenga and others of his generation strongly identified with Malcolm X's advocacy of self-defense, Black community economic and political control, as well as his view that Martin Luther King, Jr. and other activists affiliated with the Civil Rights movement were overly committed to nonviolent strategies for social change. Many of these would-be Black Power advocates differed from Malcolm X with their prior participation in the Civil Rights movement. A number of them, through personal experience, came to the conclusion that its tactics were no longer effective.

Civil Rights, Liberalism, and Patriarchy

The liberal reformism associated with the Civil Rights era argued for an equitable and just distribution of social and political rights outlined in the United States Constitution and the Bill of Rights to the entirety of the nation's citizenry. Black nationalists, however, more often than not tended to consider the nation's governing principles as being in tandem with the oppression of African Americans and other people of color. White supremacy and, sometimes, class oppression were, from this nationalist outlook, intimately connected to the core values that shape American political and economic institutions. The Civil Rights movement drew heavily from a liberal moral tradition, with a rhetorical emphasis on the contradictory disparity between the nation's stated principles and the reality of racial oppression.

Karenga, when he was known as Ron Everett, was active in the Civil Rights movement prior to his incursion into Black nationalism at UCLA. Some of his first activist experiences were "picketing at Woolworth's and raising money for SNCC and CORE and other organizations."[79] Also, while attending Los Angeles City College he helped organize rallies against nuclear proliferation and capital punishment. At that time, student-activist Levi Kingston was a leader of these campus activities.[80] Karenga, looking back at those years, thought of his transition as resulting from the failure of liberalism to provide a sense of intellectual autonomy and independence. Troubled by constant White references for democracy, civilization, and culture in his classes, Karenga felt an "alienation from an integrationist atmosphere, the sense that I don't have what I need to engage on an equal level."[81] Encounters with Black nationalist, pan-Africanist, and anticolonial literature fostered a movement away from an integrationist approach: "I'm reading Garvey, I'm reading Nkrumah, I'm reading Senghor, I'm reading Cesaire, I'm reading Du Bois, I come across Garvey's question of 'where's the Black man's place and his institutions of political and cultural power?'"[82]

After embracing a Black nationalist viewpoint, "I threw myself," Karenga said, "in the movement and distanced myself from White associates I had known in the Civil Rights movement and integration movements, as well as Black integrationists."[83] In 1963 Karenga found an outlet for his shift toward Black nationalism, the Afro-American Association, a group headed by Donald Warden, a charismatic attorney and agitator in the Bay Area of Northern California. After graduating from Howard University, Warden migrated to California in 1960, where he studied law at the University of California at Berkeley. There he rapidly immersed himself in local politics and at Berkeley and San Francisco State universities organized a weekly discussion group of African American students and visiting scholars from continental Africa. Warden and the participants in the forum "decided that an action group was needed to organize the aims and aspirations of the race and to formulate a practical framework from which both our race and nation could enjoy great progress," and thus founded the Afro-American Association in March 1962.[84]

Most of the association's activities were focused on Black economic, cultural, and community development: establishing independent cultural centers, business ventures, and schools, based on the Garveyite theme of self-help and commercial relations with African countries and the Black Diaspora.[85] At its height, the group boasted of a national and international sphere of influence, with chapters in California, Texas, Oregon, Pennsylvania, Alabama, Sierra Leone, and Nigeria.[86]

In Northern California, Warden attracted a broad spectrum of activists, many of whom would later found their own organizations, such as Ernie Allen, Huey Newton, Bobby Seale, and Ken Freeman.[87] Ayuko Babu, Tut Hayes, Akida Kimani, and Lloyd Hawkins were some of the activists in the association's Los Angeles chapter.[88] Shortly after Malcolm X visited the campus in late 1962, Warden followed and introduced an audience at UCLA to his critique of the weight that leaders in the Civil Rights movement placed on integration, arguing that efforts to "integrate a few schools or elect a few representatives" diverted African Americans from building Black institutions and thereby strengthening their own neighborhoods.[89] Warden and Karenga met around this time and Warden extended the invitation to head the Los Angeles chapter of the association. As its representative, Karenga continued the group's relentless opposition to integration.[90]

Warden had mastered the rhetoric of apocalyptic prediction and rapid-fire speech, and his comrades in Los Angeles followed suit. "I remember speaking in Watts," Karenga said, "and I was predicting a revolt—'we're gonna do this,' because there was a sense that the masses were at a breaking point."[91] A musical version of this street-speaking style appeared in the association's album *Burn Baby, Burn,* released in the aftermath of the Watts explosion. A rare artifact of Warden's views and oratory, the album features an instrumental track and layers of choruslike affirming voices, heard calling and responding to his nonstop rhythmic nationalist proselytizing.[92]

Throughout the recording, Warden castigated Civil Rights groups for not working to build an economic base in the Black community and forecast further uprisings if his organization's program were not to receive broad support. "We call upon people of good will everywhere to mobilize your resources and your energy and let's put up businesses and factories," Warden exclaimed, "so that my people can have jobs—the civil rights groups have not put up one business yet, all of the millions of dollars that have been collected has not established one business or factory."[93]

The Afro-American Association offered a secularized version of the Nation of Islam's economic plan and opposition to the mainstream Civil Rights agenda, as well as a revitalized version of the "Back-to-Africa" campaign of the Universal Negro Improvement Association (UNIA).[94] Warden, though not specifically defining the group as cultural nationalist, set in motion many of the cultural concepts and organizing principles that Karenga utilized in US. In 1964 the association established the Afro-American Cultural Center. Its activities were intended to reinforce four core values: unity, self-help, education, and dignity. "With the implementation of this motto [the four values]," as reported in *Afro-American Dignity News*, "the black man makes a distinct and dynamic contribution to the cultural life of America." Warden described the rudiments of the African American dilemma in cultural terms, maintaining that the lack of racial pride and a disconnection from the African heritage caused a general lack of motivation and achievement.[95]

Karenga remained with the Afro-American Association until late 1964 or early 1965. One former member stated that the group had difficulty working as a unit because of "strong personalities vying against each other and a lack of discipline."[96] The story of the association is understated but extremely important to the history of Black Power politics. Warden attracted a broad range of young activists and students who gained critical experience in community organizing and raising consciousness. In addition to Karenga, the founders of three California-born "Panther" formations (all of which were independent and not affiliated with one another)—the Black Panther Party of Northern

California (Ken Freemen and Ernie Allen), the Black Panther Party for Self-Defense (Huey Newton and Bobby Seale), and the Black Panther Political Party (John Floyd)—were former members of the association. Warden was a pivotal force in Karenga's political education and among other Black nationalist and radical activists in California during the early 1960s.

Karenga and other young nationalists also disagreed with many Civil Rights organizations' commitment to nonviolence as a principle.[97] By 1966, within the Civil Rights movement, younger activists in the Student Nonviolent Coordinating Committee (SNCC) and the Congress of Racial Equality (CORE) advanced to the Civil Rights line of Martin Luther King, Jr. By the summer of 1966, John Lewis had resigned from SNCC in a split with Stokely Carmichael (Kwame Ture) over the leadership's nationalist sentiments. Furthermore, during CORE's national convention in Baltimore, a resolution was passed ending its commitment to nonviolence as a policy.[98]

Karenga was sympathetic to the rumblings in SNCC and CORE.[99] Advocacy of self-defense was a central part of the US Organization's posture and was, in large measure, a lasting consequence of the Watts Revolt of 1965. By the end of that year, the California State Commission on the Los Angeles Riots released a report entitled "Violence in the City: An End or Beginning." US's response to that report unveils the ties between its early political stance and Karenga's earlier studies at UCLA.

The McCone Commission Report echoed sentiments associated with the sixties' liberal social science that tended to regard crime, familial disruption, and violence in Black urban centers as the result of Black psychological dysfunctionality born out of the history of enslavement.[100] The report constructed the explosive events that had taken place in Watts, Rochester, Jersey City, Philadelphia, Chicago, and other urban areas as a "common symptom of sickness in the center of our cities." "In almost every major city," the report stated, "Negroes pressing ever more densely into the central city and occupying areas from which Caucasians have moved in their flight to the suburbs have developed an isolated feeling of separation from the community as a whole."[101] The report considered contact with "Caucasians" as a civilizing force in the lives of African Americans. Left to their own devices in the ghetto, Blacks were accused of being plagued by a sense of "idleness" and "despair," which routinely translated into eruptions of "mass violence" as "a momentary relief from th[is] malaise."[102] The report also relied on a psychosociological explanation for the turn of events in Watts; those who participated in the "riot" were labeled criminals, lacking any moral basis for their actions. "However powerful their grievances, the rioters had no legal or moral justification for the wounds they inflicted," the report noted. "Many crimes, a great many felonies, were committed."[103]

Karenga and a handful of US members participated in a "Watts Grass Roots Community Seminar" held at the University of Southern California in December 1966. He presented a response to the governor's commission report entitled "A Black Power View of the McCone Report." Other US members and associates present were Clyde Daniels-Halisi, Tommy Jacquette-Mfikiri, Karl Key-Hekima, Sam Carr-Damu, Jimmy Doss-Tayari, and Ken Seaton-Msemaji, who also signed the document. The respondents on the panel were state assembly persons Yvonne Braithwaite, Leon Ralph, Charles Knox (who was representing Congressman Augustus Hawkin's office), Councilman Thomas Bradley, and Assemblyman Bill Greene.[104]

To a certain extent, the Black nationalist perspective—as espoused by US and others mentioned earlier—on the African American majority, or "Negroes," was shared by liberal social scientists of that period and with the McCone Report that many, if not most, were severely damaged psychologically and socially by the cumulative onslaught of American oppression.[105] The two differed in their respective proposed remedies to the problem. The liberal view, as expressed in the McCone Report, used the specter of violence as a testimony to the need for massive government economic and educational assistance to depressed urban areas and for support of political policies furthering racial integration. Karenga, on the other hand, regarded the revolt as evidence of a need for a cultural revolution led by his organization. "We are a cultural organization and thus relate everything we say to the question of culture which we define as the major problem of black people in America." The US response to the McCone Report exclaimed, "and we define culture as a composite system of ways of looking at and doing things." "We say that unless blacks create a culture of their own," the response continued, "they will always be marginal men in America, disrespected, rejected, brutalized and forced into positions of protest: vocal and physical, non-violent and violent."[106]

The response also anticipated US's clashes with the local police and eventually with the Federal Bureau of Investigation. US's "A Black Power View of the McCone Report" addressed the commission's attempt to criminalize the activities of those who participated in the revolt, and challenged the significance of law and governmental authority as they relate to African American resistance. The term "legitimacy" to the US members in the response was preferable to "legality," because it "does deal with right or wrong as decided by the people affected."[107] To define an act of revolt as illegal was limited, in their view: "To say that an act is illegal is simply to say that it is against the legal system in existence at that time." It went on to state that Black people "have had since the beginning of the Slave Revolts through the non-violent Civil Rights demonstrations to the revolts in the urban areas an expression of illegal acts against the system which were nevertheless legitimate in the eyes of black people."[108] Drawing from his studies of Frantz Fanon, Karenga and the other US advocates also took issue with the report's "refusal to accept the political and psychological relevance of the Revolt." In a manner revealing bonds between nationalist discourse and patriarchal assumptions about the male's role as leader and defender of the nation, the response asserted that the revolt was an act of "manhood" in which the Black community stood up for self-determination, self-respect, and self-defense. Karenga went on to give theoretical credence to this perspective, citing Fanon's *Wretched of the Earth.* "Brother Frantz Fanon, a black psychoanalyst," argued that "such a move [violent resistance], such action is 'a cleansing' force. It frees the native of his inferiority complex and from his despair and inaction."[109] Fanon provided movement activists with a theory that conjoined oppressed peoples' self-concept with their ability to engage in violent resistance against the oppressor. Even though the cases studied by Fanon were related to the Algerian liberation struggle, African American radicals who embraced the colonial analogy could easily accept his conclusions[110] and Karenga was among the many who did so.

Karenga and US criticized 1960s liberalist models for misunderstanding urban unrest and the Civil Rights movement's commitment to nonviolence and desegregation. However, many nationalists concurred with liberal social scientists' discussions of the state of the African American family and gender relations. Daniel Moynihan's *The Negro Family: The Case for National Action, a United States Department of Labor Report* was probably the most notorious example of a liberalist analysis of the Black family, calling for the insertion of heightened male dominance as necessary for the establishment of a healthy family based on a patriarchal model. The report dubiously contended that a key problem with the Black family was matriarchy or excessive control by women.[111]

The report's characterization of enslavement, as the basis for African American social malaise, concurred with Black nationalist claims to the same effect.[112] Moynihan's contention that the quest for African American full citizenship was, in part, contingent on thwarting a "subculture" of Black matriarchy[113] found kinship with Black nationalist rhetoric, which has traditionally equated the rebuilding of the nation with the restoration of "manhood."[114]

Karenga's own patriarchal conception of the Black family, as exemplified in the social relations of US advocates, was modeled after an interpretation of traditional African social relations.[115] Yet, the historicization of male dominance, in this context, revealed a closer affiliation with reactionary trends in the gender politics of the day than a proximity to traditional African customs. "We say male supremacy is based on three things," Karenga stated, "tradition, acceptance and reason."[116] The call for restorative male dominance, as justified by a connection with Africa, resonated with preexisting American patriarchal sensibilities and was reinforced by themes prevalent in liberal, nationalist, and Christian thought.

Kawaida: Religion and Quasi-Religion

Karenga's critique of Christianity was a consequence of his experiences as a student and activist at LACC and UCLA. The Nation of Islam, Bertrand Russell, and African cultural nationalist thought significantly influenced his rejection of and ultimate hostility toward Christianity while he was chairman of US during the Black Power years. Though the academy and urban life in Los Angeles moved Karenga away from the spiritual teachings of his parents, his own attempt to create a new religion in his organization may suggest that the Black folkways and institutions of Eastern Shore, Maryland, had a subtle yet profound impact on the US chairman's Black Power ideology.

Karenga did not eschew religion. On the contrary, his own philosophy of cultural nationalism, called *Kawaida*, "a total way of
life," had a religious dimension that expanded on the NOI dis-
missal of salvation and hereafter themes in Christian theology.
E. U. Essien-Udom noted that the "hereafter" in the Nation's cos-
mology was the "destruction of the present world and the authority of the 'Man of Sin' [the White man] to rule over it."[117]
Kawaida, during the Black Power era, also linked the transformation of power relations to its view of the "hereafter."

Karenga did not attribute the "pie in the sky" conception of
the afterlife exclusively to Christianity. In spite of his attempts to
introduce specific continental African cultural practices to African Americans, Karenga considered traditional African religions
susceptible to the problems of Christianity. "We are not interested," Karenga stated, "in spookism which is what our spiritual-
ism in Africa degenerated into. That is, invested in a spook estate
up in the sky and paying little attention to real estate on this
earth."[118] He went on to explain his organization's view of the afterlife: "We believe that children are the real life after death and
our greatest duty to them is to leave our community in better
shape than the way we inherited it."[119]

Karenga's perception of African religions may have been a
product of the state of Western anthropology during his years as
a graduate student, which tended to describe African religions as
fetishlike and inordinately ritualistic. Karenga, nevertheless, bor-
rowed heavily from the Zulu religious narrative. When asked who
is the "god-head" in Kawaida, Karenga responded, "We believe in
the first ancestor who gave us the answers to all things."[120]

The first ancestor to which he referred is Nkulunkulu, a central force in a traditional Zulu narrative of creation. "Unku-
lunkulu the old one," one study of Zulu culture observed, "is the
Creator or First Cause." "If a Zulu is asked about the origin of
man and of the world," it further explained, "he will say 'Unku-

lunkulu made all things.'"[121] "The Myth of a Beginning without a Beginning," the US Kawaida creation story, employed themes and elements of Zulu theology to fit the ideology and politics of the US Organization. The first ancestor here in this narrative was responsible for providing African people with the Seven Principles "upon which the community could prosper."[122]

Karenga and his followers were explicit in the admonition that the Kawaida creation story was indeed mythology. In fact, "mythology" was one of the US's Seven Criteria of a Culture and defined as "an answer to the origin of things and the 'chosen people' concept, necessary for a good self-concept."[123] The US leader further demystified his own religion by candidly making it clear that he was its creator. When queried about his religious beliefs, he declared, "I'm the founder of a religion called *Kawaida* . . . it's based on seven principles."[124]

The US concept of God, also borrowing from the NOI and the Moorish Science Temple, fused the creator with humanity. The Black men of US, as patriarchal heads of their households, saw themselves as possessors of divine attributes. The family, referred to as the "house," was described as the space in which their divinity was exercised. "We are Gods ourselves," a pamphlet on the doctrine stated. "Each Black man is God of his own house."[125] It was argued that this relocation of divine space mitigated against the "spookism" of Christianity and African religions. "We owe our allegiance to no one except each other," Karenga declared. "We do not pray to things in the sky because reality is here and when we achieve an astroexistence, then we will deal with that on a different level than we can discuss here."[126]

The US chairman's heterodox religion and anti-Christian rhetoric would have offended the sensibilities of the Black community that raised him in the 1940s and 1950s. Yet, US's cultural nationalist alternative, as presented in its weekly gatherings called "Soul Sessions" at the organization's headquarters, took on the tenor and feeling of the African American church that Karenga once knew. As one former US member recalled, the Sunday afternoon meetings nourished hardcore members and sympathizers just as "Christians going to church on Sunday, [were] getting their message that was going to carry them through the week."[127] Karenga's own oratorical style captured the cadence of Baptist ministry and beckoned the call-and-response participation of his audience. Though dressed in African clothing, and occasionally accenting his lecture with a chant in Kiswahili, the transformed cultural nationalist leader frequently summoned the folkways of rural Parsonsburg.[128]

Karenga in Context

Ron Everett's transformation into Maulana Ron Karenga took place within an extraordinary context. The Cold War era helped boost the academy's formal interest in African affairs and other non-Western regions, giving way to a subfield known as Area Studies. Karenga was among a small number of African American undergraduate and graduate students in the late 1950s and early 1960s interested in Africa who benefited from the expansion of Area Studies. The institutionalized study of African culture and language during that period was tied to the United States' quest for global dominance. More than likely, someone with Karenga's background would have become a State Department official, diplomat, or Peace Corps administrator and have had a professional life directed by the dictates of American foreign policy.

Karenga took a very different course. His university experience was shaped by social and political currents inimical to the Cold War agenda associated with African Studies at the time, namely, the Civil Rights and Black Power movements. Karenga's personal identity politics, as explicitly evidenced in his name change, reflected the confluence of his academic work and political activism. The academy afforded him a rare opportunity to study African culture and philosophy, while the activist impulses of the era furnished outlets for a self-styled philosophy that drew heavily from his research.

The Civil Rights and Black Power movements yielded avenues for Karenga's political career and helped mold what was to become US's cultural nationalist doctrine, Kawaida. While the Black nationalist resurgence of the late sixties is often seen as the antithesis of the liberalism associated with the Civil Rights movement, Karenga's views relating to enslavement, social relations, and gender brought to light shared readings, or misreadings, of history. This mélange of intellectual currents and social and political movements was the ground out of which the activist-scholar Maulana Karenga emerged, formulated a philosophy, and organized its practical expression—the US Organization.

3. Memory and Internal Organizational Life

Early Formation

In the fall of 1965, Maulana Karenga, Hakim Jamal, Dorothy Jamal, Tommy Jacquette-Mfikiri (Halifu), Karl Key-Hekima, Ken Seaton-Msemaji, Samuel Carr-Damu (Ngao Damu), Sanamu Nyeusi, and Brenda Haiba Karenga were among the early members a newly formed organization called "US." The term "US" was chosen as a dual reference to the organization and the community its members pledged to serve: *us Blacks as opposed to "them" Whites.*[1] According to Jamal the organization was not formed in one singular meeting. It grew out of a study group called the Circle of Seven, led by Karenga, which had met regularly at the Black-owned Aquarian bookstore in Los Angeles. Jamal also asserted that he selected the name "US" for the group. Prior to his association with Karenga, he printed and locally distributed a "magazine" called *US* intended to be "for all the black people [and] to be put in markets, free." He also noted that the US Organization's motto "Anywhere we are, US is," was originally "a caption for the magazine."[2]

Jamal had been a close associate of Malcolm X since Malcolm's days as a Boston hustler and throughout his political career with the Nation of Islam and the Organization of Afro-American Unity. Upon joining forces with the study group Jamal led a push to situate the martyred Black nationalist leader as US's main ideological and inspirational reference. The US Organization's first newspaper, *Message to the Grassroots*, which appeared in May 1966, designated Karenga as the "chairman" of US and Jamal as its "founder." The first issue introduced itself as a dedication to "Mrs. Betty Shabazz, the widow of our slain nationalist leader."[3] By the summer of 1966, Jamal had parted company with US, and Karenga stood as the organization's leader and ideologue. The split was likely to have resulted from differences over US's philosophy and leadership directions. Jamal's preference for a political program based on the teachings of Malcolm X seems to have ultimately clashed with Karenga's rapidly expanding dominance over US. By the late summer of 1966 Karenga had become the organization's central ideologue and chief leader.[4]

The iconography of this shift was evident when, sometime in the spring or summer of 1966, US members wore T-shirts that bore the image of Karenga's face, effectively replacing the ones they had previously worn showing an emblem of Malcolm X's portrait. Jamal left US shortly thereafter.[5] By 1968, he had established the Malcolm X Foundation, based in Compton, California, and emerged as a vocal critic of US and its cultural approach.[6]

Jamal found little value in US's use of African rituals and languages. Other key early members, on the contrary, responded differently to African languages, in part because they had met Karenga through his Kiswahili class. Karl Hekima and Tommy Jacquette, who described themselves as "street brothers" from Watts, had early contacts with Karenga through the class. This was also the case for Oliver Massengale-Heshimu and Charles Massengale-Sigidi. "The first real participation" that Heshimu recalled was "when Maulana was becoming very busy during the time of the Swahili classes . . . [t]here were times that he asked my brother and I to substitute for him and teach the class."[7] Jacquette and Hekima were both involved with another organization in Watts called Self Leadership for All Nationalities Today (SLANT). SLANT was successful at acquiring antipoverty funds toward projects aimed at providing jobs, training, and entrepreneurial skills for disaffected African American youth in Watts, many of whom were unemployed or involved in local gangs. Hekima remained very active with US while his comrade kept strong ties with the organization but was mainly involved in SLANT's leadership. Jacquette, upon his first encounter with Karenga, felt ambivalent about African languages: "My attitude at that time was . . . what do we need Swahili for? We need some guns and some bullets." After being exposed to the language, his attitude changed somewhat: "So I went to the Swahili class, and I liked the Swahili class! I wasn't that interested but I liked it."[8]

The centrality of Karenga's leadership notwithstanding, the US members, from the outset, had specialized and essential roles to play in the functioning of the organization. James Doss-Tayari and Clyde Daniels-Halisi were vice-chairmen. Haiba Karenga and Dorothy Jamal led the School of Afroamerican Culture. Sanamu Nyeusi was both a teacher in the school and secretary-treasurer of the organization. Samuel Carr-Damu, later known as Ngao Damu, was a key original member of US who had a great deal of influence on the US paramilitary wing called the *Simba Wachanga* (young lions).[9] He is said to have been an "ex-army sergeant," Korean War veteran, and first real "soldier" of the group. His military experience and training proved vital to the new organization's ability to survive amid the competitive and sometimes hostile world of Los Angeles's radical politics.[10] When US was featured on the cover of *Life* magazine in July 1966, a picture of Damu drilling and shouting orders to Black youth added further evidence that one of the legacies of the 1965 Watts Revolt was a radical Black nationalist trend, defiantly opposed to nonviolence.[11] James Doss-Tayari, who became vice-chairman sometime in late 1966, recalled that Damu was known as the "Old Lion" because of his military expertise.

Tayari, a tall imposing figure, was also known for his serious, tough, and robust presence.[12] He had previous experience as an activist in interracial and socialist movements in the Los Angeles area, from 1963 until 1965, such as the W. E. B. Du Bois Club, an affiliate of the Communist Party.[13]

Women were also key players in the beginning phases of US's political career. The wives of both Maulana Karenga and Hakim Jamal, Haiba Karenga and Dorothy Jamal, organized the US School of Afroamerican Culture—one of its most important institutions, serving children of members as well as those from nationalist-minded families in the Los Angeles area. Sanamu Nyeusi, who figured prominently in US's founding year, had a charisma of her own that touched several new members. In the summer of 1966, she was secretary-treasurer of US and a teacher at the School of Afroamerican Culture.[14] She recruited two brothers, Oliver Massengale-Heshimu and Charles Massengale-Sigidi, who would eventually hold prominent positions. Sanamu gave the two brothers their African names and used the names as a way of attracting them to US.[15] The practice of giving advocates African names was often the domain of Karenga, the leader, or of male advocates. Thinking back on their entry into US, Heshimu recalled that his name "is a Swahili word for honor and respect and that's the way she felt about me. This was prior to any of us meeting Maulana."[16] Sigidi, on the other hand, is a Zulu praise name traditionally reserved for the nineteenth-century Zulu head of state, Chaka.[17] One US member intimated that Sanamu's charisma and intellect was "a large reason why [she] joined."[18] Sanamu eventually left US, for reasons unknown, either in late 1966 or early 1967, and went on to work with Robaire Njuku, a local Communist activist, and also the Black Panther Party.

Another major force in the organization's early formative period was the influx of persons from Pasadena who joined US. Most of these students who attended Pasadena City College

(PCC) were the first in their families to go to college. Clyde Daniels-Halisi, one of the founders of the Black Students Union there, played a large part in drawing his friends and associates to US. Halisi remembered having first seen Karenga and Hakim Jamal on a local television program sometime in late 1965 and 1966.[19] After watching, he explained, "At that point I was convinced that I wanted to join such an organization."[20] Along with Halisi in Pasadena were James Mtume, George Subira, Joann Richardson-Kicheko, Buddy Rose-Aminifu, Amina Thomas, and a host of others. These students at Pasadena City College succeeded in attracting some of their relatives, friends, and other African American students to US's weekly forums and eventually to joining the organization.[21]

Structure and Hierarchy

By late 1966 and early 1967, the handful of people who met at the Aquarian bookstore had become participants in a major activist organization in Los Angeles. By 1967, US had moved into its own building, and its daily operations had become part of a sophisticated internal structure and hierarchy. The organization had developed several subunits: the *Simba Wachanga,* the paramilitary wing; the *Saidi,* "older" men, usually over twenty years old; a School of Afroamerican Culture, *Mwalimu,* those studying the ethical and deeper philosophical aspects of Kawaida; the *Muminina,* women of the organization; and various topical focus committees. The two main governing bodies of US during this period were the Circle of Isihlangu and the Circle of Administrators. *Isihlangu* is a Zulu word meaning "shield." That circle served as an executive committee of sorts.[22] At the end of 1967, Isihlangu's members and their ranking were (1) Maulana Ron Karenga, founder-chairman; (2) Mwalimu Jim Tayari, vice-chairman; (3) Shahidi Karl Hekima, second vice-chairman; and (4) Ngao Sam Damu, security chairman.[23] Karenga described the Circle of Administrators as "chairs over chairs" of various specific task-oriented committees.[24] Some of those listed as part of the circle in December 1967 were Reginald Endesha, finance; Clyde Halisi, advocacy-propaganda; Mwalimu Oliver Heshimu, Simba Wachanga; Shahidi Karl Hekima, labor; Mwalimu Ramon Imara, Kawaida; Ujima Imara, Muminina; Haiba Karenga, education; Ahera Msemaji, Third World; and Mwalimu Charles Sigidi, Saidi.[25]

A "List of Titles" of US, most likely written in mid-1967, cites the organization's leadership hierarchy. The highest titles and persons were those who functioned within the Circle of Isihlangu: "1. *Maulana* Ron Karenga—Master Teacher; 2. *Mwalimu* Tayari—Vice Chairman; 3. *Shahidi* Hekima—Second Vice-Chairman (Protector of the Faith); 4. *Ngao* Damu—Shield."[26] Those Saidi who were special students of the doctrine formed two groups: "*Mwalimu*—Teacher; Tayari, Imara, Sigidi, Heshimu," and "*Mwanafunzi*—Student Teacher; Halisi, Msemaji, Endesha, Chache."[27] Eventually, the high priest position Imamu came to have a distinguished rank—Halisi was the first to hold the position—rivaling only that of the Maulana. As an organization guide-booklet explained, "The title 'Imamu' which Maulana Karenga awarded first to the head of the spiritual arm of US, and later to the various affiliated temples of Kawaida nationwide, we interpret to mean 'High Priest.'"[28] The Simba Wachanga also had an internal hierarchy: "*Amiri*—Jomo, Commander; *Kaimu*—Weusi—Deputy Commander; *Sultani*—Chief; *Makamu*—Assistant Chief."[29] There were seven Sultani and Makamu in the Simba, and there were those who served within an individual Simba unit known as a tribe. The Muminina also had its own internal divisions of labor and responsibilities.

The advocate's distinct role within a structured hierarchy is best captured in a lesson entitled "A Job for Everyone," taught to children in the organization's School of Afroamerican Culture on the Kuumba—the sixth principle of the Nguzo Saba, "To do always as much as we can, in the way we can, in order to leave our community more beautiful and beneficial than we inherited it." Teachers described US's positions of power and responsibility to their young students in the following manner:

> First of all there is Maulana. There is only one Maulana. We only need one Maulana. Next we have Imamu. They are our priests. They teach us the ways of our ancestors, they teach us Kawaida. Our Amiri keeps all our warriors in line. He sees to it that they are ready whenever we need them. Our Simba Wachanga, young lions, may look alike in uniform and dress alike but each one has a special skill and each one is doing a special job.[30]

These subunits, and leadership positions within them, comprised the sum total of US. Every active member had a place somewhere within this structure and had a clear sense of his or her responsibilities. The organization was designed to be a total way of life, with seven main facets: house (family), community, revolutionary school, Hekalu (temple), congregation, revolutionary party, and nation becoming.[31]

Los Angeles was the nucleus and central locale of the organization, though in 1967 members formed an auxiliary chapter in San Diego. The chapter duplicated the structure, and fell within the chain of command, set out in Los Angeles. Karl Key-Hekima and Charles Massengale-Sigidi worked with San Diego advocates Joe and Gloria Vincent-Chochezi and Vernon Sukumu to establish a Hekalu on Imperial Avenue. Joe Vincent-Chochezi served as the founding chair whose position was filled in 1968 by Sukumu.[32]

Advocacy

US formed a series of student-teacher relationships, such as pairing the general student body with Karenga (their collective Master Teacher), the Mwalimu with Karenga, and new recruits with more experienced members. Karenga had effectively established within the organization an internal system of reverential deference to him and a system of promotions and rewards for knowledge and mastery of the US doctrine. This stress on knowledge was present in US's stipulations for active membership. An US advocate was defined as "an Afro-American" or "third world brothers and sisters" who successfully complete "a seven week doctrine course and who pledge allegiance to the organization and its leader."[33]

Wesely Kabaila's first advocacy lessons in the spring of 1967 were taught by Mwalimu Halisi.[34] For Kabaila, teachers of advocacy class were counselors or mentors during a time of personal indecision about his role in US.[35]

After a seven-week class, would-be members of US made a formal commitment by pledging allegiance to the organization. The *Kiapo*, or Oath of US, demanded not only the total commitment to the leader, organization, and doctrine, but also the recognition of a personal "salvation" of sorts:

> With sincere humbleness and gratitude, I take this oath of loyalty to US. This, I fully realize is a great responsibility, too much I fear for me alone. And so, I humbly ask for help from my brothers and sisters in my efforts to be a good advocate of US. I am emotionally, spiritually and rationally committed to US, its principles and its leadership.
>
> I accept responsibility of helping to build US, for US first, took the responsibility of building me by giving me identity, purpose and direction.

I accept the Nguzo Saba as the basis of my beliefs and actions, for it is they which have helped me begin to return to myself.

I promise loyalty to Maulana Ron Karenga who believed in us and accepted us, before we believed in or accepted ourselves, or him, who found in all our weaknesses a hidden strength, and who gave us more than he asked from us that something of value which no one can take.

I trust I shall show my worthiness by acting and speaking humbly, for we are never quite sure of our worthiness. And if I achieve any greatness or create anything of beauty, all praise is due to US: only the mistakes are mine. Moreover, I realize that if I but practice the simple things I would modestly find greatness too far away to be seriously considered. In humbleness, I promise to work to develop the strength to admit my weaknesses and to struggle constantly against myself, not my brothers and sisters.

I do not know how much I can help our people fulfill their mission of nationhood, but I do believe in the validity of our approach to victory of our cause. And to this end I offer my love, work and life in the move to change hope and belief into a reality.

For me there is no turning back. I have made my choice. For me, US shall be House and community, revolutionary school, Hekalu and congregation, a nation becoming a revolutionary party, all in one.

Therefore, I shall struggle against those who struggle against US and be at peace with those who are at peace with US. For US must endure and prevail as something of value for us and for those after us, for as long as the Sun Shines and Water Flows.[36]

The Kiapo also reinforced the idea that the demands of membership superseded any quest for individual achievement. Credit for success, within this context, had to be given to the pedagogues responsible for an advocate's Negro-to-Black conversion: the Master Teacher and US, the group embodiment of his teachings.

The twenty-one "US Cultural Organization *Kanuni* (Rules)" reveal US's view that an advocate, converted to Blackness, should exhibit behavioral characteristics differentiating him or her from the general populace:

1. Advocates shall refrain from unnecessary or loud talking or screaming in or around the Hekalu.
2. Advocates shall refrain from malicious gossip.
3. Advocates shall refrain from discussing organizational business with outsiders.
4. Advocates shall refrain from unbecoming "acts" at or near the Hekalu, i.e., smoking, drinking, profanity, horseplay, petting, arguing, and name calling.
5. Advocates shall refrain from holding side conversations during general or committee meetings.
6. Advocates shall refrain from disrespecting each other in terms of their roles as men and women advocates and officers.
7. Advocates shall not shirk responsibility to each other as brothers and sisters, advocates and officers, i.e., commitments, work and attendance.
8. Advocates shall refrain from association with open and undercover enemies of the organization.
9. Advocates shall refrain from doing anything to destroy the internal unity of the organization.
10. Advocates shall refrain from dressing in a manner that is in conflict with the organization.

11. Advocates shall refrain from representing the organization unofficially.
12. Advocates shall refrain from misusing or destroying organizational property or resources.
13. Advocates shall refrain from individual acts, i.e., those acts which place personal interest above organizational interest.
14. Advocates shall refrain from playboyism and playgirlism.
15. Advocates shall refrain from hustlerism in terms of use of references or doctrine to a personal end.
16. Advocates shall refrain from using physical force against each other in settlement of disputes.
17. Advocates shall refrain from attending meetings and places that are negative to principles of the organization, i.e., love-ins, meetings of enemies and other non-functional functions.
18. Advocates shall refrain from making statements on premature issues that affect the struggle.
19. Advocates shall refrain from neophyting and proselytizing.
20. Advocates shall refrain from beginning, developing and maintaining a divided house, i.e., that is to say a house where one party refuses to accept the principles of the organization either as a wife or husband or being lazerous or lazerene with no values and no appreciation for the principles of the organization.
21. Advocates shall refrain from talking home-spun knowledge.[37]

All US members were expected to be very disciplined and deferential to their doctrine when interacting with the wider community. Further, the Kanuni pointed out the organization's stress on conformity by discouraging close relationships with those considered "enemies" and marriage with persons opposed to US's doctrine.

Catechism and Doctrine

Karenga developed an exhaustive system of numerical catechism as a framework for teaching his philosophy. There were at least 166 doctrine points, all of which had a number of subordinate definitions and explanations—usually 3, 5, 6, or 7. Karl Hekima, who spent time with Karenga in 1965 and early 1966, while constructing elements of the doctrine, explained why certain numbers were selected for particular points. "We used the number seven," Hekima stated, "because we say that's the Black man's number."[38] He went on to point out that "[w]e gave the number six to white people, six is what we called the devil or white boy's number."[39] "If it's pro-something for Black," he noted, "most of Maulana's early writings, the doctrine, are in numbers of sevens, fives or threes, now when you talk about the negatives in terms of White folks, we usually used the number six."[40]

Long before 1965 numerological mysticism had already been deeply embedded in religious nationalist philosophical traditions. This brand of mysticism flourished among the Prince Hall Masons, Moorish Science Temple, and the Nation of Islam (NOI). The NOI's interpretation of Old and New Testament "prophesy" assigned similar negative and positive moral values to numbers. Six corresponded with 6,000 years of White (also referred to as the devil or Yakub) global rule and oppression. Seven, conversely, marked the seventh millennium, or as Elijah Muhammad stated, "the seven thousandth year after the rule of 6,000 years by the white race."[41]

The US doctrine expanded on these considerations of number and moral nature. The "Seven Principles," "Seven Aspects of US," and "Seven Basic Concepts in Brother Malcolm's Message" exemplify the use of the "Black man's number" in the US doctrine. In contrast, the devil's number finds representation in the "Six Character Types of White Liberals": (1) fadist, (2) rebel,

(3) believer in the sex myth, (4) guilt ridden, (5) paternalist, and (6) expedient.[42] There are, nonetheless, exceptions to this pattern: numbers three and four are used for diverse subject matter and are not linked to any particular theme or value.

The time and detail associated with learning each doctrine point, as well as its subdefinitions, gave a sense that mastery of the doctrine was an endless task, always leaving room for heightened expertise. For instance, the "Seven Basic Concepts in Brother Malcolm's Message" are as follows:

1. *Revolutionary Nationalism*—Revolution and nationalism are interdependent, revolution must be for nation, Mao—China; Ho—Vietnam; Toure—Guinea, and US—Afroamerica. Leftwing tried to [co-opt] Malcolm by saying he was a revolutionist not a nationalist but Malcolm said, "if you love revolution you love nationalism and vice-versa."

2. *Unity of Groups*—No hell because Baptist or Methodist or American but because you're Black. US concept of Operational Unity—Black Congress; the United Brothers (Newark, N.J.).

3. *Community Structure*—(a) Political Control—politics and politicians, Black Panther Party, Lowndes County, Control your space—Leroi Jones. (b) Economic Control—No money down, avoid destruction of family by being able to provide. Control labor in factories, eventually own factories. Cooperative economics as opposed to capitalism. UJAMAA.

4. *Human Rights Struggle*—Equal rights, equal civil privileges to be taken when giver is so inclined. Human rights what you had at birth—UN genocide convention, exposure of whiteman in UN.

5. *Afro-Asia Alliance*—Becoming majority rather than minority. Keep pushing for Bandung. Our revolution of color, people of color against the colorless. Asian-African struggle and if

we want to help South Africa move on the enemy here, he owns it.

6. *Accent on Youth*—Children life after death. Simba greater than all previous generations. Progressive perfection.
7. *Self-Defense*—(a) Internal—Shield—Simba, Mau-Mau. (b) External—white boy, adjust to the level of audience.[43]

"The Three Ends of Black Power," "Three Ends of a Culture," "Seven-Fold Path to Blackness," and "Four Areas of Political Power" received notoriety among nationalists in the Black Power movement. Most of Karenga's public speeches followed these topics and subpoints in outline form, and he would clarify them to his audience with witty anecdotes and insights.

Some rank-and-file US members, likewise, were capable of dazzling their audiences with rapid-fire recitations of this systematic and comprehensive cultural nationalist ideology. Kabaila remembered that knowledge of US catechisms gave him an advantage in public encounters: "When somebody asked us, 'Well what is this thing called Black Power?' Well, [we would respond by saying] the three ends of Black Power are self-determination, self-respect and self-defense."[44] If pushed further, Kabaila explained, US advocates would go into further detail with relative ease: "We could run it off, self-determination means that we name ourselves, speak for ourselves, and act for ourselves; self-respect means that we respect ourselves as African people and that we want to return to our traditional culture, to our traditional ways of doing things; self-defense means that we have the right and responsibility to defend ourselves against our oppressors and against enemies of those things that we hold dear and near to us as Black people."[45] This, he felt, set US advocates apart from other activists of the late sixties: "[No] one had ever come up against a young person," Kabaila maintained, "who could . . . enunciate with such command—what is Black Power."[46]

Mwalimu

An *Mwalimu* (teacher, pronounced "Emwalimu") had to rise above the average advocate's understanding of the general US doctrine, and, furthermore, possess specialized knowledge of the spiritual and religious dimension of US teachings called *Kawaida* (interpreted to mean tradition and reason). As a matter of preparation, this elite core of teachers were required to study at length as *Mwanafunzi* (student-teachers) before receiving their rank. By August 1967, Mwalimu Imara had, among his many responsibilities as chair of the Kawaida committee, to conduct the Mwalimu school and select the Mwanafunzi who would attend it.[47] Just one month earlier, Oliver Heshimu had successfully become an Mwalimu. His *Shahada*, a diploma from the Mwalimu school, was written in Kiswahili, along with an English translation. It states that "the Circle of Administrators of US, Inc. on the nomination of Kawaida Committee of the Hekalu has conferred on OLIVER MASSENGALE-HESHIMU the status of Mwalimu of Kawaida with all rights and honors related to such status."[48] The Shahada was authenticated by signatures from "Ron Karenga: *Maulana, Mwanzishi Mwenyekiti* [Master Teacher, Founder-Chairman], James Doss-Tayari: *Mwenyekiti Mdogo* [Vice-Chairman], Samuel Carr-Damu: *Mtetezi wa Katibu* [Security Chairman], Ramon Tyson Jr.-Imara *Mwenekiti wa chama cha Ukawaida* [Chair of the Kawaida Committee]."[49]

Oliver Heshimu's notes on conduct codes unveil the regulatory background for the Mwalimu distinction: "We can't backslide as Mwalimu . . . [s]et examples for punctuality and seriousness . . . [b]e zealous—do more than average advocate."[50] A shaven, bald head, like that worn by Maulana, was also an aesthetic symbol of the Mwalimu's unique standing. Heshimu understood this, not as a matter of style but as "a reminder of duty as Mwalimu."[51] Additionally, these standards spoke to a collective expectation that, as the cultural revolution moved forward, these teachers would leave Southern California eventually to build other US chapters. Imara wrote in his notes from a Circle of Administrators meeting in July 1967 that "there is a good possibility that Mwalimu Tayari and Mwalimu Heshimu will leave for a two week stay in New York. . . . Their mission will be to organize Black people and possibly set up a branch of US."[52] His notes also cite the decision to send an Mwalimu to San Diego to help establish an US chapter there.[53]

Simba

When Karenga came to lecture at Los Angeles City College, Wesely Kabaila found himself moved by the seriousness and discipline of the young men who had provided security for their leader. As Karenga walked around the campus, the unit of Simba around him regularly changed physical formations in a precise manner: "I had never seen anything like this before where young brothers, maybe 15, 16, 17 years old, acting in such unison. . . . It wasn't something haphazard, there was an actual structure and discipline to how they moved."[54] "At certain times," he noticed, "you would see a diamond-[shaped security formation around Karenga] and at other times you would see a 'U' [shape]."[55]

The discipline that Kabaila saw came from the intense level of Simba training: ideological study, martial arts, and weapons instruction. A 1968 "Simba Wachanga Weekly Schedule" lists that the group had two hours of karate instruction on Mondays and Tuesdays, and first-aid instruction and the introduction of new Simba on Wednesdays. Doctrine class, called W.P.Y. Kawaida, was scheduled for Thursdays, and Fridays were reserved for the seven Sultani, the heads of individual units, to meet. Also, Saturday mornings, from 7:00 until 12:00, the Simba received weapons training at a rifle range, and on Sundays there was physical training in the morning, followed by a Soul Session for the entire organization and the general public.[56]

Teacher-student relationships permeated the organization's paramilitary wing. Heshimu along with Ngao Damu were two main instructors in the initial stages of the Simba. "Damu was an ex-army sergeant," Heshimu said, "so as far as strategy and stuff like that was concerned, that's where Damu came in, but as far as teaching doctrine and discipline, that was my position."[57] Heshimu also had military experience in the air force and was the author of an early Simba weaponry pamphlet. "Damu," he stated, "taught us how to break down an M-1 carbine blindfolded, in the event that you end up in an alley at night or something with a jammed weapon."[58] Heshimu also planned enrichment activities for the Simba, such as horseback riding, "to build the camaraderie, to teach the brothers to work together, play together, live together, eat together."[59] His brother Sigidi added that such activities helped to "relieve some of the stress—when you have an army that's not fighting, you have stress."[60] "So we eliminated that," he explained, "by having activities, something of value."[61]

Heshimu estimated that after serving no more than six months in his position, he was reassigned to head the legal committee, and Jomo Shambulia, who was previously in charge of internal affairs, became the *Amiri*—commander—of the Simba.[62] Jomo had a look and aura about him that invoked a sense of fear and respect from his soldiers. A former Simba, Charles Johnson-Sitawisha, remembered Jomo as "a general in the truest sense."[63] Daryl Tukufu, another Simba who joined in late 1967, has an indelible impression of this Amiri: "Jomo, I thought, was the epitome of discipline in terms of his stature, how he moved and how he conversed."[64] Jomo's shaven head and stylish goatee gave him a "regal" look that commanded respect.[65]

Tukufu, though initially struck by Amiri Jomo and the overall discipline of the Simba, was ambivalent about becoming a full member. He began coming to US advocacy classes in the summer of 1967, after having graduated from high school, yet he did not join until five to six months later. Tukufu, probably like many others, thought long and hard about the lifelong commitment that came with being in US's paramilitary wing. Reflecting on his thoughts at the time, Tukufu said, "I remember someone telling me, 'Well, if you become a Simba, you're going to be in here until death.'"[66] Part of the Simba pledge at the opening of meetings contained the phrase from *The Quotable Karenga:* "We must believe in our cause and be willing to die for it . . . and stop pretending revolution and make it."[67] "I asked about that," Tukufu remembered, "and was told 'you can't leave this organization unless you die' . . . so it took me until December to say 'this is something I'm going to be doing the rest of my life.'"[68]

Just after graduating from high school, Ngoma Ali felt a need to actively participate in a revolutionary movement, as he was affected by a surge in Black nationalist consciousness in Los Angeles after the Watts Revolt. He and his group of friends were "ex–gang bangers and low riders" from South Central Los Angeles who eventually joined the Simba because they "wanted to go out and fight and be trained to do it."[69] Ali remembers two of his friends attending an advocacy class in the summer of 1967. His friends returned from the class "telling us about how [the US Organization] would teach us Swahili and they would train us in how to be urban guerrillas."[70] In addition to the combat and weapons training, Ali discovered that he and his neighborhood comrades, who joined with him, spent much of their time studying and internalizing the doctrine: "I had no time to really do anything other than the necessities; that is, study, go to work, and be down to the organization and try to learn as much as I could about nationalism because I didn't have any idea of what politics or political theory or anything was before then."[71]

Muminina

In US's initial stages, from fall 1965 until spring 1966, a large percentage of its female members were wives of male advocates, including Regina Damu, Ahera Msemaji, Ujima Imara, and Haiba Karenga. As US moved from being a small study group, located at the Aquarian bookstore, to a large local organization with its own headquarters in mid to late 1966, women members increased rapidly. The women's subunit of US, the Muminina, had representatives in the Circle of Administrators. The place of the Muminina, within the prism of US's division of labor and hierarchy, was defined by Karenga's patriarchal formulations on "social organization." The doctrine stipulated that the role of the woman was "to inspire her man, educate the children and participate in social development."[72] This role was defined as "complementary" rather than "equal" to the supreme status of the Black man. Within this framework, the School of Afroamerican Culture became one of the larger outlets for US women's activism, although women did work that was vital to the functioning of virtually all of US's committees.

Women were expected to submit to male leadership, without question, in their respective families, called "houses." A passage from *The Quotable Karenga* became a notorious example of such sexist sentiments: "What makes a woman appealing is femininity and she can't be feminine without being submissive."[73] Some women who joined US in the 1960s felt these ideas were compatible with their own patriarchal sensibilities at the time.[74] Staajabu Heshimu, looking back on her response to the notion of Black female submissiveness, stated that, upon joining in 1967, those ideas "sounded right," since "as a nation of people we needed strong male leaders."[75] Amina Thomas agreed, feeling that US women's acceptance of male dominance was shared by a wide segment of Black women who embraced nationalist patriarchal social prescriptions as a remedy for the "crisis" of the Black family. "During the Black Power movement," she argued, "what Black women did was, in the attempt to elevate the Black man, we kind of stepped back and let them come to the forefront in the US Organization. That's what happened."[76]

There were women in US, however, who did not believe in "stepping back" as a requirement for Black "liberation" or as compliance with African traditions, but saw the doctrine as the instrument of male yearnings for power and control. On several occasions Joann Kicheko was suspended from the group for arguing with the leadership over matters associated with its sexist philosophy and conduct. Reflecting on her response to the passage in *The Quotable Karenga* that equated femininity with submissiveness, Kicheko stated that "[m]y position on that particular quote, when Halisi [one of the editors] put it in there was that it didn't need to be there. I argued it with Halisi. I argued it with Maulana, because I didn't feel that Black women had to submit their will in order for a Black man to be strong."[77]

Kicheko found nothing to justify US's view of hegemonic male dominance in her studies of African culture at the time: "I had read things like Jomo Kenyatta's *Mount Kenya* and the Kikuuyu [Gikuyu] way of setting up social structure, and when I read it I didn't read it as a male-dominated society. I read it as there were things men did and women did, and things that men and women did together, but each had their power and sources."[78] South African songstress Letta Mbulu was very close to US in the late 1960s, regularly attending its forums and teaching African folk songs to women in the dance troupe. Mbulu's own experience with traditional African cultures led her to conclude, as she observed the organization, that US men had a naive or distorted view of gender relations in Africa: "What I saw [in US] was that the men wanted to be in total control—in Africa it isn't like this . . . we always give men their role but women have just as strong power as men have and that's not what I saw happening."[79]

It would not be until the early 1970s—more than five years

after the organization's birth and during the heat of its tumultuous decline as a major force in the Black Power movement—that US began to officially embrace the idea of women's equality. From 1965 to the early 1970s, US remained staunchly patriarchal in its approach to gender roles, lagging behind the Student Nonviolent Coordinating Committee (SNCC), the Black Panther Party, and others already influenced by a second wave of feminist renaissance in American political and social life. Strict gender roles and stratification were tied to the alternative "African-inspired" US way of living, but they also resonated with patriarchal social patterns that were deeply entrenched in American culture.

Identity Transformations

The US member's name change, from English to Kiswahili or another African language, relayed the seriousness of the member's conversion and commitment to "revolutionary" change to the outside world, sometimes to the dismay of family members. It also served as a defining rite in the implicit dimension of the initiation process and intra-group social order. When an advocate was given an African name, the person would either hyphenate his or her English last name with the African one, or have a totally African last name. Men in the organization were usually identified by their African last name. James Doss-Tayari, for instance, was simply known as "Tayari" by his cohort. Married women, on the other hand, were identified by their first name—for example, Ujima Imara, a woman married to Ramon Imara, was simply Ujima. The new name solidified, in most cases, a personal dedication to the leader and organization. Tayari remembered, after having been a part of the organization's rapid growth in 1966, that "Everybody had a name."[80] He told Karenga, "I need a name, Maulana, my name ain't hittin' it."[81] "He [Maulana] said, 'You're Tayari.' I said, 'Tayari?' He said, 'You're ready. That's what Tayari means.'"[82]

Active participation in US gave way to a general expectation that a name change would occur in due course. Unlike Tayari, Kicheko was less enthusiastic about receiving an African name. While meeting with Karenga after a Soul Session in 1966, her comrade Halisi told Karenga, much to her surprise: "Joann needs a new name."[83] "No I don't, I have a name," Kicheko retorted, ". . . the name I had over twenty years."[84] "Maulana said," she further recalled, "'I have a name for you . . . Kicheko,'" and I said, "'OK, what does it mean?' He said, 'One who brings smiles' and I am a person who smiles a lot." After a moment of deliberation, she conceded, "'OK, I'll use the name.' . . . He wrote it out for me and after that I became known as Kicheko."[85] James Mtume also got his name from Karenga, who found one that matched a personal trait or aspiration. At the point of deciding to become a full-fledged advocate, Mtume thought to himself, "If I'm going to be down, I'm going to be down. . . . Everybody's got these Swahili names, so I said [to Karenga], 'I'd like a name' [and] I asked him what is this name based on and he said, 'A quality.'"[86] "He said," Mtume recalled, "'What do you feel?' I said, 'I always felt destined.' He said something like, 'Yeah, I feel that in you.' He said, 'Mtume.' I said, 'Well, what does that mean?' and he said, 'Messenger.'"[87]

There were other cases in which a person's name represented a special praise or recognition of a unique sacrifice for US. After Ngoma Ali's second meeting, he was given the name "Ngoma," meaning drum, because he was a musician.[88] "Then," Ali recalled, "after I got arrested down off Slauson and Broadway where all of these prostitutes were, [Karenga] gave me the name Ali."[89] A character in the film *Battle of Algiers* inspired the name choice of Ali; "this guy had cleaned up all of the prostitution in Algiers."[90] Ngoma worked regularly to urge prostitutes in that area to give up that lifestyle. On one of those occasions, he was harassed and arrested by the Los Angeles police, who frequently targeted local Black nationalist activists. Rank-and-file members, in other cases, gave African names to persons they had recruited to the organization or were generally interested in African culture.

Family members had mixed reactions to the outwardly dramatic transformation accompanying US membership. Amina Thomas remembered her mother's resistance to using her African name, telling her, "'Look Mom, look at Cassius Clay, you guys call him Muhammad Ali now, right?'" The response to such a plea was matter of fact: "'OK, but I named you.'"[91] Charles Massengale-Sigidi also had problems with some relatives outside of his immediate family, who were less than tactful in expressing their disapproval, telling him plainly that "'you better change those damned names.'"[92] In many instances, these criticisms came from a sense that these young men and women had gotten involved in "something strange" and potentially dangerous.[93]

The advocates' natural hairstyles and African-styled clothing could provoke curiosity, if not consternation, from those outside of the group.[94] Black women's hairstyles, long before the 1960s, have been located within a complex web of American and Black discourses on femininity, racial self-esteem, socioeconomic class, and the politics of "movement" identity.[95] Membership in US, layered with its multiple symbols of personal ruptures from mainstream American and African American culture, became a powerful outlet for the period's memorable examples of youth-to-adult coming-of-age narratives. When Bobette Azizi Glover's parents took note of her dedication to the organization, her father spelled out the limits of his tolerance. "He wouldn't allow me to wear an Afro," Glover stated. "I couldn't wear an Afro until I moved out of the house."[96] Glover's experience concurs with historian Robin Kelley's assertion that Black women's Afro hairstyles were "not just a valorization of blackness or Africannness, but a direct rejection of a female beauty that many black men themselves had upheld."[97]

Members had their own labels for women who resisted the mannerisms and aesthetic of the new Black women of US, that is, deference to the men, wearing natural hairstyles and donning African-styled clothing. "Laz" or "lazerene" were derogatory terms used to describe a woman lacking the social refinement expected of a full-fledged female advocate. The disapproval that Glover faced from her father was minimal compared to what she fathomed could develop if she continued to wear her hair in a straightened style while remaining involved with US. Glover initially limited her contact with US because she "didn't have an Afro. . . . [W]omen who 'fried' their hair were called 'lazzes.' . . . That [term] was also supposed to mean that you didn't have the same [US] values."[98] She described her involvement in US as "self-limiting" until "I could make that transition, and so I moved out, then I cut my hair [and] got an Afro."[99]

Young men and adolescents in Simba also confronted the limits of parental tolerance as relatives became aware of the dangers of the group's paramilitary orientation. Ngoma Ali, a young Simba in 1967, found his heretofore successfully camouflaged commitment to US abruptly exposed when his mother demanded that he leave the house, after having "found a rifle" hidden in his room.[100] Charles Sitawisha narrowly escaped Ali's fate. As a high school student, he concealed periodic all-night security assignments by making use of his older brother's room in the adjacent garage without his parents' knowing for certain "whether I was back there or not, so I could stay out all night, and creep-in in the morning and get in bed."[101]

US welcomed participation from entire families. In fact, the problems that Heshimu and Sigidi faced with some relatives about their names contrasted with reactions from their immediate family members: their stepfathers and mothers not only took

African names themselves, Abunuwas and Maisha, but they actually joined the organization.[102] Kamili Mtume's family members responded in kind. Her mother, Sukari, joined US, and her grandfather often frequented Soul Sessions.[103] In other cases, relatives never joined but had gradually accepted the look and style of US advocates as Black nationalism became more popular in 1968 and 1969. James Mtume, whose parents lived in Philadelphia, recalled the changes in his parents' perspectives, from his first visit back home in 1967 to his second one in 1968. Upon his first return, they looked at his shaved head as an oddity and were troubled by all of his "Black talk."[104] When he arrived the following year to attend a Black Power conference in Philadelphia, Mtume was surprised to see that his "mother had an Afro and father was wearing a dashiki."[105]

Polygamy

Members of US were strongly encouraged to begin families with a mate in the organization. The doctrine stated that the house or family was "the smallest example of how the nation works."[106] Amina Thomas remembered how this internal ethic affected peoples' decisions about marriage and raising children: "Quickly all of these people who were young—twenty years old, out of high school or eighteen, going to college—everybody was trying to start these families."[107] Karl Hekima's *Arusi* was just one part of a mass wedding consisting of nine couples in US.[108] Some of these new families, however, became sites of women's resistance to the excesses that accompanied the quest for "male supremacy," especially in cases where men attempted to create polygamous households.[109]

Through the prism of the doctrine, US's experiment with polygamy extended from an attempt to "re-Africanize" Black social relations based on "tradition and reason." It had, by far, though, deeper roots in male desires for power and privilege, rationalized by a concern for Black social politics in the United States. As the myth of Black matriarchy gained popular momentum in the 1960s, men in US justified polygamy as a remedy for an "unstable" Black family and a shortage of marriage-eligible Black men. When Staajabu Heshimu was introduced to the idea of polygamy, it seemed like a practical solution to problems she experienced in her relationships with men prior to joining US. "This notion of a man dealing with other women," Staajabu stated, "wasn't so far-fetched to me because the previous two serious relationships that I had ended that way, men dealing with other women anyway. . . . [S]o the notion that maybe what we should be doing differently was to accept it and try to embrace it and try to make it work in a respectful way, made some sense to me."[110]

Unlike nineteenth-century Mormons, US members did not clash with the state over the polygamy issue, in part because the practice was shrouded in a lack of formality and overt visibility. In most cases, the first wife and the husband were legally married and lived together, and the second wife did not live in the same home with them. Amina Thomas concluded that some polygamous households were outgrowths of relationships formed prior to the US experience: "The organization legitimized relationships that might have been happening anyway."[111] "If you're a high school boy," she continued, "and you've got two girls liking you or something and somebody gets pregnant and you really like the other one—whatever the situation might be, some relationships preceded the organization."[112]

Some men in US were not at all interested in polygamy. Former vice-chair James Tayari was skeptical about its practicality. "I didn't mind having more than one woman," he conceded, "[however], I knew we couldn't manage it. . . . I said, 'Hell, I can't take care of what I got, my wife.'"[113] "I knew," he said, "it was not realistic in America, it would be more disruptive than anything."[114]

Tayari's concern about disruption manifested itself as women's pragmatic reactions to the idea of polygamy rapidly gave way to their confrontations with the organization over a series of injustices related to the family from 1967 to 1969. In one sense, the lack of legal sanction for polygamy offered men the latitude of exploitative relationships with women. In most cases, men related to the second wife in a manner characteristic of mainstream extramarital affairs. Commenting on the real consequences of nationalist experimentations with polygamy, Sandra Flowers, in *African-American Nationalist Literature of the 1960's: Pens of Fire*, observed that "only men benefited from these relationships," as their "unmarried partners" were often left with the task of raising children without the economic benefits that accompanied legal marriage when the relationship soured.[115]

In addition to legal problems, US faced serious factionalism when conflict erupted between the first and second wives. These tensions moved outside the home and into other organizational sectors. Divisions became so incisive that confrontations even emerged in the US dance troupe and in the larger Muminina body, one of which turned violent.[116] More often than not, the second wife was much younger than the first one. First wives felt especially exploited, noting that the men were giving most of their attention and resources to the second wives, who, in their view, bore less familial responsibilities and made fewer sacrifices.

Resistance to polygamy moved beyond discord among women and came to test the organization's patriarchal balance of power. The women of US held a meeting to discuss their grievances with the house system. Because the first-wife/second-wife division manifested itself, the meeting, from the US leadership's point of view, was dangerously disruptive. Some US men were even disciplined for jeopardizing the unity of the organization by practicing polygamy. "Maulana finally met with the brothers," Hekima said, "and said he would have to . . . state a law saying that polygamy is against the law. . . . Now, for those brothers that can do it and keep it together, you don't have any problems, it's not disrupting the organization, go ahead."[117] The leadership's regulatory approach could not stop women from refusing to participate in polygamous households, however. Nearly all of them by 1970 ultimately opted to discontinue their involvement in these relationships.

The explicitness with which the US doctrine opposed women's equality would make the organization a lasting symbol of sixties-era Black nationalist sexism.[118] In practice, however, and perhaps with more subtlety, the predominantly male leadership of many other political organizations that spanned the ideological gamut accepted this division. Alongside persistent nationalist calls for male dominance in the African American family, an important Black feminist trend blossomed that engendered critiques of racial and economic oppression.[119] The women of US did not officially embrace feminism until the early to mid-1970s, as the organization struggled through great turbulence and decline amid mounting government repression and internal factionalism. But earlier conflicts regarding the organization's hierarchy and doctrine of male dominance spawned women's resistance to polygamy during the height of US's prominence in the movement and laid the foundation for latter-day quests for full gender equality in the organization.

Cult of the Personality and Millenarianism

US developed a cult of personality centered around its chairman, the Maulana or Master Teacher, who presided over a program and philosophy focused on changing African American

consciousness. Karenga's status in US reached mystical proportions. The US advocate's reverence for the Maulana was akin to
the leadership paradigm found in African American messianic
religion and in social and political movements where a charismatic figure is given responsibility for the conversion or salvation
of the followers.[120] Some members' testimonies about their nationalist conversions refer specifically to Maulana Karenga as a
personal source for self-understanding and a newfound identity.[121] The "Introduction of Maulana," a text sometimes used as
a guide for an Mwalimu or others in the position of introducing
Karenga before a lecture, captured the protocol and collective
sentiment in US, calling for an explicit acknowledgment of its
leader as the basis for identity transformation. It begins by stating
that "Maulana Ron Karenga possesses a presence and personality
that gives US peace [and] . . . [h]e possesses a message that
makes 'Negroes' forget their misery and lose their madness."[122]
In addition to Karenga's superior knowledge, the "introduction"
cited the US chairman's genuine and deep commitment to his
people: "He possesses a love that opens the eyes of those who before have found life unbearable and unexplainable."[123]

Leaders who systematically fostered systems of deference that
patronized them, were prevalent in the newly formed, or transformed, "revolutionary" states of Africa and Asia during the late
1950s and 1960s—for example, Chairman Mao Zedong, Kim II
Sung, Kwame Nkrumah, and Julius Nyerere. Mystification of
these leaders revolved around "histories" of personal sacrifice,
courage, and narratives of superior intellect. Tanzanian president Julius Nyerere embraced the praise name *Mwalimu,* meaning teacher, and Kwame Nkrumah added the praise name
Osagyeyfo, the redeemer, to his list of titles. Written political
manifestos served to confirm these men's positions as supreme
philosophers for their respective national and international
constituencies.[124] The "Maulana" was a continuation of older

African American messianic leadership styles (Moorish Science Temple, Nation of Islam, and other pre-sixties formations) and post–World War II international trends among left-leaning revolutionary philosopher-leaders. US's self-conscious emulation of this tendency is evidenced in the shaping of Karenga's own early manifesto, *The Quotable Karenga*. James Mtume, who along with Clyde Halisi edited the text, remembers why they chose the color green for the booklet: "We had seen the Red Book because everybody was running around with Mao, then there was the *Black Book* of Nkrumah, so we said, 'The green book: Red, Black, and Green.'"[125]

US doctrine advanced its own millenarian-like Seven Year Calendar that Karenga advanced: 1965, Year of the New Generation (Watts Revolt), *Mwaka wa Uasi*; 1966, Year of Black Power, *Mwaka wa Uwezo Mweusi*; 1967, Year of the Young Lions, *Mwaka wa Simba Wachanga*; 1968, Year of the Black Panther, *Mwaka wa Chui Mweusi*; 1969, Year of Reconstruction; 1970, Year of Splitting Apart, *Mwaka was Dabuka;* and 1971, Year of the Guerrillas, *Mwaka wa Gaidi*.[126] More than likely, this calendar was created in late 1966 or sometime in 1967 in that Karenga's designations for the years 1965 through 1967 were historical interpretations, based on what he deemed most significant to his organization's birth and growth. On the other hand, the descriptions for 1968 through 1971 represent his predictions at the time. The Year of the Black Panther, 1968, anticipated the rise of a mass African American independent political party,[127] followed by a year in which African Americans would look inward and reorient their values, sense of identity, purpose, and direction. In 1970, Karenga foresaw African Americans separating themselves from White society. This act of autonomy and self-determination would culminate the following year in a guerrilla war.

The Seven Year Calendar followed the pattern of long-range social and economic central planning schemes, popularized by

Third World nationalists and socialists during the late 1950s and 1960s, exemplified by Jawaharlal Nehru's five-year plans in India, Gamal Abdel Nasser's Arab socialism in Egypt, and Indonesia's use of Chinese economic planning methods.[128] Karenga discussed each year as a target for particular focus points. In the fall of 1968 he stated that "next year . . . will be the year of reconstruction, or re-evaluation of what took place this year. . . . Nine[teen] Seventy will be the year of separation and 1971 the year of guerrillas, in which defense instead of development will be stressed."[129] This presentation for the general public does not convey the millenarian dimensions of the calendar's meaning to those inside the organization.

For some US advocates, the calendar represented the forthcoming path of a new Black nation.[130] Throughout the late sixties, George Subira, a Saidi, looked forward to 1971, the Year of the Guerrillas, and he forecast "a big fight between US and L.A. police and whoever . . . [whereby] some people would die and some people would go to jail."[131] Subira accepted his potential martyrdom to the extent that it undermined his enjoyment and participation in US's musical and artistic programs and activities: "If that was the real deal of what to expect, I never absolutely got overjoyed about anything because I knew that wasn't what we were together for."[132]

Kwanzaa and Alternative Rituals

US's revolution of alternatives inspired the establishment of a new system of holidays and rituals for members and for the wider Black community. The key annual US holidays during the late 1960s were *Kuanzisha*, September 7, celebrating the founding of US; *Kuzaliwa*, May 19, the celebration of Malcolm X's birthday; *Uhuru* Day, August 11, commemorating the 1965 Watts Revolt;

Dhabihu, in February, recognizing Malcolm X's martyrdom; and *Kwanzaa,* a seven-day occasion based on traditional African harvest festivals, December 26 until January 1.[133] Other rituals were related to life-cycle transitions, such as the *Arusi,* a wedding ceremony; *Akika,* a "nationalization ceremony for children"; and *Maziko,* the funeral ceremony.[134]

Kwanzaa has become, in recent decades, a holiday celebrated by a broad range of African Americans from diverse religious and political persuasions.[135] The overwhelming majority of those who embrace the holiday have little or no knowledge of its organizational roots. In *Kwanzaa: A Celebration of Family, Community and Culture, Commemorative Edition,* whose 1998 publication corresponded with the United States Postal Service's issuance of the Kwanzaa stamp, Karenga stated that "*Kwanzaa* was not created to give people an alternative to their own religion or religious holiday . . . [a]nd it is not an alternative to people's religion or faith but a common ground of African culture."[136] Karenga's statement and other more recent US positions on Kwanzaa address the widespread religious and political diversity among the millions of Kwanzaa celebrants worldwide. During the era of Black Power, however, the holiday was closely tied to US's own cultural nationalist ideology and its political allies throughout the United States.

When US established Kwanzaa in 1966, the holiday coexisted with several newly developed practices that fit into the organization's mandate to initiate a cultural revolution of alternatives. At that juncture, the organization's ideas about the holiday and its audience were far more exclusive than what came to be in recent years. Christianity was seen by US, at the time, as the handmaiden of a pathological Negro identity and an obstacle to a new reconstructed Black nationalist consciousness: "Christianity is a white religion," Karenga stated. "It has a white god and any negro who believes in it is a sick negro. . . . How can you pray to a white man?

If you believe in him, no wonder you catch so much hell."[137] Christmas was, thus, seen as an extension of a pathos necessitating criticism and, more importantly, the construction of a culturally and psychologically healthier alternative.[138] Karenga remarked at a speech given at Howard University in 1968: "If we ask people not to celebrate Christmas then we must be prepared to give them an alternative . . . [s]o we did some research and found a Zulu custom [the Zulu harvest festival, *Umkosi*] where people came together to celebrate for about a week around the first of the year."[139]

The dates chosen for Kwanzaa might also have been influenced by the example offered by the Nation of Islam's pre-1970 practice of celebrating Ramadan in December, a departure from the Islamic calendar for the purpose of accompanying Christmas holiday celebrations.[140] The term Kwanzaa and its spelling was a fusion of Kiswahili language and US's own organizational history. While the word "Kwanza" literally means "first" in Kiswahili, an extra letter "a" was added to the name of the holiday as a result of the circumstances surrounding US's first celebration in 1966. Karenga recounted that "at the very beginning of US, seven children in the organization wanted to put on a program in which each of them represented and explained a letter of *Kwanzaa.*" "Since *Kwanza* (first) has only six letters," he went on to explain, "we added an extra 'a' to make it seven, thus creating *Kwanzaa.*"[141] The number seven has further significance for the holiday in that each day was set up to give tribute to one of the principles of the Nguzo Saba: (1) *Umoja* (unity), (2) *Kujichagulia* (self-determination), (3) *Ujima* (collective work and responsibility), (4) *Ujamaa* (cooperative economics), (5) *Nia* (purpose), (6) *Kuumba* (creativity), and (7) *Imani* (faith).

Karl Hekima has vivid memories of the very first Kwanzaa in 1966, which took place in an US supporter's apartment near Washington Street and Tenth Avenue in Los Angeles, crowded with about fifty people.[142] Reflecting on the night of the big feast, the *Karamu*, which took place at the close of the week-long celebration, Hekima recounted "we did the whole traditional thing —you bring your food, you brought your pillows and stuff to sit on the floor, you didn't eat with utensils, you used your hands."[143] The festive and communal spirit of the first Kwanzaa left an indelible impression on him: "We did African dances. We told African stories. . . . It was very festive. . . . I've never been to a Karamu greater than that."[144] Elizabeth Softky's father, W. D. Campbell, brought her along with him to an early Kwanzaa celebration in the late sixties. Looking back on her experience as a nine-year-old, she remembers being moved by the holiday's festive and communal spirit: "During one celebration I saw for myself what made Ron Karenga special."[145] "I was used to seeing Karenga lecturing from a podium, looking so stern in his black clothes, dark-rimmed glasses, beard and goatee," she continued, "but now he was on the dance floor, enjoying himself with everyone else. I was surprised to see someone so serious—a big shot—down with the folks, relaxed and having a good time."[146]

Letta Mbulu's encounter with an early Kwanzaa celebration in 1966 or 1967 was seen through the lens of her South African upbringing. For her, this African American–invented tradition provided a connectedness with the aesthetic of her homeland and African communal traditions. "There were fruits, baskets and baskets of fruits all over the place and candles in the national colors of the African people," she stated, describing the affair. "It was so beautiful what they had done, I think they had thrown some white sand around, it looked like a beach area—it was so beautiful."[147] Kwanzaa also fostered a spiritual link with African Americans and their unique struggle for cultural renewal and identity. Mbulu remembers a point during the Karamu where the events induced childhood memories of her grandmother's teachings about enslavement of African Americans:

It was a very emotional moment for me. . . . My grandmother told me about my people. So when I came to the United States I knew what went down. I knew about slavery. Just before she died she used to talk about—because she was a teacher—African people who were taken away from the land and brought here [to the United States]. So when I came here I was already geared up. So when I saw all of these wonderful things happening, that's why the whole [US] organization became so important to me. My grandmother lived. I saw my grandmother's words. I heard them for the second time like the affirmation that this is what my grandmother was talking about.[148]

She surmised that "these are the African people that she was talking about—look at them really holding on to who they are—for me it was very, very emotional."[149]

Kwanzaa, during US's sixties years, was part of a matrix of rituals, holidays, and social praxis that effectively comprised a nationalist counterculture capable of attracting a diverse body of Black Americans to the organization: first-generation students from working-class families, former gang members, older activists, and working-class area residents. Like Marcus Garvey's UNIA, US offered its advocates an alternative system of rewards, hierarchy, and special positions countering the outer world's restrictions. The Hekalu became a space in which a diverse group of African Americans had access to African languages, international politics, and an ideology that explained "Blackness" in concrete terms. As Master Teacher, Maulana Karenga succeeded in bringing a university-style classroom to an urban cultural center. Karenga captured the hearts and minds of his followers as much through the mystification of his knowledge as through his oratorical ability.

While US posed radical challenges to the politics of racial dominance, it also advanced retrograde forms of authoritarianism and sexism. E. Frances White points out this duality in an article, "Africa on My Mind: Gender, Counter Discourse and African-American Nationalism." White contends that Black nationalist and Afrocentric ideologies "can be radical and progressive in relation to white racism and conservative and repressive in relation to the internal organization of the black community."[150] This duality or contradiction would find itself at the center of conflicts and tensions within US and its political alliances.

To some outside observers, US's counterculture may have looked cultish at best. From the vantage point of US members, however, their lifestyle was a blueprint for African American sociocultural life in light of a coming cultural revolution. As one former advocate stated, "I never remember thinking we were in a cult. I believed we were part of a movement, we were nationalists, [and that] we had the right view with respect to what Black people needed to be doing and thinking."[151]

4. The Politics of Culture

The US Organization and the Quest for Black Unity

The lifestyle of the US advocate was not thoroughly consumed by internal organizational dynamics. The parochial new world inside the Hekalu reinforced a political mandate to function as organizers of organizations in the thrust toward cultural revolution. Specifically, US sought to "programmatically influence" political and cultural projects within the Black community in a nationalist direction—leading interorganizational caucuses (e.g., Temporary Alliance of Local Organizations and Black Congress); working for self-determination, regional autonomy, and Black representation in electoral politics; agitating against United States military aggression in Vietnam; and organizing a series of local and national Black Power conferences to spread Black nationalism and build united fronts.

Recent scholarship on the Black Power era has largely overlooked or misunderstood US's political legacy.[1] The group's approach to organizing, which resisted mass recruitment into its ranks, may have abetted this trend. US leaders saw no need for a large membership. Their goal was to ideologically influence other organizations with its united-front approach, and thus direct the course of the coming "cultural revolution." This strategy took place in concert with the organization's direct involvement in urban uprisings, school walkouts, student strikes, and underground violent resistance. Also, a keen eye cannot escape noting that US's activism brings additional focus to the linkages between collective rituals and resistance in the historical understanding of oppositional movements. The bulk of the public holidays initiated by US were tied to the struggle for local Black community control and Black nationalist alliances, spanning across the country.

The Politics of the Holidays

Kwanzaa remains the most well known US creation with origins relating to a flourishing African American autonomist and anti-commercial sentiment in the 1960s. Other holidays instituted by the organization were more closely tied to local manifestations of Black Power politics. On February 22, 1966, US convened its first public event, a memorial observance for Malcolm X, who had been assassinated the previous February. US called the event a *Dhabihu* (sacrifice) service and declared the day a special holiday to pay homage to Malcolm X's sacrifice of his life for the cause of Black liberation.[2] Karenga was featured as the keynote speaker at the service, which was attended by about two hundred people.[3] The Dhabihu gave Karenga a platform to introduce the organization's political views to a larger audience, especially the basis for what would become US's opposition to the Vietnam War.

The anti-imperialist service included a candle-lighting ritual, an activity also associated with the first Kwanzaa celebration that would occur some ten months later. An account of the ceremony noted that "two candles burned at the foot of the lectern." It continues to note that "they were blown out and re-lit, but not before onlookers were informed that one burned for Malcolm X and the other for Patrice Lumumba."[4] US and other local nationalists were openly defying the Nation of Islam (NOI) by organizing this public event since the Dhabihu took place at a time when the NOI vehemently argued that Malcolm X was a fallen traitor. Just over a year after US introduced the first Dhabihu, its second annual celebration of Malcolm X's birthday, called *Kuzaliwa* (birthday), stood at the center of student protest in Los Angeles.

By early 1967, US had achieved significant momentum after having conducted its first Kwanzaa celebration. Those who attended the week-long festivities, culminating in the Karamu (feast) held on December 31, remember them as intimate yet powerfully inspiring gatherings. At the beginning of spring 1967, US members had reason to rest faithfully assured that diligent activism would bring forth a mass acceptance of their new Black culture. This is evidenced in US's 1967 call for African Americans not to go to work or school on May 19 or the closest weekday to it in observance of the new Black national holiday Kuzaliwa, Malcolm X's birthday. The response in Los Angeles was overwhelming and partly responsible for US's growing appeal to African American youth in Los Angeles.

The *Los Angeles Sentinel* reported that "a wave of absenteeism hit Los Angeles in response to a call from Ron Karenga, of US, to make the birthday of the late Malcolm X a national Negro holiday."[5] One high school faced a walkout by an estimated 1,500 students.[6] After leaving school, students from all over Los Angeles assembled at a park, for what the *Sentinel* described as "a peaceful day of picnicking."[7] Kamili Mtume was a senior at Washington High School during the spring of 1967. Her first contact with US, prior to joining the organization later on that year, came as a result of her actively working to garner support for US's call for a student and worker strike in honor of Malcolm X's birthday. "I was active in getting and encouraging other kids to not come to school that day or walk out that day," she recalled, "so much so, that the principal of the school came to me to try to get the kids to come back—of course I wasn't interested in doing that."[8]

In the spring of 1967, Charles Johnson-Sitawisha was an eighth grader at Horace Mann Junior High School. Following the example of his older brother, who had been attending US community forums and lectures, Sitawisha decided not to attend school on May 19. Reflecting on what transpired when he returned on the following school day, he stated that "the teacher asked me for an absence slip. I told her I didn't have one and she asked why." "I said," he continued, "'because it was a holiday yesterday,' and the whole class laughed at me." He remembered remarking to his classmates, "'If it's funny to you, that's fine, but I choose to do that as a Black man,' and I told the teacher if she wanted to mark me truant, that's fine, but I stand by that."[9] The following year Sitawisha joined the Simba Wachanga, the young male wing of the US Organization.[10]

The challenge that the mass walkouts presented to public school administrations in the Los Angeles area did not stop with the Malcolm X holiday. Other community demands for increased responsiveness from the public schools to local African American concerns persisted throughout 1967. In August of that year, Kenneth Hahn, the Los Angeles County supervisor, warned in an internal memo that "[m]ilitant forces seem intent on trying to disrupt every university, college and high school campus."[11] Urging a countywide crackdown, he declared, "We cannot have anarchy existing in California."[12] That fall, a coalition of concerned parents and community groups organized protests demanding the ouster of Robert Dehamy, the principal of Manual Arts High School. Among the various grievances was the charge that he routinely expelled or suspended students without consulting or adequately advising parents.[13] An article on a particular demonstration at Manual Arts is accompanied by a photo of Karenga, who is present at the rally, alongside a woman toting a placard that stated, "We are sick of Our children Being Mistreated!!"[14] The demonstrations went on for months. The cover of the November 17, 1967, issue of the US Organization's newspaper, *Harambee,* displays a photograph of a police officer chokeholding a Black female. The police were in the process of breaking up a protest at the school. The front-page headline of the newspaper read, "Another View of Manual."[15]

The heyday of US's effectiveness from mid-1966 until early 1969 reflects the strength of the renascent Black nationalist movement of those years. The excitement generated by the movement's growth gave rise to a sense of cooperation and shared purpose among Black Power organizations. Uhuru Day, another holiday created and celebrated by US, became a building block for the organization's alliances and relationships with other activists during the group's early years. The holiday, first celebrated on August 11, 1966, commemorated the Watts uprising.[16] Since US came into existence, in part, as a result of the rise in the popularity of Black nationalism in Los Angeles following the Watts Revolt, Uhuru Day had a special significance for US advocates and community activists.

The 1967 Uhuru Day rally revealed the growing political consensus and commitment to alliance-building among Black nationalist organizations. H. Rap Brown, national chairman of the Student Nonviolent Coordinating Committee (SNCC), and Huey Newton, Minister of Defense of the Black Panther Party for Self-Defense, joined Karenga as keynote speakers for the event. Newspaper reports indicated that between 3,000 and 5,000 people attended the event, which was held outside of the US headquarters.[17] US, SNCC, and the Black Panther Party for Self-Defense were united in support of the Uhuru Day theme, advocacy of the right to self-defense, and by Malcolm X's vision of a Black united front based on the principle of Black unity. From a historical perspective, Newton's presence at the rally was particularly significant given that the US Organization and the Black Panther Party would embark on a violent feud within two years. In 1967, however, the rally exemplified an early tendency for both organizations to work together on projects that reflected a mutual commitment to fulfilling Malcolm X's vision.

Rap Brown's appearance at Uhuru Day, while he was the focus of national controversy over the use of violence within the Black movement, is even more of a testimony to a sense of unity among Black nationalists at that time. A couple of weeks before the rally, both federal and Maryland state authorities had issued warrants for his arrest in connection with a speech he delivered in Cambridge, Maryland, which was followed by an outbreak of violence.[18] Just days following his appearance at the rally in Los Angeles, Brown was arrested by federal authorities in Washington, D.C.[19]

Local Umbrella Organizations: Electoral Politics, Freedom City, and the Temporary Alliance of Local Organizations

As young militants joined the US Organization and as radical Black Power groups aligned themselves around the revolutionary legacy of Malcolm X, Karenga and his associates paid close attention to their philosophy of organizing. US's distinctive organizational structure and new Black culture were complemented by extensive usage of Malcolm X's united-front approach to politics as exhibited in his Organization of Afro-American Unity. Malcolm X modeled the framework for this coalition organization after the pan-African structure for governments, the Organization of African Unity.[20] US's early activism underscores a quest to actualize this united-front ideal, urging the advocates to engage and transform existing sites and venues that affect public discourse—schools, conferences, and community rallies. It also functioned as a mandate to continue providing new spaces for African Americans to discover their "Blackness." The task of changing African American minds and culture carried with it a political struggle for control of the instruments and institutions that impact Black consciousness.

US members had long expressed a great deal of reverence for SNCC and its leaders for their efforts to build independent African American political organizations in the South. Black nationalists in the North and West were struck by the bold efforts of the Lowndes County Freedom Organization, a SNCC-organized political group that had been challenging White political control in the heart of the Alabama Black Belt since 1965. In 1966, Clifford Vaughs, director of the Los Angeles chapter of SNCC, attempted to build a Black political organization in Watts to lead a campaign to secede the area from Los Angeles and establish an independent municipality called "Freedom City."[21] Karenga served as the movement's "public relations director."[22] Watts had, in fact, been an independent municipality, prior to 1926, when, as Raphael Sonenshein has noted, discriminatory housing practices elsewhere in the area inspired thousands of African Americans to move to Watts. As a result, the municipality "was quickly incorporated into Los Angeles . . . thereby preventing a Black-dominated local government."[23]

The Freedom City movement received a significant amount of national attention as the media focused on Watts during the first anniversary of the 1965 rebellion. Several feature articles on Watts in national news magazines portrayed Black nationalism as the ominous specter of the gloom yet to come.[24] Among the Los Angeles Black nationalist activists and groups discussed in these articles, US was seen as especially dangerous. The cover of the July 15, 1966, issue of *Life* magazine shows Ngao Damu, US's first head of security, drilling four young boys, lined up in single file, with serious and stern looks on their faces. In the *Saturday Evening Post,* a similar photograph appeared, with the following description: "A member of US, an extremist group, drills two Negro boys."[25]

Journalists, inspired by an alarmist White backlash against Black Power, interpreted US's role in the Freedom City movement as further evidence of the rising Black nationalist peril.[26] While Karenga wrote press releases for the initiative, US members did door-to-door canvassing in the election precincts. This political experience proved valuable later when Karenga and the US Organization advised younger organizations that were beginning voter registration and electoral work. Ultimately the advocates of Freedom City failed to acquire the 217,543 signatures on a petition necessary for initiation of the secession process. Historian Clayborne Carson regarded this result as indicative of the failure of SNCC's northern activists to transform their Black Power rhetoric into "actual political power."[27] For US, however, the Freedom City movement established what would be the hallmark of the organization's Black Power legacy—its constant effort to participate in, form, or lead African American umbrella organizations modeled on Malcolm X's united-front ideal. Throughout the late 1960s US would go on to serve in various cooperative and leadership capacities with the Black Congress, the planning committees of the 1967 and 1968 Black Power conferences, the Republic of New Afrika, and the Committee for a Unified Newark (which eventually helped spawn the election of the city's first Black mayor in 1970).

Beyond the effort to form an independent Black-governed municipality in Watts, US members worked to bring about the 1966 election of Yvonne Braithwaite Burke to the California State Assembly. Ken Msemaji, the head of community relations for US, coordinated the group's participation in neighborhood canvassing, literature distribution, and other precinct work. Likewise, US members helped to bring about state assemblyman Mervyn Dymally's 1967 election to the California state senate. US regarded electoral politics as critical terrain in the struggle for Black self-determination and community control. Msemaji recalled that when talking to potential voters at the time, he was "trying to emphasize why it's important to get Black people elected to office and not be represented by Whites."[28]

During the summer of 1966, US joined another coalition called the Temporary Alliance of Local Organizations (TALO). It was described as "a loose coalition of individuals in the Black organizations of Los Angeles: CORE, Central LA NAACP, SLANT [Self Leadership for All Nationalities Today], US, the United Civil Rights Committee."[29] Among TALO's major achievements was the partial funding of the Community Alert Patrol, a group formed to monitor police activities in South Central Los Angeles. US pulled out of TALO that fall, because Karenga felt "TALO didn't have a program beyond the Community Alert Patrol." He also criticized the alliance for its ineffective decision-making procedures.[30]

As the organization became increasingly steeped in Karenga's own unique ideology, US sought coalition arrangements in which his ideas could dominate. This juncture presaged the explosive tension between the organization's political aspirations and self-conception. As a self-declared representative of the progressive Black future, the US Organization frequently clashed with other constituent member groups in several umbrella formations, including the Black Congress, tragically leading to the violence at the UCLA campus, and then a confrontation at the 1970 Congress of African People that only narrowly escaped a similar decline into wanton sectarian strife.

The Black Congress and Vietnam

In the fall of 1967, US joined forces with the Black Congress, a newly formed alliance of African American organizations, businesses, and associations. Black Congress chairman Walt Bremond, an experienced activist and student of Saul Alinsky's protest strategies, had previously led a Los Angeles organization, called the Social Action Training Center, which "taught two alternatives to violence—community organization and community development."[31] The Black Congress had over twenty participating groups, including the Afro-American Association, Afro-American Cultural Association, Black Anti-Draft, Black Panther Party, Black Resistance Against Wars for Oppression, Black Student Unions of California State University at Los Angeles, Compton City College, Los Angeles City College, Black Unitarians for Radical Reform, Black Youth Conference, Citizens for Creative Welfare, CORE, Freedom Draft Movement, Immanuel Church, L.A. County Welfare Rights, NAACP, Operation Bootstrap, Organization of African Studies, Parent Action Council, Police Malpractice Complaint Center, SLANT, Social Action Training Center, Underground Musicians Association, United Parents Council, US, and Watt's Happening Coffee House.[32]

The Black Congress embraced the US doctrine of "operational unity" as a guide for its effort to promote cooperative activism and brought together Black organizations of diverse ideological perspectives under one umbrella. In fact, most of the participating organizations moved their headquarters to the Black Congress building or had auxiliary offices there. The programs or services offered by an individual organization functioned within the framework of the congress's larger united-front agenda.[33] Using a model similar to that of the United Nations, representatives from member groups took part in specific subdivisions in the congress called councils, such as the finance council, education council, or security council. Those involved with the housing council, for instance, were charged with the task of "aggressively and ruthlessly mov[ing] against all 'slumlords' with legal, political boycotts, 'rent strikes' and any other means necessary."[34]

That structure inspired supplementary and interorganizational support for initiatives previously seen as the domain of a
specific group or individual, making the congress an extraordinary force in the balance of political power in Los Angeles. For
example, Margaret Wright, a persistent advocate for Black community control in the school system and head of the United
Parents Council and the Black Educators, received additional
support for her efforts from the attorneys and legal rights advocates of the legal council. Mwalimu Oliver Heshimu, who represented US on the legal council, reported that during one meeting, he and others discussed launching retaliatory legal measures
should the Board of Education "fail to approve teaching of Black
History as [United Parents Council and] Black educators have
demanded."[35]

US identified completely with this alliance, moving its Hekalu
to the Black Congress building and transforming its own newspaper *Harambee* into the organ of the congress. Whereas Karenga
had been the paper's editor in 1966, by the fall of 1967 *Harambee*'s leadership and content had changed. John Floyd of the
L.A.–based Black Panther Political Party (entirely different and
unaffiliated with the Panthers in Northern California) became
the editor, and Elaine Brown, later a prominent leader in the
Oakland Black Panther Party, served as one of the paper's report-
ers. Under Floyd's editorship, *Harambee* described the paper's
mission in the same terms as the US organization's definition:
"HARAMBEE, a Swahili word that means, 'let's pull together,' is a
black community newspaper published by the Los Angeles Black
Congress."[36]

In addition to collective local projects in community development, the congress fostered a policy consensus on key national and international issues such as alliances with people of
color and opposition to the Vietnam War. On October 22, 1967,
US was among a group of organizations in the Black Congress

that signed the "Treaty of Peace and Harmony, and Mutual Assistance" with the Spanish-American Federal Alliance of Free City States, a consortium of Chicano activists and organizations seeking political autonomy in the Southwest. Reies Tijerina, a leader in the alliance, also attended the treaty signing in Albuquerque.[37]

The US Organization's involvement in the "Treaty of Peace and Harmony, and Mutual Assistance" also underscored its ideological concurrence with ideas popularized by the Bandung conference—that nations of color should form an international political bloc, or Third Force (neither capitalist nor communist). This perspective figured prominently in the US Organization's positions on domestic and international issues and extended to the Black Congress's opposition to the Vietnam War. The antiwar consensus brought numerous organizations in accord with the congress's united-front agenda. A 1967 article in *Harambee* described an antiwar rally at which Karenga shared the rostrum with representatives of the Black Panthers, CORE, and the Black Student Union Alliance.[38]

Using the Seven Principles as an explanatory framework, a 1967 "US Statement on the Viet Nam War" relates its opposition to the war with the assertion that African Americans and Asians share a common quest for self-determination. Indeed, some members of the US Organization's Kawaida faith were conscientious objectors to the war in Vietnam:

> As members of the Kawaida faith we oppose the war because it violates two basic principles upon which our faith is based. (1) It violates the sixth principle KUUMBA which is creativity. As members of the Kawaida faith we are pledged to be creative rather than destructive. We consider creative that which promotes human life and development; and we consider destructive that which is negative to human life and development.

(2) The Viet Nam war also violates our second principle KUJI-CHAGULIA which is self-determination for it is a war that denies people of color of Asia their right to choose their own form of government and to promote human life and development in the way they see is beneficial to them and to their own needs and desires. We, ourselves, are struggling for the right of self-determination on every level. We would be against ourselves if we fought to deny others of the same right.[39]

The antiwar position of the US Organization and the Black Congress inspired a group of Black marines to form an affiliate division of US, located in Vietnam. In late 1967, some Black marines temporarily stationed at the aviation squadron at El Toro, California, attended the US and Black Congress meetings during their off-duty time.[40] Marine Joseph Harris-Askari, a relative of US members Oliver Massengale-Heshimu and Charles Massengale-Sigidi, introduced the US doctrine to members of his own squadron and neighboring ones. Before leaving California for Da Nang, Vietnam, they formed an auxiliary unit of the Simba, known as the Fulani tribe.[41]

A primarily Black and Latino temporary barracks in Chu Lai, Vietnam, doubled as a Hekalu (temple), modeled after the US headquarters in the Black Congress building. Fulani tribe members conducted Soul Sessions there, which typically featured lectures and discussions led by Sultani (chief) Askari or the second-in-command of the tribe, Makamu (assistant chief) Randolph Abunuwas-Stripling.[42] US was among a series of radical organizations, along with the Mau Mau and the Black Panther Party, that had sympathizers or corollary chapters among Black soldiers and marines stationed in Vietnam. By 1970, as Wallace Terry, the Black military journalist and author of *Bloods: An Oral History of the Vietnam War by Black Veterans*, noted, "Ron Karenga's Swahili-speaking *US* movement for black culture, pride and self-defense, has spread to at least four Marine bases in the I Corps."[43] Black marines' use of African names, special handshake greetings, hairstyles, and other outward expressions of solidarity with elements in the Black Power movement became a major concern to military authorities. Gary Solis, in *Marines and Military Law in Vietnam: Trial by Fire*, noted that by 1969 "Many white NCOS and officers viewed Afros, dapping, and passing power [various types of handshakes] as threats to authority and challenges to leadership."[44] In a recording of interviews with African American marines and soldiers, *Guess Who's Coming Home: Black Fighting Men Recorded Live in Vietnam*, Wallace Terry described the Hekalu in Chu Lai as a place where "Black marines and soldiers meet . . . a barracks where they are free to talk about the man. No officers are present, no whites are present, only brothers."[45]

The Fulani tribe's association with the US Organization bolstered Black resistance to racism in the Marine Corps. US's cultural nationalism, alongside other radical ideologies of the late 1960s, may have even influenced the choices of some African American marines to rebel. During the late 1960s and early 1970s—the height of the Black Power movement and its subsequent impact on Black servicemen—the marines, as other armed forces, were confronted with an abnormal amount of fraggings, that is, attacks against officers by lower-ranking service men. A significant number of these incidents were a product of racial tensions in the military.[46] In his book, Solis noted that an internal marine report showed that "between April and June 1969 there was an average of one 'large scale riot,' per month," and a number of judge-advocate trials relating to the occurrence of "racially motivated fraggings, armed confrontations and even intramural small-arms firefights."[47] Thomas Nrefu-Belton, a marine who assisted in establishing the Fulani tribe, felt that activism in the US Organization forced him to question the morality of the war and White military authority.[48]

Armed Struggle and Underground Resistance

While US and the Black Congress contributed to the consolida-
tion of widespread African American opposition to the Vietnam
War, challenges to the discipline of interorganizational unity
emerged while the alliance peaked in its effectiveness. The early
months of 1968 marked a high point both in the Black Congress's public profile and in US's ability to position itself as the
leading organization within that united front. On February 18,
1968, an estimated five thousand people attended a Black Congress–sponsored rally at the Los Angeles Sports Arena to support
the incarcerated Minister of Defense of the Black Panther Party,
Huey Newton, who had been arrested and charged with murdering a police officer. The range of speakers at the rally—Maulana Karenga, Kwame Ture (Stokely Carmichael), the Reverend
Thomas Kilgore, H. Rap Brown, Bobby Seale, and Reies Tijerina
—revealed a continued sense of unity, albeit fragile, that Newton's case had generated among nationalists and other radicals
around the issue of self-defense.[49] On one hand, the rally was a
practical expression of Karenga's vision of operational unity, yet
it also housed US/Black Panther Party in-fighting as differences
over security matters led each group to view the other with distrust and suspicion.[50]

Throughout the latter half of 1968, rivalries and internal dissension consumed the Black Congress, US, and the Panthers.
The rift between the congress's two most powerful member organizations disrupted any sense of "operational unity." From
early 1968 through 1970, US and the Black Panther Party com-
peted for dominance in the public sphere—from community
meetings and street corners to college campuses. The rivalry had
grave explosive potential from its inception, given both organizations' penchant for violent resistance.

Clayborne Carson, in *In Struggle: SNCC and the Black Awakening
of the 1960s*, asserted that "[t]he major line of cleavage within the

black nationalist militant community was between cultural nationalists, who urged blacks to unite around various conceptions
of a black cultural ideal, and self-defined political revolutionaries who were more likely than cultural nationalists to advocate
armed struggle to achieve political or economic goals."[51] This
type of distinction, based on perceived differences in how these
two tendencies relate to violent resistance, is also presented in
Alphonso Pinkney's *Red, Black and Green: Black Nationalism in the
United States*. Pinkney argued that "[u]nlike the revolutionary nationalists, the cultural nationalists do not advocate at the present
time the use of revolutionary violence or even the stockpiling of
arms."[52] US's experience with armed struggle invariably challenges a historical view invested in the bifurcation of the two organizations' respective approaches to violent resistance.

Resisting the 1960s trend among militant radicals of embracing Che Guevara's guerrilla warfare theories as a model for revolution in the United States, Karenga was skeptical of the idea
that a small insurgency could instigate a revolution. He was convinced, however, that successful and protracted armed struggle
necessitated a preexisting, broad-based African American consensus and will to make great sacrifices in support of the revolution. "What we should concentrate on is not the weapons but
the people," Karenga stated. "How can we win the people? It is
not a question of how can we kill the enemy, for the people
must decide that that is necessary themselves, or the vanguard
will vanish and the revolutionary party which has placed itself
in a front position will fall flat on its face and history will hide all
of them."[53]

The US chairman, amid mounting tensions at the Los Angeles
"Free Huey" rally, publicly compared his organization's inclina-
tion toward underground violence and guerrilla warfare with
the Black Panther Party's above-ground armed monitoring of
the police and vocal threats of violent retaliation against the
state. Karenga felt that elements in the movement had become

accustomed to substituting grandiose violent rhetoric for military training and readiness. The contrast was somewhat misleading, as the Black Panther Party had an active underground wing as well. The language of military preparedness, nonetheless, persisted in Karenga's pronouncements and writings in the late sixties.[54] "You never hear," Karenga declared at the 1968 Los Angeles "Free Huey" rally, "us [members of the US Organization] say, 'We're going to get this man and blah-blah-blah.' . . . We always say, 'Yeah, we're against violence,' but after sundown anything might happen."[55]

Trouble after dusk came from an inner circle of members from the ranks of the Saidi and the Simba who took part in regular underground activities: bank robberies, raids of armories, the development of explosive materials and devices, and so on. Those involved in the US underground were motivated by a drive to raise funds for the organization and prepare for a coming apocalyptic Black confrontation with the government, led by US. Karenga's Seven Year Calendar envisaged 1971 (the final year) as wrought with massive Black uprisings and, thus, completing a cycle of African American preparation for a storm of unforeseen mayhem.

Former Simba Ngoma Ali, discussing some of the tactics used by the underground, insisted that the cadre chose to conduct "hit and run" operations and did not focus on defending territory or protecting buildings against police raids.[56] "You create havoc, you run maneuvers," Ali explained. "You do things that incite the masses that put harm on the enemy."[57] "In all respects," he continued, "you don't get caught. That's why you had to train because sometimes you may have to run a long ways or you may have to do sacrifices [and remain in] strange positions in strange places for long periods of time."[58]

The circumstances in which US members did "get caught" created opportunities for outsiders to catch a glimpse of the scope and range of their clandestine operations. Throughout the late sixties and early seventies, members of the Simba, Saidi, and even high-level leadership circles in US were arrested and, in some instances, served prison sentences for armed robberies of banks, stores, hotels, and other establishments.[59] A police raid of the US headquarters in early 1970 uncovered a stockpile of weapons, ammunition, and pipe bombs.[60] An FBI memo alerted the director and other agents that "[t]he 'US' organization has approximately 20 militant, hardcore members, a number of whom have been arrested for possession of incendiary devices, attempted arson, armed robbery and burglary."[61] In 1968 and 1969, local police and the FBI intensified their counterintelligence measures to disrupt US and effectively posed an obstacle to the continuation of US's underground activities. Most harmful, however, to the proactive functioning of the underground and US's day-to-day programs was the brewing violent feud with the Black Panther Party, which, at the bureau's behest, threatened to shatter any prospect of Black operational unity in Southern California.

Operational Unity and the US/Panther Conflict

In April 1968, the Black Congress organized several events immediately after the assassination of Martin Luther King. Violent revolts occurred in several American cities in response to King's death, but the Black Congress succeeded in directing the collective rage felt in the Los Angeles African American community away from retaliatory violence and toward a plan for organized, antiracist community action—a plan based on US's concept of operational unity. Although the Black Congress as a whole had taken the position against violent retaliation, some media had incorrectly attributed this solely to the US Organization. An extensive profile on Karenga that appeared on the front page of the *Wall Street Journal* in July 1968, "Black Enigma: A West Coast Militant Talks Tough but Helps Avert Trouble,"[62] claimed that "Karenga's prestige also rose after his open participation in an 'operational unity steering committee,' formed by the Black Congress only hours after King's death." "The committee's main purpose," it continued, "was to prevent Negro rioting here."[63]

The article raised two other specific issues that would subsequently fuel charges that the US Organization was either committed to diverting mass-radical sentiment or was a direct operative of the United States government. The first allegation cited was that Karenga had "met clandestinely with Los Angeles Police Chief Thomas Reddin after Mr. King was killed."[64] This assertion supported the article's thesis that Karenga was a master manipulator who used the language and imagery of militancy to mask his own personal accommodation with traditional White-dominated centers of political power. Without revealing its sources, it contended that "[c]ivil rights observers agree that Karenga is typical of many militants who talk of looting and burning but actually are eager to gather influence for quiet bargaining with the predominately White power structure."[65]

Karenga never denied meeting with the police chief. He did, however, remind his critics that the meeting was *not* clandestine and that it occurred with the presence of other members of the Black Congress.[66] When asked about this matter in an interview, Karenga said that "[w]hen we met with Reddin we were meeting as the Black Congress, as a collective group with Walt Bremond, with Reverend Edwards and other people who were on that committee."[67] He also rejected the taboo against meeting with elements of the "white power structure," adding that the objective of the meeting was to thwart police misconduct. "That is necessary at times," he argued, "for us to meet with different factions in society and try to ease the oppression and repression that's going to constantly occur."[68] As far as the result of the meeting was concerned, he concluded that "we were able to change the amount of police in the community for a while."[69]

More difficult for Karenga and US to defend, however, was another issue raised in the *Wall Street Journal* profile—Karenga's going to Sacramento "a few weeks after the assassination of Martin Luther King" for "a private chat with Gov. Ronald Reagan, at the governor's request."[70] By the time of King's assassination, Governor Reagan, elected in 1966, had already earned a reputation for repressive "law-and-order" politics. Radicals and Black nationalists throughout California found him an easy negative symbol, representing the very worst of the state's right-wing constituency.[71] In any case, Karenga conceded that he attended the meeting and expressed regret, retrospectively, at having done so. "Reagan called my house," he explained, "and I had a lot of people [from the US Organization] in jail and in prison and I thought that was an outlet where we could get some of our people out of prison."[72]

Karenga conceded that his meeting with Reagan was "the wrong move."[73] For him the mistake was tactical and, in a vague sense, ideological, although he maintained the position that the very notion of conferring with the governor did not pose any inherent ethical problems. He eventually concluded that the way in which the meeting transpired added to accusations that he and US were collaborating with reactionary government agencies: "It [the meeting] was wrong," he reflected, "because I did it by myself. . . . I did not take any other people."[74] The decision to meet unilaterally with the governor without representatives from other congress organizations is a likely indicator of the arrogance that accompanied US's vanguard sense that it could operate as the leading group within a supposedly cooperative alliance. In any case, reports of the meeting increased the already mounting tensions in the Black Congress.

Apart from its clash with the Black Panther Party for Self-Defense, US was notorious for using violent strong-arm tactics against dissenting individuals and organizations that disagreed with the US position within the congress's internal deliberations.[75] The Black Panther Party also used force and intimidation to get its way with the congress, especially with respect to the L.A.–based Black Panther Political Party that included Angela Davis, John Floyd, and Ayuko Babu.[76] In fact, SNCC's James Forman ventured to Los Angeles on a number of occasions in order to mediate both the US/Panther conflict and the strife between the two Panther organizations.[77] The Federal Bureau of Investigation took note of these independent efforts to quell the feud and intensified its campaign to destabilize both organizations. The atmosphere in the Black Congress grew particularly tense when a series of FBI-created anonymous letters were sent to leaders and rank-and-file members of both groups, some of which urged the Black Panther Party to "take over" US, and others concurrently warned US about a planned takeover.[78]

In late September 1968, the Los Angeles branch of the FBI stated that it had been informed that "there is considerable friction between the Black Panther Party and the 'US' organization headed by Ron Karenga," and that, as a result, the Black Panther Party had recently withdrawn from the Black Congress.[79] The memo also mentioned that "information has been received that the BPP has issued instructions that Ron Karenga, Chairman of 'US,' is to be killed."[80] Two months later, on November 29, the Los Angeles office made the director aware that it was "currently preparing an anonymous letter for bureau approval which will be sent to the Los Angeles Black Panther Party (BPP) supposedly from a member of the 'US' organization in which it will be stated that the youth group of the 'US' organization is aware of the BPP 'contract' to kill Ron Karenga, leader of 'US,' and they, 'US' members in retaliation[,] have made plans to ambush leaders of the BPP in Los Angeles."[81] The special agent in charge made the objective of this operation ominously clear: "It is hoped this counterintelligence measure will result in an 'US' and BPP vendetta."[82] There may have been no truth to the bureau's "information" about an actual assassination plot. It is quite probable that as a war of words escalated between these groups, the climate of heightened rhetoric yielded that kind of "talk" among rival partisans. Even more disturbing, however, is the FBI's apparently gleeful enthusiasm and coldly deliberate inaction with respect to a prospective murder conspiracy.

By early 1969 the conflict had moved onto the UCLA campus. Throughout the 1968–1969 school year, members from both US and the Black Panther Party were taking preparatory and regular classes at UCLA through the "High Potential Program," which provided opportunities for Los Angeles–area African Americans and Mexican Americans with what the university considered "less than customary entrance requirements," to gain access to higher education.[83] By late 1968 and early 1969, the UCLA Black Student Union became a major forum for both groups to compete for influence.[84] A very contentious issue ensued relating to the selection of the director for a forthcoming Black Studies program. Many in the BSU regarded Karenga as the dominant member of a university Community Advisory Committee, which selected Charles Thomas, a psychologist and the education director of the Watts Health Center, as the candidate for the position, without getting adequate student input or representation.[85]

The students' perception that US was attempting to muscle its own self-selected candidate into the position was intensified by a confrontational meeting with Karenga—accompanied by a large and intimidating contingent of Simba—and members of the BSU on January 15.[86] Elaine Brown recalled the sense among the students that US was attempting to bully them, even though Karenga came as a representative of the advisory board. Brown and

Alprentice "Bunchy" Carter, and a host of other students, openly challenged Karenga. The Black Panther Party took the position that the process was a breach of students' right to self-determination; the BSU responded by setting up its own committee on the Black Studies program which included party members John Huggins and Elaine Brown.[87]

Efforts to resolve these tensions took a tragic turn moments after the adjournment of a student meeting on January 17. In a fracas that ensued after the meeting, Bunchy Carter and John Huggins, both leaders in the Black Panther Party, were shot to death, and Larry Watani-Stiner sustained a gunshot wound to the shoulder. How the exact turn of events transpired is not altogether clear. Eyewitnesses testified that Claude Hubert-Gaidi (also known as Chochezi) shot Carter and Huggins while the two were in an altercation involving an US member, Harold Jones-Tawala. Apparently the two Panther leaders were involved in a violent struggle with Tawala, who, just moments before, was engaged in a heated argument with Elaine Brown.[88] It was reported that during the melee, Huggins also fired shots before he fell dead. Larry Watani-Stiner may have gotten caught in the crossfire.[89]

Former deputy minister of defense Geronimo Pratt, now a celebrated and freed political prisoner of the movement, was Carter's head of security at the time, but there are contradictory reports of his exact whereabouts after the BSU meeting.[90] Looking back on this sad turn of events, he insisted that rather than a conspiracy, the UCLA incident was a spontaneous shootout. Pratt stated that the altercation with Huggins, Carter, and Tawala "caused one of the Panthers to pull out a gun, and which subsequently caused US members to pull out their guns to defend themselves."[91] "In the ensuing gun battle," Pratt continued, "Bunchy Carter and John Huggins lay dead."[92] Karenga and US members have described the UCLA tragedy with an emphasis on some of the same points mentioned in the version articulated by Pratt.[93] In any case, shortly after the deaths of Carter and Huggins, the Black Panther Party maintained an official position that what had transpired was, indeed, a planned assassination, orchestrated by Karenga in fulfillment of a government directive.[94] Problematically, many historical accounts of the UCLA incident accept this partisan view without question or scrutiny.[95]

The view that the deaths were the result of a planned conspiracy was also advanced by Los Angeles district attorney's prosecutor Stephen Trott in his case against three US members of the Simba on trial for the shootings.[96] Shortly after the UCLA incident, George Ali-Stiner, his brother Larry Watani-Stiner, and Donald Hawkins-Stodi surrendered to the police, who had issued warrants for their arrests. The three were subsequently tried and convicted for conspiracy to commit murder and two counts of second-degree murder.[97] The person who allegedly did the shooting, Claude Hubert-Gaidi, was never found, and neither was Harold Jones-Tawala. Ali and Watani (the Stiner brothers) both received life sentences whereas Stodi, because he was only twenty years old, served time in California's Youth Authority Detention.

In 1974 the Stiner brothers escaped from a minimum-security family visitation unit at San Quentin prison.[98] In 1978 the FBI claimed that it knew that Hubert (Gaidi) was in hiding in Guyana, but that the Guyanese government rejected requests for his extradition. At that point, the bureau was concerned that he might attempt to return to the United States, posing as a survivor of the Jonestown massacre.[99] In 1994, a destitute Larry Watani-Stiner turned himself in to American authorities after twenty years in exile. At that time, he had been living in Surinam. He was immediately returned to San Quentin prison, where he remains to this day.[100]

Karenga first got word of the shootings on January 17, 1969, as he was preparing to give a major address for a fundraiser organized by the Committee for a Unified Newark at the Rockland Palace in Harlem, which also featured Olatunji, SunRa, and the Myth Science Arkestra, Imamu Amiri Baraka, the Spirit House Movers, and the Soul Merchants.[101] Baraka described Karenga as very shaken by the news:

> The place was packed, perhaps a thousand people. . . . At the height of the program Karenga received a long distance phone call backstage. . . . Karenga questioned the caller, talking furiously and almost hysterically. There had been a shootout at UCLA. . . . Karenga was frozen by what he had heard on the phone. . . . He was scheduled to speak very shortly and it was obvious he could not. . . . Finally, he did go out to speak, surrounded on all sides by the security, the L.A. brothers, and our own people.[102]

Wesely Kabaila was one of the Simba who had traveled to New York for that speaking engagement and also recalled Karenga's response after receiving the call: "I can remember the expression on his face, he just froze for a moment and he just stared off . . . he went into a deep, kind of meditative state for a few moments."[103] Among the multitude of thoughts that may have passed through his mind, one incontrovertible fact had to have been clear: things would never be the same in his organization, nor in its relationship to the movement.

Other US members were also shocked by the turn of events, especially with the notion that Carter and Huggins had been killed —particularly because it had seemed that they were among those in the leadership of the Southern California chapter who were making an effort to calm the brewing tensions.[104] Most of the serious clashes between the two groups up to that point were among the younger troops and did not involve the leadership or older members. Daryl Tukufu was a Makamu (deputy chief) in the Masai tribe of the Simba at the time. He could have been among the Simba who went to UCLA on January 17 but was assigned to security duty at the Hekalu instead. "The thing I really hated about it—it still saddens me to this day," Tukufu said, "is that those two individuals, Bunchy and Huggins, they were the guys that were the friendliest to members of the US Organization, to me they were trying to keep the peace between the two organizations. I really liked and had a lot of respect for both of them."[105]

The shootout had an immediate crippling effect on the Black Congress at the outset of 1969. Shortly afterwards, congress chairman Walt Bremond resigned.[106] Even more damaging, another group of organizations, some of which had belonged to the Black Congress, formed a counter united-front coalition called the Black Alternative.[107] By the spring of 1969, the Black Congress was effectively defunct, and the US quest for a united front in Los Angeles had come to an end.[108] Ironically, throughout the period in which US experienced opposition to its version of united-front politics in Los Angeles, the organization received appreciation from and acceptance by local activists in New Jersey.

The New Ark Laboratory: The Black Power Conferences and Electoral Politics in Newark

Long before the shootout with the Panthers, Karenga and Amiri Baraka (then LeRoi Jones), the literary genius and activist, met for the first time in late 1966 or sometime in early 1967. Karenga was in New Jersey for meetings with Nathan Wright, which resulted in the Newark Black Power Conference of July 1967. Soon thereafter, Baraka took a look at the US Organization while on a visit to Los Angeles. The alliance between these two leaders and their respective groups led to a series of concrete political achievements in Newark, the most noteworthy of which was the election of the city's first Black mayor in 1970. Alphonso Pinkney, exploring these developments in *Red, Black and Green: Black Nationalism in the United States*, posited that "Karenga's influence on the black community in Los Angeles has been minimal when compared to that of Baraka in Newark."[109] Pinkney further explained that "[a]s a theoretician of cultural nationalism, Karenga's contribution is notable but as a community organizer his abilities appear to lag behind those of Baraka."[110] On the surface, the demise of the Black Congress looks potentially supportive of this view. However, a deeper appraisal must acknowledge the comparatively more receptive terrain in Newark for US to implement its blueprint for building a united front and achieving Black political power. The nationalist political successes in Newark were, furthermore, the result of collaborative efforts as opposed to personal ones.

Komozi Woodard's *A Nation within a Nation: Amiri Baraka (LeRoi Jones) & Black Power Politics* maintains that the goals of independent politics and black nationality formation were key developments in Black Power–era cultural nationalism. A centerpiece in this process was the launching of what Woodard has termed the Modern Black Convention Movement—the 1966, 1967, and 1968 Black Power conferences, the 1970 and 1972 Congress of African People conventions, the 1972 National Black Political Convention in Gary, Indiana, and a series of other major political gatherings. Through networks established with East Coast nationalist organizations, far away from the contentious regional struggles for power in Southern California, US was able to assume a dominant role in this budding convention movement. The US political relationship with Newark began with planning the first National Conference on Black Power. As a participant in

the Black Power Planning Conference on September 3, 1966, organized by Representative Adam Clayton Powell in Washington,
D.C., Karenga emerged as one of the five members of the Continuations Committee who would play a leading role in planning
the 1967 conference.[111] This conference brought together 169
delegates from thirty-seven cities, eighteen states, and sixty-four
organizations.[112]

The Continuations Committee decided that the National Conference on Black Power should be held the following year in
Newark, New Jersey. This decision would have an unanticipated
level of political importance given that the four-day conference
was scheduled to begin July 20, 1967. On July 11 of that year, a violent rebellion erupted in Newark, as it had in Watts in 1965, that
raged on for almost a week. As a result of this turn of events,
twenty-six people were killed and over one thousand were injured.[113] The committee was pressured by numerous city officials
to postpone the conference, but they decided to go ahead with it
as originally scheduled.[114] As a result, the conference became not
merely an avenue for creating a strategy for Black Power on a national level, but also a forum to address the local political and
economic bases for the rebellion.[115]

The conference consisted of a series of workshops and general
sessions where participants voted on specific resolutions. Nathan
Hare, Hoyt Fuller, Ossie Davis, Faye Bellamy, James Farmer,
Vivian Braxton, William Strickland, and Cleveland Sellers were
among those who facilitated workshops.[116] Significantly, Karenga
was the coordinator for one called "Black Power in World Perspective: Nationalism and Internationalism."[117] As had been the
case with the Black Congress, Karenga emerged as a central theorist who provided a model for the conference's participating organizations on how diverse ideological positions could function
cooperatively. Conference chairman Nathan Wright of the Epis-
copal Diocese of Newark noted that "[t]hose who had attended

the 1967 National Conference on Black Power in Newark were impressed by Maulana Ron Karenga's emphasis upon the need to develop what he called 'operational [unity].'"[118] Wright went on to explain his understanding of how operational unity functioned at the conference: it "did not require the creation of a new organization. All groups keep their own identity. A coalition of leaders is, however, created to conduct a dialogue and make decisions for work in parallel and mutually supporting ways."[119]

The conference resolution calling for a political task force to assist in unseating Newark mayor Hugh Addonizio became a focal point of an emerging alliance between US and various political forces in Newark.[120] Baraka, who had been injured in a police beating, became even more active in Newark politics after the rebellion. He was in close contact with, and in certain instances a leading member in, a few key organizations that would collectively ignite a campaign to increase African American political representation in Newark: the United Brothers, Black Community Defense and Development (BCD), and a collective of local artists called the Spirit House. Eventually, these forces merged and became a sort of East Coast affiliate chapter of the US Organization. Baraka recalled that "[i]t was Karenga, who on one of his visits, suggested that we formally bring together the United Brothers, BCD, and the Spirit House forces. . . . Karenga suggested the name Committee for a Unified Newark (CFUN)."[121]

Apparently even before these groups came together, the BCD, whose members were predominately from East Orange and Montclair, New Jersey—as Baraka remembered—"had formed a group [styled] after the US people and regarded Karenga as their leader."[122] Even though the BCD segment of CFUN had already accepted the US Organization's doctrine, some of the moderate elements in the United Brothers were more resistant to the notion of accepting this new alliance. Baraka stated that

"Karenga's influence came to dominate the entire CFUN." He went on to note, however, that this had "alienated a few of the older political brothers in United Brothers, all of whom would certainly not become Karenga cultural nationalists."[123]

This new alliance's first major public effort toward organizing in electoral politics was the Black Political Convention in Newark on June 21–23, 1968.[124] Karenga spoke at a plenary session. His effectiveness was bolstered by an ability to expose convention participants to a theoretical model that assisted them in conceptualizing a strategy for gaining political power.[125] His own doctrine's catechisms specified various objectives and steps for achieving political power. Most noteworthy are the four areas of political power: (1) political office, (2) community organization, (3) coalitions and alliances, (4) disruption.[126] The convention was a major step in launching CFUN's electoral campaign that ran Ted Pinkney and Donald Tucker for city council seats for the November 1968 election. This effort was called the "Peace and Power" campaign. Baraka recalled that "Karenga came to town especially to help with the campaign." He went on to mention that "[i]t was he [Karenga] who named the campaign 'Peace and Power,' hoping to capitalize on the peace movement that was one aspect of the anti-Vietnam protests as well as the Black Power movement."[127]

In August 1968 the National Conference on Black Power presented CFUN with an opportunity to gain national support for the Peace and Power campaign. "The 1968 Newark convention," Baraka stated, "later used the Black Power conference of that year, held in Philadelphia, as a sounding board, getting not only a hearing for the issues in the Newark black convention platform, but also getting endorsement for the candidates."[128] By that time, Karenga was the head of the Black Power Continuations Committee. The conference further solidified the alliance between US and CFUN. A large contingent of US members attended the conference.[129] Wesely Kabaila, a former US member who attended the Philadelphia conference, recalled that just afterwards, a group of them "left Philadelphia and went directly to Newark to help organize."[130] Kabaila also remembered his contingent of US members staying in Newark for nearly one month assisting with the campaign and teaching the US doctrine to the BCD and CFUN members.[131]

In addition to direct input from this cadre, Karenga personally assisted CFUN in the development of its day-to-day organizing efforts, especially voter registration and fund-raising. Historian Komozi Woodard cites interviews with former United Brothers member Russell Bingham and Peace and Power candidate Donald Tucker that support the conclusion that "[a]s far as the political veterans in the United Brothers were concerned Karenga was well-schooled on political organization, and he gave Baraka training in how to effectively organize precinct work."[132] Evidently, Karenga and US's experiences with voter registration drives in the Freedom City movement and other organizing efforts in Los Angeles informed their ability to play an advisory role at the beginning of their relationship with CFUN.

The Peace and Power campaign fell short of achieving the election of its candidates to the city council. However, this entree into electoral politics laid the basis for CFUN's electoral triumph in its 1970 mayoral campaign that produced the election of Newark's first Black mayor, Kenneth Gibson. Baraka, reflecting on the relationship between the two campaigns, noted that "[t]he first one . . . we lost but it was good because it gave us our first taste of it."[133] Baraka also mentioned that after the Peace and Power loss, Karenga suggested the use of an African proverb—"to stumble is not to fall but to go forward faster"—as a slogan for CFUN to continue its efforts.[134] Indeed, Newark provided room for US to attain the political vanguard status it so diligently sought in Los Angeles.

US's participation in united-front politics declined in the early 1970s when sectarian conflict and government repression undermined the organization's overall effectiveness. The internationalization of the Modern Black Convention Movement continued without the US Organization's participation during the mid-1970s, giving way to the African Liberation Support Committee and an extensive African American presence at the 1974 Sixth Pan-African Congress in Tanzania.

The story of US should remind students of the 1960s that resistance is almost always multidimensional and complex. Not only did US challenge White power, it was a central force in the Black Power movement and at the core of the series of local and national conferences and alliances that effectively comprised the Modern Black Convention Movement. African American leadership has a long tradition of establishing Black interorganizational umbrella formations. The US Organization attempted to fulfill united-front ideals articulated in Malcolm X's blueprint for the Organization of Afro-American Unity.

US's strategy of "programmatic influence" effectively contributed to the budding Modern Black Convention Movement and to the electoral political action of Amiri Baraka's Committee for a Unified Newark, yet it did not establish a lasting Black alliance capable of enduring ideological and political conflict—an objective that *remains* to this day beyond the grasp of African American activism. During the Black Power period, many other organizations and factions similarly regarded themselves as vanguard leaders and ultimately challenged US authority in the movement. Quite fascinating, nonetheless, is the degree to which these potentially explosive united-front efforts helped forge and solidify a consensus on critical issues of the time: community control in schools, the right to Black self-defense, adequate Black representation in urban politics, and opposition to the Vietnam War. Indeed, the zeal with which US members embraced a new nationalist inner world, replete with alternative rituals and institutions, mirrored their larger effort to transform the outer one. The multiple spaces in which power, conflict, disheartenment, vision, and collective sacrifice flourished is best captured in the US Organization's own motto: "Anywhere we are, US is."[135]

5. Sectarian Discourses and the Decline of US in the Era of Black Power

By 1969, US and the Black Panther Party had grown to become certain about their respective standings as leading Black Power organizations. US sought to lead a cultural revolution transforming Black consciousness, group identity, purpose, and direction—which would lay the foundation for a collective African American political decision.[1] The Black Panther Party defined itself as the vanguard party in the national liberation struggle to free the "Black colony" and simultaneously to unite with other progressive forces to combat racism, capitalism, and imperialism.[2] Actually, the broad objectives of both organizations were complementary. The Black Panther Party's goal of bringing about a "United Nations supervised plebiscite to be held throughout the black colony . . . for the purpose of determining the will of black people as to their national destiny"[3] required a consensus born of African American political will and sense of collective identity.

Beyond the simple contest for power, the US/Panther conflict was also the end product of conflicting organizing styles and priorities. The Black Panther Party was much more of a mass organization than US, rapidly establishing chapters nationwide after the 1967 armed protest in Sacramento. The party made use of populist organizing strategies, flamboyantly displaying its armed monitoring of local police and setting up free-breakfast programs and clinics in urban areas. US, on the contrary, was comfortable with being a small elite force, directing the program and philosophy of other mass organizations. "We do not expect US to be a mass movement," Karenga asserted in a 1969 interview, "we are not a mass movement, we are an organization that mobilizes, organizes and nationalizes because we believe that we must first have a revolution of alternatives, before we can make revolution."[4]

US's leadership did not adequately appreciate the party's successful populist community organizing. This is evidenced in Karenga's dismissive view of the breakfast programs and free clinics. "That's not a revolutionary act," Karenga stated, "to set up a kitchen and put out food for people, the welfare does that, the bureau of public assistance."[5] He further diminished the significance of the Panthers' free clinics: "To set up a free clinic is no novel idea, Medicare has preceded that with much more money and much more technical organization."[6] Ultimately, Karenga felt that these programs would pacify African Americans. He declared, "Let us not be diverted to duplication of programs that the people who have tried to divide us have already set up to disillusion us and create illusions for tokenism, as Brother Malcolm X said."[7] Remarks of this sort illustrated the US leader's failure to grasp how these programs fit into the movement's mandate for community control and self-determination. The Black Panther Party successfully administered these services—galvanizing resources from a network of allies—for the purpose of politicizing and empowering scores of Black urban communities.[8] This was truly a very different project from that imagined by liberal reformers.

The Black Panther Party's formidable social service efforts, activism, and effective use of American mass media gave them a strong base of popular support in many urban areas. US did not pursue the kinds of activities that helped the Panthers become a popular icon of Black resistance, putting Karenga's organization at a decisive disadvantage as the US/Panther conflict reached violent proportions. For many African Americans outside Southern California and nationalist circles, their initial introduction to US came as a result of the UCLA shootings. US, though a major force in the Modern Black Convention Movement, lacked the kind of far-ranging popular base that the Panthers developed and was less equipped with defenders of its image, as the feud would generate a barrage of anti-US allegations and mischaracterizations in 1969. C. R. D. Halisi recognized that the Black Panther Party was more effective at gaining community support. "They [the Black Panther Party]," Halisi asserted, "weren't asking people to give up pork. We were asking people to make a total life-conversion in order to be a part of the organization."[9] "That is not," he concluded, "something that lends itself to wide acceptance even though people could see the value."[10]

Whites and "The Lumpen"

US and some other Black nationalist organizations were leery of the alliance the Black Panther Party forged in 1968 with White radicals such as Students for a Democratic Society and the Peace and Freedom Party. US maintained that the central role of White progressives was to "civilize" racist and reactionary elements in their own communities and make financial contributions as "foreign aid" to Black organizations.[11] The Black Panther Party, on the other hand, argued for a much closer alliance with White progressives, especially toward garnering economic and political support for the effort to free those in the party's leadership who were imprisoned.[12] US members and sympathizers incorrectly equated this position with an assimilationism and overlooked the

Black Panther Party's genuine and deep-rooted relationships with important segments of African American urban communities throughout the United States.

These differences gave way to a view among the US leadership and members that the Black Panther Party had been co-opted by the White left and no longer represented the aspirations of African Americans but those of a privileged interest group seeking influence in the Black community.[13] Karenga himself referred to the Black Panther Party as a "front group."[14] Imamu Amiri Baraka concurred, and accused Minister of Information Eldridge Cleaver—who had gained a large influence on the party's policies in 1968—of plunging the party into a state of dependency. "Frankly the Panthers," he stated, ". . . are extreme examples of PimpArt gone mad." "With the incarceration of Huey, and the move by Cleaver into the chief strategist's seat," he declared, "the Panthers turned left on Nationalism, and turned left on Black people."[15] Baraka proceeded to launch an ad hominen attack, linking Cleaver's alleged romantic proclivities with his politics, "the love of Beverly Axelrod has left terrible Marx on the dirty Lenin Black people have been given by some dudes with some dead 1930's white ideology as a freedom suit."[16]

Also, Karenga's own remarks added fuel to allegations that he and his organization were rightists. Using terms that did not greatly differ from red-baiters, he often referred to the Black Panther Party's allies as "the left."[17] An article in the *Los Angeles Free Press* made note of this problem, noting that Karenga "was beginning to sound like [Los Angeles] Mayor [Sam] Yorty," a notoriously virulent anticommunist, "when he said, 'the oldest technique of the left is to use front organizations.'"[18] These kinds of statements gave the impression that Karenga's own group was not a part of "the left," even though it rejected capitalism and advocated communalism and African socialism.[19]

Criticism of the Black Panther Party's alliance with White radicals was not restricted to the rivalry with US. In July 1969,

Stokely Carmichael (later known as Kwame Ture) publicly re-signed from his position as the Black Panther Party's prime minister. An article reporting on his resignation mentioned that the turn of events brought "into the open the constant division among revolutionary blacks over the issue of white alliances."[20] He had already disagreed with the party's position in public during the series of West Coast "Free Huey" rallies in February 1968.[21] Reflecting on his views at the time, Toure stated, "I told [Cleaver] that there was nowhere in history that I know of where the economically insecure, in this case Africans, had made an alliance with the economically secure, in this case white liberals, and that both of them could fight for some kind of economic advancement that he was proclaiming."[22]

In the San Francisco Bay Area, the issue of the Black Panther Party's alliances became even more contentious as threats of violent retaliation against local nationalists opposed to the involvement of White people in the Black liberation struggle emerged in the *Black Panther* newspaper in 1968. The ultimatum, entitled "Warning to the So-called 'Paper Panthers,'" ordered "Black brothers" to "stop vamping on the hippies."[23] It went on to impose the party's own conception of ally and enemy:

> Your enemy right now, is the white racist pig who supports this corrupt system. Your enemy is the Tom nigger who reports to his white slavemaster everyday. Your enemy is the fat capitalist who exploits your people daily. Your enemy is the politician who uses pretty words to deceive you. Your enemy is the racist pigs who use Nazi-type tactics and force to intimidate black expressionism. Your enemy is not the hippies. Your blind reactionary acts endanger the BLACK PANTHER PARTY members and its revolutionary movements.[24]

"WE HAVE NO QUARREL WITH THE HIPPIES," the warning declared, threatening dire consequences for those who do not adhere to this policy: "LEAVE THEM ALONE. OR—the BLACK PANTHER PARTY will deal with you!"[25]

US and Black Panther Party members had disparate notions of revolutionary conduct and praxis. US and other Kawaidists, in the tradition of the Nation of Islam, operated from the standpoint that the conversion to cultural nationalist advocacy demanded new habits and mannerisms, a certain revolutionary *savoir vivre*. Irrespective of their class origins, new Kawaidists were expected to be polite, calm, disciplined, and intellectual. These attributes, born of an internalization of a new value system, were counterpositioned against the behaviors of "Negroes" or African Americans without values.[26] US advocates often viewed Black Panther Party members as promoters of the very behaviors that cultural nationalists were seeking to change. Continuing with his "pimp art" theme, Baraka assailed Eldridge Cleaver's leadership and philosophy, calling the Black Panthers "misguided dudes who think by saying 'Pick Up the Gun,' that the devil will wither up and die, or just by picking up that literal gun . . . using the same sick value system of the degenerate slavemaster, the same dope, the same liquor, the same dying hippy mentality, that they will *liberate* all the slave peoples of the world. NO."[27]

Conversely, the Black Panther Party, especially during the height of Cleaver's leadership, valorized the revolutionary potential of the African American lumpen proletariat, whom they referred to as "the brothers and sisters off the block," or "street niggers."[28] This perspective did not condemn but embraced a raw and rough street attitude shunned by US members. Cleaver, in fact, positioned the brothers and sisters off the block against those in the movement with an academic background, who he felt lacked the capacity for revolutionary commitment. He described educated leaders in the movement as inherently weak and cowardly. "All of these freaks with college educations," he stated, "from Jimmy Garrett, Ron Karenga, LeRoi Jones, to Sir

Stokely [Carmichael], saw the sky falling in upon them and felt the carpet under their feet when the Black Panther Party . . . came on the scene."[29]

A *Black Panther* newspaper article's description of Karenga suggested his academic background detracted from his authenticity as a community leader: "Karenga is not a street brother, although he has learned some street tongue just as he has learned Swahili."[30] "Ron Karenga," it continued, "is an intellectual who has advanced and promoted black culture in the ghetto through his personal acquaintance with Black Studies, the program he followed at UCLA."[31] Some activists in Los Angeles held the same type of suspicions about Angela Davis, who also had academic credentials. Davis's and Karenga's parallel circumstances as well-educated activists in the midst of a popularized anti-intellectualism was perhaps best dramatized by Elaine Brown's memory of having been taken aback when she encountered Karenga and Davis conversing in French together at a party.[32]

The US Organization's internal culture discouraged behaviors and mannerisms attributed to "street life," and inspired a common fascination with education out of emulation of its leader.[33] There was a general perception among US advocates that elements in the party celebrated a lifestyle unfit for revolutionaries.[34] As the heat of the feud intensified, both US and the Black Panther Party gravitated toward simplistic impressions of their rival as Other.

Vilifying Cultural Nationalism

Uniform and caricaturized depictions of cultural nationalists had a profound impact on the image of the US Organization. Black Panther Party leaders and commentators described cultural nationalism as diversionary, discouraging its adherents from violent resistance or a protracted struggle for political power. Party leaders charged that US manipulatively used the veneer of African rituals to disguise a real preference for Black capitalism and reactionary politics.[35] Minister of Defense Huey Newton juxtaposed cultural nationalism with the Black Panther Party's self-styled revolutionary nationalism. He rejected the idea of returning "to the old African culture" and proclaimed that "culture itself will not liberate us[.] We're going to need some stronger stuff."[36]

The idea that cultural nationalists were inherently weak and unwilling to "pick up the gun" had direct political implications for how the Black Panther Party would interact with Bay Area activists and organizations, even prior to the violent conflict with US. Both Bobby Seale and Huey Newton recounted, with much self-congratulation and masculinist bravado, anecdotes of their use of crude strong-arm tactics on the cultural-nationalist Black Panther Party of Northern California. Newton, Seale, and Cleaver, leaders of the Black Panther Party for Self-Defense, would derogatorily label them, and some other local activists, "Paper Panthers."[37] In their memoirs of conflict with the Black Panther Party of Northern California and other groups, both Seale and Newton stressed the Black Panther Party's use of violence as a final solution to disagreements. From their standpoint, this readiness to use force stood at the heart of what distinguished them from the cultural nationalists.[38]

A shortcoming of the Black Panther Party's official characterizations of cultural nationalism was the neglect of US's anthropological view of culture, which contained the politics of self-defense and socialism as constituent components of culture. As a result, Panther denunciations of cultural nationalism tended to distort US's ideology, defining it as a nonpolitical aesthetic preoccupation. This error was ever present in the Black Panther Party's most elaborate statement on the subject by Linda Harrison entitled "On Cultural Nationalism." After the assertion that "[t]hose who believe in the 'I'm Black and Proud' theory—believe that there is dignity inherent in wearing naturals; that a buba makes a slave a man; and that a common language, Swahili, makes all of us brothers," Harrison went on to declare that "cultural nationalism ignores the concrete, and concentrates on a myth and fantasy."[39]

The image of the weak cultural nationalist was part and parcel of the Black Panther Party's own vanguard self-perception. In various editorials and interviews, Panther leaders and spokespersons positioned the practical and fearless revolutionary nationalist as the correct alternative to the nonthreatening cultural-nationalist escapist. In fact, there was an attempt to displace US's self-styled African American culture with the party's own invented "revolutionary culture." In keeping with this idea, the Black Panther Party offered its own essentialist conception of Africa. "The True Culture of Africans," in the *Black Panther* newspaper, described contemporary anticolonial wars in the Congo, Mozambique, Angola, Guinea-Bissau, and Zimbabwe and supplied several photographs of African soldiers and guerrilla fighters brandishing weapons or in the middle of training for the battlefield.[40] This ever-fighting image presented an answer satisfying Harrison's query: "How can a cultural nationalist claim to love and be proud of a country—and a continent that has suffered hundreds of years in colonialism and slavery, and is still suffering in all the cleverly disguised and open forms of these institutions?"[41]

The rivalry between the two organizations set in motion a binary discourse grounded on false assumptions. The choice between African culture as represented by images of military resistance and a central value system and rituals is a manufactured one. US also saw itself as an ally of anticolonial liberation struggles in both Asia and Africa, and actively supported these movements. However, nuances of this sort were replaced by sectarian allegations as the US/Panther conflict became intensified by violent clashes in the late sixties and as power politics within the Black movement came to supplant an initial focus on struggle with the state or White cultural hegemony.

Former SNCC activist Julius Lester was one of few to critique the vilification of cultural nationalism and, by extension, US. On March 30, 1969, Students for a Democratic Society—a predominantly White group within the New Left and antiwar movement —boldly declared that "[w]ithin the black liberation movement the vanguard force is the Black Panther Party."[42] During the heat of the US/Panther conflict, the SDS resolution also gave weight to the Black Panther Party by denouncing cultural nationalism as reactionary.[43] The entirety of the resolution was printed in *The Guardian* on April 19, 1969. Lester responded to this turn of events in his editorial column, "From the Other Side of the Tracks." He contended that revolutionary nationalism was dependent on cultural nationalism as a broad ideological base necessary to inspire African Americans to advocate fundamental change in American society. "It is cultural nationalism that has laid the foundation for revolutionary nationalism," Lester asserted, going on to state that "[i]t is cultural nationalism that has, more than any other ideology, brought a common consciousness to blacks."[44] He also recognized the underlying political consequences of static ideological mischaracterizations: "To condemn cultural nationalism outright is to divide the movement and create the conditions for warring factions."[45]

Kathleen Cleaver, then secretary of communications for the Black Panther Party, answered Lester's remarks. Finding it unprincipled that Lester would challenge a White organization for supporting a faction in the Black movement,[46] she considered the SDS resolution declaring the Black Panther Party the vanguard an appropriate recognition of "the objective reality of the black colony."[47] Cleaver also reinforced the party's position on

revolutionary and cultural nationalism as "classic distinctions between ideological principles."[48] Throughout her remarks Cleaver
compared Lester's editorial with the United States government's
repression of the Black Panther Party. After noting that "the
entire apparatus of the U.S. pig law enforcement, coordinated
out of Washington by the FBI, CIA, Department of Justice and
Department of Defense, is waging a full-scale campaign to destroy the leadership and organization of the Black Panther Party
across the country," Cleaver stated, "Now Julius Lester raises his
whine in chorus with the opposition."[49] After calling Lester a
"counterrevolutionary," a "fool," and a "disservice to the people,"
she went on to retort: "So exactly what's over there on that side
of the tracks I don't know, but I have a feeling it's a bunch of
punks, sissies and cowards, so fuck them and fuck Julius Lester."[50]

Stokely Carmichael's (Kwame Ture's) resignation statement
echoed themes highlighted in Lester's remarks. "The party," he
stated, "has become dogmatic in its duly acquired ideology—all
those who disagreed with the party line are lumped into the same
category and labeled cultural nationalists, pork chop nationalists, reactionary pigs. . . . It is dishonest and vicious."[51] Looking
back on the sixties, Ture—in one of his last interviews in the
United States prior to his death—remained opposed to a polar-
izing view of cultural and revolutionary nationalism. "The Panthers made the position so extreme," he stated, that "automatically if you were what they called a 'cultural nationalist,' you're a
reactionary . . . so in order for you to get away from the stigma,
you had to denounce cultural nationalism."[52]

The Black Panther Party experienced bicoastal splintering
and in-fighting in the late sixties and early seventies. The Oak-
land-based leadership faction often used the label "cultural nationalist" to vilify and indict members targeted by the central
committee. Mumia Abu-Jamal discussed this trend and its impact
on members of the New York chapter: "In a party as ideologically

hostile as the BPP became to any smattering of cultural national-ism, the New York chapter with its Muslims, Yorubas, and Puerto Ricans (and probably a few Santerios), while thoroughly New Yorkers, were seen as somehow suspect."[53] "Culture nationalist," in this strange context, became a signifier for insider/outsider identification and ultimately the term, within party leadership circles, evolved into "one of the most damning epithets imagina-ble."[54] "I understood," Kwame Ture remarked, "that it [cultural nationalism] was a struggle of African culture coming to the fore and certainly, I was 100 percent for this . . . so the positions as they were defined politically were incorrect."[55]

Some scholarly attempts were made at the time to unravel the assortment of ill-defined terms and sectarianism plaguing the US/Panther conflict. In 1970, Harold Cruse, in a speech given at the University of Texas at Austin, did not accept the definitions of cultural nationalism emanating from the intergroup rivalry. He saw the phenomenon as a broad trend of the movement at large, in which specific organizations and the general populace expressed new interest in African and African American culture, history, aesthetics, and so on. He even included the Black Pan-ther Party within this broad cultural-nationalist thrust, and de-scribed the Panther and US leadership quarrels as expressions of cultural nationalist heterogeneity.[56]

The ideological dimensions of the US/Panther conflict went far beyond the classic coalitionist/self-determinationist tensions in the history of African American political thought and activism. The intergroup feud was complicated by differing ideas about or-ganizational strategy, revolutionary conduct, the role of educa-tion, and mass participation—as well as the role of progressive Whites in the movement. Black Panther Party leaders were, nonetheless, quite successful at redefining and ridiculing cul-tural nationalism, frequently referring to cultural nationalism as "pork chop nationalism." Most striking, however, is the notion that this antagonism between the Black Panther Party and cultural nationalists appears to have been limited to California. In other parts of the country, notable Black Panther Party chapters struggled alongside strong cultural nationalist contingencies—as in Chicago, New York, and New Orleans—and experienced neither the ideological nor physical conflict that existed in Oakland, Los Angeles, and San Diego.

Clashes between US and the Black Panther Party began within the contentious terrain of Los Angeles Black nationalist politics. The fluid, town-hall atmosphere wherein much of the local Black nationalist and radical activism took place encouraged the transition from a war of words to a war of guns. The sectarian discourses of both groups had destructive consequences, as most of the clashes between US and the Black Panther Party occurred during or after a public political gathering of some sort such as Black Congress meetings, "Free Huey" rallies, and student meetings.

Residual memories of the US/Panther conflict, through the prism of reflections by US and Black Panther Party leaders, tend to overlook the experiences of rank-and-file members of both organizations who had grown up with each other, attended school together, and had relationships preceding the violence at UCLA.[57] Beneath the presentation of US and the Black Panther Party as ever-feuding forces on the UCLA campus in *A Taste of Power* is the reality that Elaine Brown was the roommate of an US member, Bobette Azizi Glover, in the residence hall for High Potential students. The two were said to have gotten along "extremely well" until their friendship was suddenly disrupted when Brown departed from the dorm room after the shootings.[58] Charles Johnson-Sitawisha was fifteen years old in January 1969 and a dedicated Simba active in both US and the Black Students' Union at Crenshaw High School. He watched as the US/Panther feud imposed rigid battle lines that tore through friendships at school. In due course, Sitawisha had resigned to leave the group that he had come to know as a family: "I didn't join an organization to be fighting other Black people."[59] It had become clear to him that the aims of the organization were being rerouted toward internecine warfare and fighting within its own ranks. If premonition lured Sitawisha away from his comrades at that moment, it barely moved him out of the pathway of a turbulent period, from 1969 through the 1970s, that permanently altered the very foundations and makeup of US.

Contested Memories, US's Black Power–Era Decline

The year 1971, according to US's Seven Year Calendar, would set in motion an apocalyptic struggle against the state, with the US Organization leading a guerrilla war. In reality, the year brought forth US's leadership breakdown and sealed the decline of the group as a major force in the Black Power movement. In June 1971, Karenga was convicted of assault and false imprisonment and was sentenced to a one- to ten-year prison term. The charges were that he, along with three other US members—Fred Sefu-Glover, Louis Sedu-Smith, and Luz Maria Tiamoyo (now Tiamoyo Karenga)—had subjected Gail Idili-Davis and Brenda Jones to various forms of torture in May 1970. Glover was convicted on only the false-imprisonment charge while the other three codefendants were found guilty of both charges. Key testimony against the US chairman came from his estranged wife, Brenda (Haiba) Karenga; the former head of US's Simba George Weusi-Armstrong; and his wife, Carletta Weusi-Armstrong.[60]

During the trial, Karenga's wife testified that her husband had come to the conclusion that Idili and Jones were engaging in an assassination plot to poison and drug him, and he therefore ordered as well as participated in their beating and torture. The goal was to get information from them about the location of "pills" and "crystals" he believed were present in his food and drinks. Jones also testified that she and Idili were held captive at Karenga's residence in May 1970, beaten, and tortured with a water hose, soldering iron, and caustic chemicals.[61] Gail Idili-Davis did not testify at the trial.[62]

Karenga maintained his innocence, testifying that his organization was against violence and that he had neither participated in nor had any knowledge of the alleged acts against Jones or Idili.[63] His attorney, Richard Walton, argued that the state's case against Karenga was a frame-up.[64] US's official statements asserting Karenga's innocence were made by Imamu Clyde Halisi in "Maulana Ron Karenga: Black Leader in Captivity," published in *Black Scholar* in May 1972; he had assumed chairmanship of US either just prior to or shortly after the conviction.[65]

Gail Idili-Davis's recollections corroborate much of the testimony at the trial. Her silence at the time of the trial, she stated, was a response to an US ultimatum threatening violent retaliation against her and family members. She found solace in the fact that Jones's testimony—along with that of others—succeeded in convicting Karenga. While Idili also believed that the organization had been infiltrated during the course of a government campaign to destroy US, she noted that Karenga's own destructive response to this pressure brought about a terribly horrific ordeal. She recalled that Karenga, succumbing to paranoia and drug abuse, accused her and Jones of being agents. As she remembered the events, Karenga ordered and directed others at the Sun House to brutally torture the two of them in an attempt to extract nonexistent information. "That's how the torture started because he was trying to get me to talk: who sent me. I'm naive and I'm saying, 'I don't know what he's talking about.' All I know is that he's trippin'."[66] After barely escaping with her life, Idili sought refuge among family members in the Bay Area.

Paradoxically, former Black Panther Party members and others recounted that Karenga's nemesis, Huey Newton, had, likewise, abused drugs and similarly brutalized party members during the 1970s.[67]

Events at the Sun House did not occur in a vacuum. From January 1969 onward, a series of upheavals and conflicts in US had taken place that would have easily been fertile soil for the violence of the spring of 1970. This period came to be known in US lexicon as "The Crisis." The taxing combination of the threat of retaliation from the Black Panther Party alongside police and FBI surveillance, disruption, and attacks had a transformative impact on the organization's structure and internal operations. Most striking was US's rapid militarization. Every facet of US—the Simba, the Saidi, and even the Muminina—had to shift its main activities to ones relating to protecting the organization's leader from the immediate threat of an attack from the Black Panther Party or the police. For instance, Daryl Tukufu's life as a Simba changed drastically; the time he spent doing community relations, studying the doctrine, and performing with the Taifa Dance Troupe was replaced mostly by security work at Karenga's personal residence. "It was," he recalled, "like twenty-four-hour security: bullet-proof barricades were put up on the side and back [of Karenga's house], it was wired so if someone tried to approach the home, it was alarmed."[68] "Some [Simba]," he continued, "had to sleep outside, some slept on the side in the living room, some would be in the garage, and so everything seemed to be centered around protecting Karenga."[69]

The Saidi, Mwanafunzi, Mwalimu, and Imamu all recentered their duties, from administration and pedagogy to various duties relating to security. Oliver Heshimu's tasks on the legal committee were greatly intensified: "We had a lot of illegal search and seizures on our property and persons, a lot of arrests due to concealed weapons and so forth."[70] During The Crisis, many Saidi had responsibilities similar to those in US's paramilitary wing. James Tayari, who was vice-chair at the time, feels that the organization had developed a "siege mentality."[71] The reality of shootings at members' homes, the constant police harassment, and the flood of FBI misinformation certainly contributed to US's paranoia and siege mentality during The Crisis.[72]

Cadres of women in US had also been mobilized into paramilitary formations, one of which was called the *Matamba* tribe, named after an African nation that vigorously resisted Portuguese colonialism under the leadership of Queen Nzingha in the seventeenth century. The Matamba reported to the commander of the Simba and had an extensive system of independent units.[73] Like the Simba, members went through an elaborate martial arts and weapons training program.[74] The Matamba paramilitary wing became a key piece in US's overall military strategy during The Crisis, since many of US's men were well known and regularly searched and harassed by the police. Participation of women in US's security apparatus had a progressive impact on the organization's eventual move away from a doctrine of male supremacy to its acceptance of gender equality in the early seventies.[75]

The combination of US's militarization and the general perception, after the UCLA shootings, that it had become a violent-prone menace undermined the organization's community support. The image of US as a group of assassins produced a sense of fear and distrust on the part of African American communities in Southern California, whereas the Black Panther Party —because of the deaths of Carter and Huggins as well as the highly publicized police repression its members and leadership faced throughout the country—was largely seen as a victim. Even though US maintained some of its regular community activities, the level of popular enthusiasm and participation had drastically decreased. US had become increasingly isolated and vilified.

Ngoma Ali remembered how disturbing it was to move from feeling like a celebrated community hero to being a shunned villain: "You started seeing where we used to go to Simba meetings and people would be honking at us and giving us the [Black] Power sign—we started having that fade, and people started having more negative things [to say], 'What's happening with y'all and the Panthers?' . . . It was very disheartening."[76]

By the summer of 1969, J. Edgar Hoover's ultimate objectives manifested themselves in US as the pressures on the organization had begun to have a deleterious impact on its internal stability. At this point, large portions of the organization began to have doubts about the leader who, according to their doctrine, was "infallible."[77] Likewise, Karenga questioned the overall strength and loyalty of many in the organization. As a result, there is a great disparity in the memories of US's decline during these troubling times: the perspectives of the former members interviewed for this study sharply conflict with Karenga's sense of the past. These contested memories, nevertheless, constitute an important window illuminating how an organization with a stellar structure and discipline can fall apart and lose the very base of its internal cohesion.

Many former US members interviewed for this study, as well as Amiri Baraka, also remember observing the steady deterioration of Karenga's capacity to lead after the UCLA shootout, asserting that he was overcome by fatigue, abuse of medication, paranoia, and reckless authoritarian conduct.[78] Others maintained that Karenga surrounded himself with sycophants and uncritical voices, thereby exacerbating the problem.[79] Some former US members recounted a foiled attempt, among a group of Saidi, to convince Karenga to leave California temporarily, or even kidnap him if necessary, to force him to rest and recover from drug addiction and extreme fatigue.[80] The culmination of these internal contradictions, coupled with outside disruption from the FBI and police, was said to have created the context for not only the torture of two US members, but a wave of other violent and repressive acts on the part of the leadership.[81] A mass exodus of US members in the Circle of Administrators, Saidi, and a segment of the Simba erupted sometime around the summer of 1969. A contingent of them moved to Newark, New Jersey, to work with the Committee for a Unified Newark and the Congress of African People under the leadership of Imamu Amiri Baraka. Some remained active in other ways, and others had become disillusioned with the movement as a whole. Ngoma Ali, a Simba who served time in prison from 1968 until early 1970, was shocked to see such a drastic change in US upon his release:

> When I came out everything had changed. It was as different as day and night. The Panther conflict was dying out but it was still a problem at that time. . . . All of the old circle of people that we had looked up to are gone. They've broken off from the organization. You've got a different organization and you don't have the sharpness, in terms of intellect, underneath Karenga and the state of mind that you had before. Now you have some rank-and-file people assuming positions that I thought they were unqualified for and didn't have the tenacity [either]. You had people around Karenga that were basically "yes men."[82]

James Tayari saw the organization's undoing as partly a product of its autocratic leadership structure. "The problem," Tayari maintained, "when you have an organization based on a charismatic leader, if you don't watch out you'll develop the cult of personality, and that's what Maulana developed." "He developed," Tayari continued, "too much power, and he had too many people in there that weren't going to speak up and couldn't present an alternative view to things, to make the group go."[83]

Karenga does not see himself as fundamentally responsible for the excesses of 1969 and 1970, arguing that his conviction and the US in-fighting were the products of COINTELPRO.[84] Furthermore, Karenga asserted that internal conflicts between the Saidi and Simba grew out of the demands of the necessity for rapid militarization, rather than his own personal manipulation and shortcomings. "The more we militarized the more we needed Simba," Karenga argued, "and the Saidi had become what one would say in the movement, comfort corrupt, and they are used to ordering and telling things to do and they became more and more weary of the military aspect."[85] He also believes that an agent had infiltrated the leadership of the paramilitary wing and had "misdirected the Simba in [his] name and also in the name of the organization itself."[86]

Baraka made other claims that US's leadership had become dangerously self-absorbed and militaristic. Paradoxically, as US's community and political organizing declined while it was in the midst of the US/Panther conflict and internal strife, Baraka was on the road to leading CFUN and the Congress of African People (CAP) to unprecedented levels of Black nationalist participation in electoral politics, international alliances, and urban reconstruction planning. One of the high points of this trend was the 1972 Black Political Convention in Gary, Indiana.[87] During the early seventies, as CAP began to assume a leadership position in the cultural-nationalist movement, eclipsing US in the public political sphere, it also began to clash with US. CAP's 1970 conference in Atlanta became the setting for a near deadly showdown between Baraka's security forces and a group of US Simba that were sent to intimidate the conference organizers. As soon as the US members appeared at the conference site, tension permeated the event. Armed CAP security people stood poised for a shoot-out that fortunately never occurred. Part of CAP's security force consisted of the former US members who had recently left

California, further increasing the chances of fratricidal violence at the conference.[88]

This group of former US members remained in CFUN for two or three years but eventually collided with the leadership over issues associated with their own adventurism, polygamy, and Baraka's own cult of personality. They had difficulty accepting the specificity of Newark's brand of cultural nationalism and tended to view themselves as the true bearers of the Kawaida tradition. A couple of former US Simba clashed with Baraka as they engaged in illegal underground activities that he felt endangered the organization.[89] Further, by the early seventies, the CFUN leadership circle, especially Amina Baraka, adamantly discouraged polygamy. Some of the former US members continued to live in polygamous households and were seen as setting a bad example and precedent for others.[90] Finally, differences were provoked by Baraka's cultish elevation of his own status as Imamu to proportions that the former advocates felt surpassed even what they experienced with Karenga in Los Angeles. The major point of contention was a "high holy day" that CFUN set up in honor of Imamu Baraka called Leo (blessed) Baraka Day.[91] Over time, those who had ventured eastward to continue the Kawaida mission went their separate ways, breaking ranks with CFUN and CAP.

CAP executive council members Baraka, Balozi Zayd Muhammad, and Imamu Vernon Sukumu responded by labeling the former US advocates "agents" and "paid traitors" committed to sowing the seeds of disruption after having been rightly purged by Maulana Karenga.[92] This development conveyed the instability and rapidly shifting alliances in a movement suffering from infighting and weariness from external repression. Ironically, the very group that had left Los Angeles to join forces with Baraka, designated as agents, had just previously been instrumental in preventing their former US comrades from disrupting both the 1970 and 1972 CAP bi-annual conferences.[93]

In any case, CFUN and CAP went on to play a major role in advocating Karenga's release from prison. He was denied parole in 1973 on the grounds that he "accepted only partial responsibility" for the offenses and "evades the seriousness" of the crime.[94] Some in the movement felt that Karenga's fate was a part of the U.S. government's campaign of political repression aimed at imprisoning and driving underground radical leaders throughout the United States.[95] While in prison, Karenga was restrained about pronouncing himself a political prisoner. When asked in a 1974 interview if he saw himself as such, he responded "That's such a facile phrase, I know one thing, that I'm innocent, that it was convenient for those people to do that to me and I understand why it happened and the adverse opinions that I got as a result of it. . . . With regard to my own case what I would like is for me to give the details of it and let other people decide and define the nature of my captivity."[96] Throughout his four-year stay at the California Men's Colony in San Luis Obispo, Karenga did not release a detailed public statement on his case, but he did author several critical and insightful articles relating to class, gender, and new directions for the movement in the post-1960s era, published in *Black Scholar.*[97]

After serving his four-year prison term, Karenga was paroled in 1975. During Karenga's stay in prison, Imamu Clyde Halisi served as chairman of US. The organization experienced an even further steady decrease in membership and scale of its activities during the early 1970s. By 1974 its ranks had dwindled to only a handful of committed members, and most of its activities were centered around maintaining an independent school, the Kawaida Educational and Development Center in Pasadena.[98] The group's decline in the early seventies had a lasting impact on what would become US in its contemporary form.

After his parole in 1975, Karenga reunited with his second wife, Tiamoyo Karenga (formerly Luz Maria Tamayo), who had

been convicted along with him. Together they joined with supporters in San Diego, one of whom was Ken Msemaji, one of US's
original members, then active in the Nia Cultural Organization,
formerly a cadre of CAP. Imamu Sukumu, also a former US
member, was Nia's main leader before CAP's ideological shift
in 1975.[99] Karenga now swiftly began organizing again in his
new cultural-nationalist formation called the New Afroamerican
Movement, while simultaneously completing doctoral studies in
political science at U.S. International University in San Diego.

From 1975 to 1980, Karenga renewed close links with former
CAP cadres in Brooklyn, Chicago, and New Orleans that had
maintained a nationalist position.[100] This alliance became a key
component for Karenga's successful post-1975 reentry into Black
nationalist activism. It provided national and international audiences and publication venues for a presentation of an updated
Kawaida theory, void of its quasi-religious emphasis and rede-
fined as a secularized ideology of social change based on pan-
African, nationalist, and socialist thought.[101] Many nationalists
found in Karenga's return a voice of clarity and a fresh analysis in
a period wrought with conservativism and a lack of popular support for Black nationalist initiatives.[102]

By the 1980s, after forming another interim group called the
Kawaida Groundwork Committee, Karenga had reestablished US
as a small but highly dedicated community-based organization in
Los Angeles. Only a few members who were active in the sixties
returned to US in the late seventies, and almost all of those active
while Karenga was in prison, including Halisi, chose not to remain. A couple of them attended meetings with Karenga in Pasadena and San Diego shortly after his release and gave serious
consideration to participating. But ultimately they decided that
he had not taken adequate personal responsibility for leadership
failures they felt had greatly contributed to the organization's demise and upheavals.[103] For most former US advocates, however,

the question was about moving on with their lives. Oliver He-shimu captures this sentiment in his reflections on why he could not return to US in its new form in the late seventies: "I don't know if [one] know[s] what it's like to put your life, your future, your every belief, your hope, everything that you have, into something and see it fall apart like that."[104] "I don't know what type of person it takes to just go back into that again," he continued, "but I wasn't that type. . . . It was just too painful."[105]

6. In the Face of Funk

US and the Arts of War

Maulana Karenga's essay "Black Art: Mute Matter Given Force and Function," originally published in 1968 as "Black Cultural Nationalism" in *Negro Digest,* was an influential treatise on the role of Black art in the "revolutionary" struggle during the era of Black Power. Using concepts introduced by Leopold Senghor, Karenga sought to explicate a criterion for evaluating Black art. "Black Art" captured resounding themes articulated in the cultural renaissance known as the Black Arts movement—often considered the artistic corollary to the Black Power movement. The Black Arts inspired many African American musical, literary, and visual artists with its emphasis on nationalist themes such as community control, self-defense, the institutionalization of a Black aesthetic, and use of working-class African American vernacular. US's cultural-nationalist philosophy thus found natural allies among many of the artists, activists, and cultural workers associated with the Black Arts movement.

Nationalist influences on the arts in the late sixties and early seventies gave rise to a close bond between creative production and political agitation. US's view of cultural revolution contributed to debates on the meaning of the new "Black aesthetic."[1] The search for unconventional conceptions of Black creative expression in this period augured well for US to position its doctrine, Kawaida, as a "new" Black revolutionary philosophy.[2]

Movement artists, from the standpoint of the US Organization, were charged with drawing their source of inspiration from the "masses" and simultaneously offering a transformative realization of their revolutionary potential. US activists frequently doubled as performing and visual artists themselves in the quest to bring forth public encounters with their vision of the Black post-liberation order—in effect, the red, black, and green at the end of the rainbow of struggle. Throughout US's tenure as a premier Black Power organization, the arts were a most effective outlet for the introduction of its alternative Black culture to African American audiences. There were multiple facets to US's efforts in the arts; woodcarving and fashion, for instance, powerfully captured and conveyed the group's sense of aesthetic to those outside of the organization. But this chapter focuses primarily on the cultural work of US members, and those sympathetic to Kawaida, in the areas of African dance, jazz music, and literature.

Taifa and Pan-Africanism

The US Organization's Taifa Dance Troupe (Taifa means "nation" in Kiswahili) exposed African Americans in Los Angeles to colorful African-style clothing, festive folk songs, and traditional South African dances. From 1967 until 1969, the dance troupe operated during the high point of US's prestige and effectiveness. As such, these years encapsulated the organization's "peacetime" ethos, prior to a critical mass of government repression, war with the Black Panther Party, internal dissension, and leadership breakdowns.

Shortly after US formed Taifa in 1967, the participants in the troupe received a creative boost by attending a performance of South African songstress Letta Mbulu and her husband, musician-composer Caiphus Semanya, at the Watts Summer Festival.[3]

Karenga, interested in South African culture, was already study-ing and speaking Zulu himself when he met Mbulu and Se-manya. Semanya recalled that, not long after the 1967 Watts Summer Festival, Karenga "asked us at one meeting that he had with us, if we could help them—the US Organization—with some music and dances from the 'motherland,' that's how he put it."[4] A relationship then ensued whereby these two and other South African artists taught traditional South African songs and dances to the Taifa Dance Troupe. This relationship was not merely that of teachers and students. US grew to become a fam-ily away from home for Semanya and Mbulu, who were political exiles. Mbulu remembered that, in a time of dire need, later in 1968, this relationship enabled them to raise funds to hire a lawyer so they could escape deportation.[5]

The dance troupe was comprised of different subgroups that performed specific dances. Members of the Simba Wachanga did the traditional miners' boot dance, another contingent of male and female dancers specialized in the traditional Zulu dance, and a segment of women dancers focused on a rain dance with vocal accompaniments taught by Letta Mbulu. Caiphus Semanya taught the Simba the boot dance and Ernest Thuso Mohlomi, John Sithebe, and Philiman Hou were the instructors of the Zulu dance.[6] The creative outcome of this collaboration was a cultural product of pan-African character. US members learned the ori-gins and meanings of the songs and dances but, consistent with their cultural nationalist ideology, did not regard African tradi-tions as static or unworthy of adjustment to their own African American cultural sensibilities. Reflecting on Taifa's view of tra-dition, Joann Kicheko, who co-led the troupe along with Ngao Damu—remarked, "Our perspective was that you go back to Africa and learn—you bring it forward and then you re-create it." She went on to note that "there was no sense that we didn't feel that we could change it or redirect it."[7]

The dances themselves, filtered through the life experiences and worldview of these US members, were distinct from their South African counterparts. The boot dance, performed by the Simba, was exemplary of this pan-African mélange. Kicheko understood the origins of this dance as follows:

> The boot dance is a dance that came out of the diamond mines and other types of mines that are in South Africa. The men . . . had to walk to and from the mine area. They didn't have bus transportation. It was from what I understand a pretty fair trek for you to walk in the morning. . . . They had different shifts. They had 24-hour shifts. So you would be trekking through the sand or the dirt and you would have on your rubber [mining] boots. So Africans being creative are not going to walk any distance without any rhythm going on, so they created the boot dance. I think the miners, to this day, do either the boot dance or something else to and from the mines as they are walking and that's how this came about.[8]

A televised Taifa performance in 1968 shed light on the linguistic, theatrical, and musical mixture that went into this dance. During the show, the leader of the seven Simba performing the boot dance emerged and shouted the following Zulu phrase: "*Ninga Mabuthu* [Are You Warriors]?" The others responded, "*Yebo* [Yes]!" In another instant, the Simba, as they stepped, called on a Yoruba warrior deity, "*Willy, Willy, Shango!*"[9] When counting off the beginning of a different pattern in the step, the dancers did so in the US Organization's lingua franca, Kiswahili. Interestingly enough, the Kiswahili numbers "moja, mbili, tatu" were changed to a monosyllabic form making the numbers fit into an African American rhythmic pattern—1, 2, 3. This count replaced "moja, mbili, tatu" with the utterance of the last syllable of each number—"ja, li, tu."[10]

Maulana Karenga and Hakim Jamal. Early US literature designated Jamal as the group's founder and Karenga as its chairman. Jamal was a close friend of Malcolm X. He left the US Organization in early 1966 apparently as the group became steeped in Chairman Karenga's own ideology rather than Malcolm X's. (Courtesy of the Harry Adams Collection, Center for Photojournalism & Visual History, Journalism Department, California State University, Northridge)

US member Vernon Sukumu wearing a Malcolm X sweatshirt, frequently worn by US members in the group's early years. The US members considered themselves heirs of Malcolm X's legacy. Sukumu went on to chair US's affiliate chapter in San Diego. (Courtesy of Vernon Sukumu)

Early US circle meeting with Maulana Karenga. To the left of Karenga: Tommy Jacquette-Halifu, Ken Msemaji, Ngao Damu, Thomas Henson-Hakika, and Karl Key-Hekima. (Courtesy of Terry Damu)

Brenda Haiba Karenga, Maulana Karenga's first wife and founding member of US, teaches children at the Aquarian Center, US's initial meeting place. (Courtesy of Terry Damu)

Sanamu Nyeusi, secretary-treasurer and charismatic presence in the formative months of US. (Courtesy of Terry Damu)

US members pause from distributing literature at a conference. Sitting, left to right, are Clyde Halisi and James Mtume. Standing, left to right, are Melvin Mabadiliko, Asali Halisi, Diama Hekima, Ngao Damu, Subira Dhani, and William Dhani. (Courtesy of C. R. D. Halisi)

Early Kwanzaa set in the home of Ngao Damu, a founding US member. The *Kinara* (candle holder), *Mishumma* (candles), *Kikombe cha Umoja* (unity cup), *Mkeka* (mat), *Zawaidi* (gifts), and *Mazao* (crops) are shown above. At a different location from the one shown above, approximately fifty people attended the first Kwanzaa Karamu feast on December 31, 1966. The event was held at the home of an US supporter, Noble Hanif [?], near Washington Street and Tenth Avenue in Los Angeles. (Courtesy of Terry Damu)

Brenda Haiba Karenga being escorted after taking her marriage vows in a mass
1967 US Arusi (wedding ceremony) officiated by Maulana Karenga. James and
Carmelita Tayari, Karl and Diama Hekima, Ngao and Imani Damu, Ray and
Ujima Imara, William and Subira Dhani, Oliver and Hasani Heshimu, Melvin
and Constance Mabadiliko, Joe and Diane Jomo, and Frank and Rene Kudumu
were other couples married at this ceremony. (Courtesy UCLA Library, Department of Special Collections)

Group of US women at the 1967 US wedding. Women in US (Muminina)
worked in an organization that embraced male dominance as part of its doctrine. They, nonetheless, were extremely active and essential to US's day-to-day
functioning and political outreach in the Black community. (Courtesy UCLA
Library, Department of Special Collections)

Amiri Baraka, Maulana Karenga (left, below), Ken Msemaji (left, standing),
H. Rap Brown, presently named Jamil Amin (right, sitting), Imamu Halisi
(right standing), and Floyd McKissick (far right, sitting) at the 1967 Black
Power Conference. The conference took place in the wake of a massive urban
uprising in Newark, New Jersey. Baraka was still wearing head bandages from
wounds sustained by a police beating. At that point Baraka was in the process of
developing a close alliance with the US Organization. Later on in the early
1970s, Baraka's Congress of African People and Committee for a Unified
Newark eclipsed US as the foremost cultural nationalist force in the Black
Power movement. (Courtesy of C. R. D. Halisi)

Members of US's paramilitary wing, Simba Wachanga (young lions), demonstrating their form of martial arts called *Yangumi* (the way of the fist). The Simba trained extensively in weaponry and martial arts. Some of them participated in underground guerrilla activities against government authorities and private institutions. Standing in the back, from the left to the right, are Walter Williams-Jadili, Robert Butler-Chochezi, Earl Evans-Giza, and Fred Sefu-Glover, seen demonstrating a stance and movement in the front. (Courtesy of Rosalind Goddard)

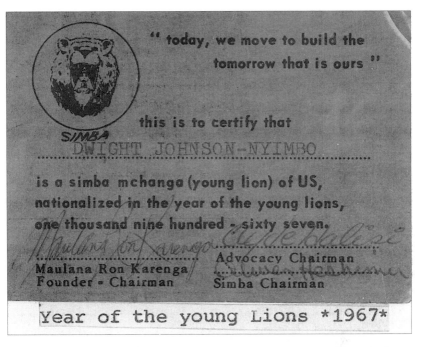

"today, we move to build the
tomorrow that is ours"

this is to certify that

SIMBA

DWIGHT JOHNSON-NYIMBO

is a simba mchanga (young lion) of US,
nationalized in the year of the young lions,
one thousand nine hundred - sixty seven.

Maulana Ron Karenga
Founder - Chairman

Advocacy Chairman

Simba Chairman

Year of the young Lions *1967*

1967 Simba Wachanga certification card of Dwight Johnson-Nyimbo. Nyimbo was among the first group to join US's paramilitary wing. (Courtesy of Charles Johnson-Sitawisha)

Members of US's Taifa Dance Troupe performing the Zulu dance. The troupe learn traditional African folk songs and dances from South African artists: songstress Letta Mbulu, her husband songwriter and musician, Caiphus Semanya, Ernest Thuso Mohlomi, John Sithebe, and Philiman Hou. (Courtesy of Charles Johnson-Sitawisha)

Sometime in late 1967 or early 1968, Black marines in Vietnam formed a division of US, known as the Fulani tribe of the Simba Wachanga. Joe Harris-Askari, founder of the Fulani tribe, speaking to his comrades in their headquarters, known as the Hekalu (temple), located in Chu Lai, Vietnam. (Courtesy of Charles Johnson-Sitawisha)

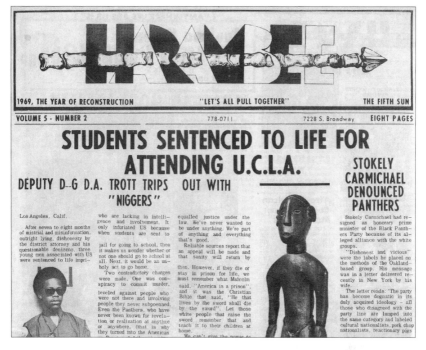

Front page of *Harambee* with the headline "Students Sentenced to Life for Attending UCLA." US's newspaper was reacting to the conviction of Larry Watani-Stiner, George Ali-Stiner, and Donald Hawkins-Stodi for the killing of Black Panther Party leaders Alprentice "Bunchy" Carter and John Huggins at UCLA in January 1969. The tragic events marked the beginning of the end of US's tenure as a premier Black Power organization. Throughout 1969 and 1970 US was plagued by the violent feud with the Black Panther Party, alienation from the Black communities of Southern California, internal factionalization and violent in-fighting among its own ranks, and eventually a leadership breakdown.

Gail Idili-Davis recounted a horrific ordeal of torture and confine-
ment that occurred in the spring of 1970. She was one of the two
women that Karenga and three other US members were convicted
of assaulting with intent to do great bodily injury. (Courtesy of Gail
Idili-Davis)

Above: Karenga along with Wesely Kabaila (left) and attorney Richard Walton (right) leave the courtroom after the assault conviction in May 1971. (Courtesy UCLA Library, Department of Special Collections)

Left: Maulana Karenga at the Men's Colony at San Luis Obispo where he served four years, from 1971 through 1975. Imamu Clyde Halisi chaired the US Organization throughout the period in which Karenga was incarcerated. (Courtesy UCLA Library, Department of Special Collections)

Maulana Karenga and his current wife, Tiamoyo Karenga (left) and educator Denise Lee (right) pause for pictures after a Kawaida wedding (Arusi), which Karenga officiated in 1994. By the 1990s Maulana Karenga had acquired the status of a renowned scholar of Black Studies, having earned two doctoral degrees and authored numerous books and scholarly articles on African philosophy, Black Studies, and African American politics. (Courtesy of Scot Brown)

US, now called the "Organization Us," houses regular cultural and educational activities, an independent school, and a publishing company in its current headquarters, the African American Cultural Center, located in South Central Los Angeles. Members, supporters, and allies of the current Organization US attended its 30th anniversary celebration in 1995. Standing from the left to the right, after participating in anniversary festivities, are Karen Malina White, Brian "Chambuzi" Sales, and Shadidi Turner. (Courtesy of Scot Brown)

Throughout the boot dance, certain steps honored leaders in the US Organization, such as the military commander Amiri Jomo and Maulana Karenga. At times these steps were fashioned to fit personality traits or habits attributed to the heroic figure to whom praise was being given. Kicheko, after viewing the Simba's step for the Maulana (Master Teacher), stated that "they had a step they did for Maulana which was a slower step because Maulana never danced fast. . . . he did not kick up his heels and wiggle. It was a slow movement. So they created a step for him in acknowledgment of him."[11]

The musical accompaniment to the boot dance also veered away from tradition. James Mtume, Charles Sigidi, and George Subira played congas and other percussive instruments while the Simba performed.[12] However, as Caiphus Semanya noted, the boot dance in South Africa did not use percussive instruments: "There are no congas in the boot dance. It's one guitar and the boot dancers."[13] Semanya regarded this hybridity as consistent with his own interest in pan-African musical exchange and considered the mixture akin to the cultural mélange found in Cuban and Brazilian music.[14] The troupe's interpretations of South African dance and song were consistent with the US Organization's overall approach to tradition and culture. Collaborations with Caiphus Semanya and Letta Mbulu granted US members access to the fundamentals of traditional African dances and songs, though their own conception of themselves as a political and cultural vanguard mediated against a purist notion of African cultural practice.

The troupe was one of the most effective recruiting mechanisms for US, performing at festivals, high schools, conferences, and rallies throughout Southern California and beyond.[15] A large portion of US members' initial fascination with the organization came from watching the colorful movements and chanting voices of Taifa. The troupe presented an inspiring representation of the motherland and the pan-African elements of a new Black culture in the United States, an accomplishment that US members felt distinguished their group from other African American activist organizations. Karenga boasted that his organization was "the first time that Blacks have gotten together to create a new culture based on revolution and recovery."[16]

The Taifa Dance Troupe's ability to function as a platform for the cultural revolution depended on a receptive African American community and access to public space, both of which were in abundance at the peak of the troupe's prominence from late 1967 until early 1969. The shootings at UCLA shattered US's normative and proactive activities and programs. Most of Taifa's members, men and women, rapidly had to shift their energies away from recruitment to defense, security, and other paramilitary-like duties. The aftermath of this tragedy undermined the US Organization's rapport and credibility in Black communities in Southern California.[17] As C. R. D. Halisi, the former Imamu (high priest) and chairman of US during the 1970s, noted, the conflict "forced a tremendous militarization of the organization . . . and the community became afraid."[18]

US and Jazz

While the US/Panther conflict subverted the efficacy of the Taifa Dance Troupe, it helped catapult the organization's brief, but nonetheless significant, influence on several key jazz musicians and their works. The seeds for this development were planted before the deadly events of January 1969 took place. James Mtume, who had become an US advocate in 1966, along with a group of fellow students from Pasadena City College,[19] is the son of renowned jazz saxophonist Jimmy Heath and was raised by James "Hengates" Forman, a jazz pianist, and his mother, Bertha Forman, a jazz enthusiast.[20]

As an US advocate in the late 1960s, Mtume embraced the group mandate of spreading Kawaida by influencing others to accept the doctrine. His personal acquaintance with many jazz musicians, because of his family background, offered opportunities to introduce them to his cultural-nationalist philosophy. "When jazz groups would come and perform at Shelly's Manhole or The Lighthouse [jazz clubs in Los Angeles]," Mtume recalled, "I would go out and talk to them."[21] Sometime in 1968, Mtume began to have a major impact on the Herbie Hancock sextet in which his uncle Albert Heath was the drummer. These musicians' interest in US's ideology was further extended when they decided to take on Kiswahili names that Mtume provided for them.

Like all US members who accepted African names, Mtume gave each musician a new name based on the translation of a term describing a personal quality. "For us to have a Swahili name," said Albert Heath, "that was something exciting and new." Mtume "told us why we needed to have these names and we needed to redefine ourselves and that the names we had didn't really suit our personalities." Having the new names, Heath added, "gave us this connection with Ron Karenga's organization . . . although we did not belong to the organization."[22] Other musicians allied with the sextet who went through this identity change were Herbie Hancock, who was renamed Mwandishi (master composer); Buster Williams, who became Mchezaji (the player); Albert Heath, who became Kuumba (creativity); Jimmy Heath, who became Tayari (ready); Eddie Henderson, who became Mganga (the healer); and Billy Bonner, who was renamed Fundi (the craftsman).[23]

Amiri Baraka's Committee For a Unified Newark (CFUN), an East Coast affiliate of the US Organization, grew in stature after the UCLA shootings while US was declining.[24] Having visited Los Angeles in 1969, Baraka stated that "[b]ecause of the constant shootouts and military encounters with the Panthers and the police . . . US was not able to do much in the way of community organizing. The whole function of the organization now was security and defense, all development was on hold."[25] CFUN came to be regarded by some as a possible heir to the US Organization in promoting Kawaida and continuing the proactive community organizing that had come to a halt in Los Angeles. James Mtume was among a group of Saidi who had left the organization to join forces with CFUN in Newark—in the hope that they could continue their cultural-nationalist mission there.[26] It is within these stormy circumstances that Albert Heath, Herbie Hancock, Jimmy Heath, Mtume, Billy Bonner, and Don Cherry recorded an album entitled *Kawaida* on December 11, 1969, in New York, which promoted US's Kawaida cultural-nationalist ideology through jazz music.[27]

Mtume wrote all of the songs on *Kawaida* except for one, entitled "Dunia," which was written by his uncle. This was unique given that Mtume was a relative musical novice, recording with some of the greatest jazz figures at that time. Albert Heath obtained the record deal and had the contacts to bring in other acclaimed musicians. He allowed Mtume to bring the philosophical concept to the project as well as compose the music. "I was the 'whipper-snapper,'" Mtume stated. "I'm in here with all of these great artists. I was just overwhelmed to be sitting there giving them their parts and their taking those parts very seriously and letting me do my thing."[28]

The first song on the *Kawaida* album is entitled "Baraka" in recognition of Imamu Amiri Baraka, who came to be the major cultural-nationalist political and artistic voice in the early 1970s. Not only did Mtume have a particular affinity for Baraka because of the view that the US Organization's mission would be continued by CFUN, it was further enhanced by Baraka's work as a jazz critic and interpreter.[29] In addition, Baraka frequently used music as a creative motif and theoretical reference in his poetic and scholarly works. When describing an aesthetic blueprint for a Black nationalist societal alternative at a speech in San Francisco, Baraka did not differentiate between jazz and soul, asking the audience to "dig the idea of buildings that look like John Coltrane's solos or automobiles that look like James Brown's singing."[30] Baraka was also viewed as a spiritual leader in the Kawaida movement. Sometime around 1968, Karenga gave Baraka the name/title "Imamu," for "high priest."[31]

The spiritual aspect of Baraka as an Imamu was at the center of the song "Baraka." It opens with several voices chanting a popular Kiswahili phrase among US advocates: "Sifa Ote Ina Mtu Weusi," which means "all praise to the Black man" in Kiswahili. The backdrop of soft flutes, chimes, a gospel-like humming voice, and periodic interventions from the piano and bass give these chants an added sense of being a call to invoke a mystical transcendent force.[32] "We were trying to convey some spirituality, a prayer," Heath said. "We were opening the ceremony, like the opening of most African ceremonies start with a prayer." "This," he went on to say, "is why we're rejoicing and praying . . . [t]hen we got into the music which was the offering."[33]

After the opening chorus of sounds and voices slowly diminish, Buster Williams's (Mchezaji's) bass line begins to orchestrate a commanding melody driven by the horns. Midway into the song, Heath's voice is heard summoning Baraka's presence, calling "Ameer, Ameer, Ameer."[34] This song, like all of the songs on the album, is a modal piece, and there is a steady groove throughout, complemented by solos, slight variations, and breaks. Both Mtume and Heath felt this arrangement made jazz music more accessible and sensitive to African Americans' musical aesthetic. "What the mode does," Mtume argued, "it creates a certain fiber that runs through the composition as opposed to many different chord changes." "One of the things that makes jazz inaccessible to a lot of Black people," he contended, "is the chord changes constantly moving. . . . Repetition is not boring."[35] He considered repetition or "the groove" as a central part of Black people's musical sensibilities and argued that its basis can be found in continental African drumming.[36]

Heath concurred with Mtume's views about jazz but felt this arrangement sometimes went against the tendencies of many musicians who had, in his view, become elitist and disconnected from the African American masses. He also said, "Jazz musicians have a tendency to play over everybody's head and to play faster than anybody can pat their foot. They play so fast you can't dance to the music or they play so many chords that you can't sing the song."[37] There was a clear sense that Mtume and Heath were self-conscious about making jazz on this recording, which appealed to the very sensibilities that could give their music a larger audience.

The album's title track "Kawaida" connects these musicians to the US Organization's cultural-nationalist ideology in a most extraordinary manner. The only instruments in this song are wooden flutes that each of the musicians plays freely without any sense of rehearsed structure. The listener's attention is forced to focus on the voices of each musician taking turns reciting the definitions of the Seven Principles (Nguzo Saba): Umoja (unity), Kujichagulia (self-determination), Ujima (collective work and responsibility), Ujamaa (cooperative economics), Nia (purpose), Kuumba (creativity), and Imani (faith). For instance, Herbie Hancock (Mwandishi) instructs the listener that Ujima means "collective work and responsibility: to build and maintain our community together and to make our brothers' and sisters' problems our problems, and to solve them together."[38]

After they finish reciting the Seven Principles, Mtume and others follow with phrases from the US manifesto, *The Quotable Karenga:* "To go back to tradition is the first step forward," and "We don't borrow from Africa, we utilize that which was ours to start."

A voice responds to these phrases saying, "Teach! Learn!" Toward the end of the composition, these different voices peak by coming together, and various Kiswahili chants and calls are layered on top of one another. It ends with the fading of the flutes, whose sounds move wildly in the background.[39]

The wooden flutes were chosen to create a spiritual, temple-like atmosphere and an "eastern sensibility."[40] The flutes also inspired a sense of camaraderie among the musicians. "The other reason for the flutes," Mtume stated, "is that we all could do that. We couldn't all jump on the piano. We couldn't all jump on the bass."[41] This granted the musicians freedom from constraints associated with their regular instruments. Mtume noted that the flutes had "no tonal center, there's no chord, it's all free form."[42]

"Kawaida" projects a religious or spiritual feeling. Indeed, the musicians' reading of the US doctrine gives the impression that, for at least that moment, they shared a belief in Kawaida as a philosophy. Heath, however, was skeptical about the extent to which this indicated a larger commitment. When asked whether or not they really believed in the doctrine that they celebrated in this song, Heath suggested that a less profound relationship to these ideas took place: "I think some of us were reading," he replied.[43] Mtume, on the other hand, felt that the session produced an intense yet brief spiritual consensus among them: "For that moment in time we all felt a collective truth, it was the time and circumstance of that period."[44]

The album has, in addition to "Baraka" and "Kamili"—a song dedicated to Mtume's wife—another commemorative piece, entitled "Maulana." By 1969, praise of the Maulana or Master Teacher had long since become standard practice in various forms of artistic expression among US and Kawaida advocates. US members often ritualistically expressed reverence for their leader's intellect and oratorical ability. Halisi's poem "Maulana and Word Magic" gives praise to Karenga's speaking style, which the advocates cherished during their Sunday evening gatherings called "Soul Sessions."[45] Amiri Baraka's poem "For Maulana & Pharoah Sanders" links Karenga's rhetorical abilities with the sounds and images created by Pharoah Sanders' saxophone. For Baraka, both shared an equal capacity to create images that satisfied a human need to experience a higher level of interaction with beauty.[46] The instrumental dedication to the Master Teacher was in some respects the continuation of an organizational trend involving jazz musicians who were, with the exception of Mtume, at best only peripherally connected to the cultural-nationalist movement.

The song entitled "Maulana" begins with a soft and lengthy piano introduction by Herbie Hancock (Mwandishi) that ends with Hancock playing the song's melody on the bass keys, leading the way to the entry of the other instruments, as in "Baraka." For a couple of moments, Heath's singing voice, accompanied by a melodic horn line, summons the Master Teacher. Trumpeter Don Cherry (Msafari) is the first soloist in "Maulana."[47] By the time of this recording session in December 1969, Mtume had already departed from US and had been assaulted by a group of his former comrades. He had serious doubts about the quality and conduct of US's leadership during this period of strife.[48] Nevertheless, the song ends with his voice humbly giving thanks to the Master Teacher, Maulana.[49] This gesture, Mtume said, was "my way of saying thank you for some very positive things that were given." By this point he had shed his exaggerated reverence for Maulana and begun to "separate the principles from the person. That to me was my farewell."[50]

The farewell did not thwart a continuing effort to apply and explicate Karenga's theories through jazz music. His attempt to provide an expanded definition to the Kawaida perspective on jazz began before his departure from US and continued through the early seventies. In 1971, the Mtume Umoja Ensemble recorded a second attempt at creating a revolutionary Kawaida jazz form, the live album *Alkebulan: Land of the Blacks*.[51] The ensemble was made up of a broad range of jazz artists: Carlos Garnett, Ndugu, Leroy Jenkins, Gary Bartz, Stanley Cowell, Buster Williams, and Billy Hart (Jabali). Also featured were vocalists Eddie Micheaux, Joe Lee Wilson, and Andy Bey as well as two poets, Yusef Iman and Weusi Kuumba.[52] *Alkebulan* was recorded live at the cultural center The East, a Brooklyn-based cultural-nationalist organization led by Jitu Weusi. At that time, it was a member organization of the Congress of African People.

Both albums, *Kawaida* and *Alkebulan,* rely heavily on speech or vocal narratives to assist the listener in gaining a sense of the music's message. In fact, the first piece on *Alkebulan* is called "Invocation" and has no instrumentation. Only Mtume's voice is heard, preaching his cultural-nationalist ideology and informing the listener about the political purpose of the music, for three or four minutes. Looking back at how the use of vocal narratives supported his creative and political agenda, Mtume stated, "If you're dealing with a music that has no words, instrumental music, which is basically what jazz is, then one must create a context to explain the source and dimension of that music. Once the ear digests the information in terms of what the spoken word is, what the dedication of this stuff is, then you hear the music differently."[53] The "Invocation" is explicit in its attempt to make the listener aware of the artist's ideological orientation and political objectives. "The music retained in this album," Mtume declared, "is the humble offering to the unity of the entire Black nation and all those who through Kawaida have tasted the nectar of its totality."[54] "The sounds which are about to saturate your being and sensitize your soul," he continued, "is the continuing process of nationalist consciousness manifesting its message within the context of one of our strongest natural resources, Black music."[55]

None of the musicians involved in these projects was as fully dedicated to propagating the Kawaida doctrine as Mtume. Without a direct relationship with US or CFUN, they eventually moved on to take different musical paths. As the Black cultural-nationalist movement waned in the mid-1970s, Mtume began to write songs that appealed to the popular Black market in funk and dance music. Close links, nevertheless, persisted between jazz artists and Black nationalist ideologies, and they continue in multiple forms today. US's connection to jazz, during the Black Power years, was not the result of official pronouncements or seemingly predictable tendencies of cultural nationalism. These developments were part of a way by which an US member, along with many others, sought to reconcile a deep commitment to the organization's ideals with its decline, alongside the wider repression of political dissent in the United States.[56]

Imamu Amiri Baraka and Poetry

The process by which US's ideas began to influence cultural-nationalist writers in the late sixties and early seventies also grew out of direct personal relationships. In 1967, Karenga visited the Spirit House in Newark, New Jersey, a Black theater/arts collective run by Baraka. Baraka was already a premier literary figure of the Black Arts movement—a celebrated poet, playwright, musicologist, critic, and social commentator. Karenga was interested in revealing his own views in poetry and would sometimes end a speech with "Sheeba Revisited," a piece he had written. He believed that writers had a special role in the liberation struggle.[57] "We must make warriors out of our poets and writers," he declared in the *Quotable Karenga,* "for if all our writers would speak as warriors our battle would be half won. Literature conditions the mind, and the battle for the mind is the first half of the struggle."[58]

When Karenga arrived at the Spirit House along with two other US members, he was eager to discuss Baraka's works, particularly *Home* and *Blues People.*[59] Baraka, for his part, was impressed by the US Organization's discipline and structured, systematic approach to knowledge, but he was initially bothered by Karenga's "arrogance."[60] However, "What Karenga brought with him," Baraka noted, "was a total freshness and sense of formal commitment that I hadn't seen before."[61] This approach appeared to be a remedy for the general lack of discipline in the Black Arts movement: "They [US members] were straight and convinced they were correct, and it then seemed healthy, in the sense that they were not too hairy, atavist, weed-smoking culturists that I had known and was an eminent part of."[62] By the end of the meeting, Baraka stated, "I had been stirred to reevaluate where I was coming from, and definitely where I was going."[63]

James Doss-Tayari, then vice-chair of US, felt the meeting produced an instant intellectual camaraderie: "Their positions complemented each other."[64] However, they held opposing views in their respective assessments and appreciation for blues music.[65] Baraka recounted that Karenga "thought the blues were reactionary. That blues were talking about slavery and submission. I blinked and politely disagreed."[66]

In the quest for a comprehensive theory of Black art, Karenga referred to blues music to demonstrate the evaluative dimension of his cultural-nationalist doctrine and its capacity to designate certain art forms as invalid. "Art," he stated, "will revive us, inspire us, give us enough courage to face another disappointing day." The blues, he felt, were locked into a discourse of suffering and oppression, rendering it incapable of inspiring revolutionary change. "We say the blues are invalid," Karenga concluded, "for they teach resignation, in a word acceptance of reality—and we have come to change reality." This focus on transformative art, Karenga argued, distinguished previous generations of

African Americans from the Black Power era's cultural-nationalist refusal to "submit to the resignation of our fathers who lost their money, their women, and their lives and sat around wondering, 'What did I do to be so black and blue?'"[67]

Karenga felt that the blues had historical validity as a Black expression of the past but had exhausted its revolutionary utility. The blues, he stated, are "a very beautiful, musical and psychological achievement of our people, but today they are not functional because they do not commit us to the struggle of today and tomorrow, but keep us in the past."[68] While Baraka and many other nationalist-inspired writers of that era agreed with the notion that art should serve the revolution, they often still had a great affinity for the blues.[69]

Some poets, such as Nikki Giovanni, concurred with negative assessments of the blues,[70] while others clearly dissented and saw Karenga's cultural nationaslim as a new form of elitism. Sam Greenlee's poem "Soul Brothers" equates Karenga's position with the anti-folk hostilities of Black conservative and reactionary leaders.[71] James Cunningham's response to "Black Cultural Nationalism" highlighted the narrowness of Black cultural nationalist art criticism. Although motivated by "a sincere desire for unity," cultural nationalism's excessive advocacy, Cunningham argued, easily degenerated into dogmatism. He then challenged nationalists to cultivate a sensitivity for a range of individual experiences, including personal resignation, in their discussions about the role of art in the Black freedom struggle.[72]

The quarrel over the blues contrasted, paradoxically, with a consensus between Baraka and Karenga that Black literature lacked a revolutionary tradition. In fact, prior to his meeting with Karenga in 1967, Baraka described the African American literary tradition as mainly an expression of "mediocrity" and a "spectacular vapidity."[73] This, he claimed, resulted from the middle-class status of the writers and, by extension, their preoccupation with escaping Blackness and becoming assimilated Americans. According to him, the only Black art form to escape this tragedy was music, specifically blues and jazz:

> Negro music alone, because it drew its strengths and beauties out of the depth of the black man's soul, and because to a large extent its traditions could be carried on by the lowest classes of Negroes, has been able to survive the constant and willful dilutions of the black middle class. Blues and jazz have been the only consistent exhibitors of "Negritude" in formal American culture simply because the bearers of its tradition maintained their essential identities as Negroes[;] in no other art . . . has this been possible.[74]

Baraka's stance positioned music as a barometer that determines the status of African American literature and other Black arts. His understanding of the blues, as produced by artists in solidarity with working classes, was in part responsible for his ability to agree with Karenga's contention in 1966 that Black literature "is only now being made."[75]

Early dialogues between Karenga and Baraka on music and literature, in 1967, when US had not yet faced the brunt of repression, aided a rising bicoastal cultural-nationalist alliance.[76] Ironically, Baraka's ascension to cultural-nationalist priest "Imamu" peaked in the face of funk, when US had been stifled and its own leadership was imploding. In this context, Kawaida functioned as a Black gospel from 1969 through the mid-1970s, guiding the poetry, theatrical creations, and criticism of a premier African American writer.

Baraka's Kawaida writings aimed to fulfill Karenga's mandate to (1) expose the enemy, (2) praise the people, and (3) support the revolution. At certain points, one of these three priorities would take precedence or would even conflict with the other

two. The US Organization's portrait of "the enemy" was not restricted to White supremacy and its institutions, but also to African Americans (Negroes or, mockingly, "knee-grows") who refused to relinquish a self-destructive value system.[77]

Baraka's poem "Who will Survive America / Few Americans /
Very Few Negroes / No crackers at all," a vision of a Black revolutionary society in the United States, describes character types
incapable of enduring the aftermath of the Black uprising. Paradoxically, the types of "Negroes" that supposedly would not survive were very much common folks or "everyday people"; church-
goers and old people represented a backward past to be left
behind.[78] "The stiff backed chalklady baptist," Baraka wrote, "in
blue lace / if she shrinks from blackness in front of the church
. . . will not survive." He added, "She is old anyway, and they're
moving / her church in the wind / Old people. No. / Christians
No."[79] The combined refutation of Christianity and "old" unde-
sirable Black folkways exemplified Baraka's effort to expose the
enemy within the Black community—the adoption of counterrevolutionary values.

Though "Who will Survive America" casts a negative light on
African Americans who have no Black nationalist consciousness,
other works center on praising the people and find majesty and
grandeur in the masses, irrespective of their political affiliation.
The collection of poems and photography by Baraka and Fundi
(Bill Abernathy) *In Our Terribleness: (Some elements and meaning in
black style)* invokes "Terrible" as an aesthetic descriptor: "*Terribleness*—Our beauty is BAD cause we bad," Baraka wrote, "Bad
things. Some bad bad bad ass niggers."[80] The concept embraces
the language and the survival strategies of the Black working class. "Who will Survive America" concerns itself with fore-
casting Black people's ability to survive a forthcoming apoca-
lypse, the Black revolution. *In Our Terribleness* praises African
Americans for surviving oppression and remaining "beautiful
throughout."

The book is filled with pictures of common folk doing common things: riding the bus, walking down the street, standing on the corner. The accompanying prose assigns a sense of grandeur and divinity to the images as if to project common folks as gods and goddesses. The book even contained a removable mirror with the phrase "In Our Terribleness" inscribed on it. The mirror was flexible so that one's image can be changed and altered. The reader could see his or her own "terribleness." Baraka regarded praise of the people's beauty as part of his responsibility as an Imamu. The book's dedication was "FOR ALL THE ADVOCATES OF KAWAIDA / FOR THE ADVOCATES— / TEACH KAWAIDA!!"[81]

"Come See about Me," a poem published in the 1972 collection *Spirit Reach*, expresses Baraka's sense of spiritual obligation as priest, asking, through prayer, for divine assistance for the Black liberation struggle.[82] Its tone shifts from that of a humble plea for God's help to that of an official grievance, presented by the representative of a people whose need for mass exodus (either cultural of physical) had been overlooked.[83] "All in the Street," also in *Spirit Reach*, situates Baraka as a prophetic voice in conversation with future generations of Black people who are completely liberated from oppression. These futuristic Black people, through Baraka, assure African Americans of a coming victory. "We know the struggle / you go thru now. / We know how hard it is to be black / in that primitive age. But do not / naaw . . . do not ever despair / We won / We here / . . . We still baddest thing on the planet."[84] As the Imamu, Baraka was the only one capable of having contact with these future generations. He explained this to his audience, noting: "They [the Black people of the future] would appear right here to / say these things but do not want to / frighten you / instead / they speak thru / me."[85]

Baraka also provided imagery for millenarian dimensions of Kawaida's Seven Year Calendar, which predicted the process by which African Americans would become liberated. US members looked to 1969 as the "Year of Reconstruction" wherein Black people were collectively to focus on internal rebuilding before separating from the American nation-state the following year, and have an eventual all-out war with White America.[86] The poem "In the Year" details the process by which African Americans who turned inward would chart out a new cultural identity and a forthcoming political struggle.[87]

> In the year of reconstruction, 1969, we turn again
> to look at our selves, turn again to old understanding
> experience colors the landscape reality color, curtains of words
> trap dreams like objects as suicide name America
> breathe farts on our momentary conclusions
> so turn again
> rear up again
> the thing we need, is each other
> if we could find completion as sand lays cool for the rising
> wave
> a natural
> though the tide returns each night
> and the earth speeds through space
> they hook up just the same.[88]

Poems of this sort were especially faith-inducing to Baraka's organizational audience—at the Hekalu in Newark and in other independent nationalist-cultural centers nationwide.

By the mid-seventies Baraka shifted from a cultural-nationalist concept of revolution to a Marxist-Leninist-Maoist one. With this change, Baraka zealously disavowed Black cultural nationalism. The transformation alienated him from poets and activists committed to cultural nationalism and pan-Africanism, such as Haki Madhubuti and Kalamu ya Salaam. In his autobiography, Baraka recalled an incident in March 1974 that became a turning point in his relations with other cultural nationalists:

At a meeting in Chicago a midwestern regional meeting of CAP [Congress of African People], I read a speech, "National Liberation and Politics," which ended by calling for the inclusion of Marx's theories and the teachings of Lenin and Mao as part of Revolutionary *Kawaida*. The speech was more of a bombshell than I anticipated. At the end of the meeting, both Jitu Weusi of The East and Haki Madhubuti of IPE [Institute of Positive Education] resigned.[89]

Ironically, Baraka, once a scathingly vociferous critic of Black Marxists, had, by October 1974, declared CAP "a Marxist-Leninist organization."[90] Karenga, after his release from prison in 1975, viewed Baraka's ideological change as a hasty conversion replete with religious overtones. "Baraka's tragedy is not his transformation," Karenga lamented in 1977, "but the toll it is taking on the Movement as a result of the counterproductive form it has assumed . . . the bridges burned and the boats sunk now that he has crossed Jordan into the illusive promised land."[91] Baraka's ideological changes in the mid-1970s marked the end of a period in which one of the greatest literary figures in the United States was the key propagandist for an African American nationalist organization and philosophy. His tenure as an advocate of US's philosophy was a unique occurrence in African American history (analogous to the idea of James Baldwin operating as a spokesperson for the Nation of Islam).

Haki Madhubuti and Kalamu ya Salaam

Poet, activist, and publisher Haki Madhubuti was among a group of poets influenced by Baraka's literary style and political views. When Baraka became a Marxist, placing a greater emphasis on the class struggle as opposed to Black cultural revolution,

Madhubuti vigorously objected. His essay "The Latest Purge: The Attack on Black Nationalism and Pan-Afrikanism by the New Left—the Sons and Daughters of the Old Left" (published in 1974) criticizes defectors to the Marxist camp, contending that "communism and capitalism are the left and right arms of the same white body."[92] The essay sparked an extensive debate in *Black Scholar.* Unlike Baraka's broadsides, Madhubuti's criticism of Black Marxists was devoid of any personal attacks. "The Latest Purge" signified Madhubuti's movement away from poetry, toward essays and political commentary in response to Marxist and feminist challenges to Black nationalism. He felt a need to formulate new positions capable of explaining issues relating to class and gender that had been previously ignored.

Madhubuti had written collections of political commentary before 1974. *From Plan to Planet, Life Studies: The Need for Afrikan Minds and Institutions,* published the previous year, is a blueprint for the establishment of independent African American institutions: schools, book publishers, and general communications apparatuses. Madhubuti regarded the Nguzo Saba (Seven Principles) as an ethical glue and core value system necessary to solidify these institutions and their leadership:

> The Seven Principles are the basic values of the US organization founded by Maulana Ron Karenga. The Nguzo Saba in its righteous direction and Pan-Afrikan scope has moved across this nation like honey giving energy to the brain. Of all the concepts that Maulana Karenga has initiated, the Seven Principles is the most used. Most of the independent black institutions and all black nationalist organizations have used the Nguzo Saba in one way or another. However it must be understood that the Seven Principles are only part—a major part— of an entirely new revolutionary movement: Kawaida.[93]

He also explained his view of Nguzo Saba's corrective potential:

We need a people who think, act, live and relate to each other on a higher and much more functional level. This re-definition will by definition change our relationship to the western world. . . . Study and adjust to the Black Value System—it is a major step toward the unification and empowerment of Afrikan people.[94]

Kawaida, from Madhubuti's standpoint, promoted African American unity and the development of a cultural basis for liberation. Consistent with positions advocated by US, he argued that the primary task for accomplishing Black freedom hinged on an extensive change in Black consciousness. The African American's "behavior pattern," he stated, "will be more 'American' than 'Afrikan' even if he consistently tries to be 'Afrikan,' because to be 'Afrikan' requires more than color and desire." "It requires," he continued, "a complete re-education. . . . This is not an overnight process. . . . This is why *Kawaida* . . . which stresses Afrikan language and the NGUZO SABA are so necessary."[95]

Madhubuti, though not officially tied to US, was an active force in the Congress of African People. Along with his wife, Safisha Madhubuti, he ran the Institute of Positive Education, an independent Black school, and the Third World Press publishing company. When discussing the Seven Principles, he resisted presenting himself as the authority on the Kawaida doctrine: "With my limited knowledge, it is not for me, at this time to attempt to teach the Kawaida movement."[96] Madhubuti also differed from Baraka in that he did not use poetry to promote the doctrine. Many of his poems fall within what Carolyn Rodgers called the "covers-off" category, which she defined as poems that "hip you to something, pull the covers off of something, or run it down to you, or ask you to just dig it—your coat is being pulled."[97] Like Sonia Sanchez, he responded to the Black Arts movement's thrust toward writing for a Black audience by taking the "covers off" of the internal contradictions in everyday Black community life. "The REVOLUTIONARY SCREW (for my sisters)," for instance, captures his lament that sexist attitudes of Black men adversely affected the quality of relations between male and female activists in the movement.[98]

Madhubuti exhibited a level of humility and self-interrogation uncharacteristic of many of his nationalist contemporaries. When Baraka and other writers ridiculed the "backward" habits of Negroes and refused to act "Black," as defined by cultural nationalists (wearing wigs, taking drugs, eating pork, worshipping Jesus, etc.), there was a distinctly corrective tone, suggesting the writer's removal from these issues. The poem "Malcolm Spoke/ who listened? (this poem is for my consciousness too)" reveals that Madhubuti was aware of his own vulnerability to the corrupt and superficial behavior underscored in his writing.[99] Madhubuti's attraction to Kawaida and the Nguzo Saba was born of a profound concern about the ethical conduct accompanying the didacticism of Black nationalist rhetoric and pronouncements. His poetry and commentary demonstrate that, in terms of sensitivity and temperament, he may also have been suited—if not best—for the title "Imamu" within the leadership circles of the cultural-nationalist movement of the early 1970s.

Kalamu ya Salaam, like Madhubuti, was a leader in a cultural-nationalist stratum heavily influenced by Kawaida and a member organization of CAP, Ahidiana. Based in New Orleans and founded in the early 1970s, it defined itself as pan-Africanist and nationalist. Ya Salaam and his comrades were actively supporting African anticolonial and anti-imperialist struggles in Mozambique, Guinea-Bissau, Angola, and South Africa.[100] In New Orleans, Ahidiana engaged in local political issues and operated an independent school and a poetry/music ensemble.[101] Ya Salaam's literary contributions included service as an editor of several progressive journals and an impressive list of prose and social commentary. Two of his books, *Hofu Ni Kwenu (My Fear Is for You)* and *Pamoja Tutashinda (Together We Will Win)*, provide, alongside a range of other insights, an independent explication of Kawaida's call for new values and alternative family forms.

Hofu Ni Kwenu (My Fear Is for You) contains poems, two short essays, and an array of visual images and symbols. This work offers a Kawaida interpretation of African American male and female relationships using Karenga's patriarchal "complementarity" model. Even though ya Salaam brought his own interpretations to this task, the doctrine served as an overarching authority: sections of the book open with passages from *The Quotable Karenga.*[102]

Like Madhubiti, ya Salaam entered a dialogue on the nature of revolutionary conduct and the movement's internal contradictions. He evoked imagery intended to elevate the place of the Nguzo Saba in people's everyday lives, arguing that the value system "is not a dogma not rhetoric / in fact it is nothing unless we live it."[103] The poem "SUN-PEOPLE/SUN-RISING a getting up poem in this age of our awe inspiring terribleness being collected" comment on each principle of the Nguzo Saba and on mindsets and behaviors understood to be compatible with the values. With respect to Umoja, for instance, he intimated that dogmatic vanguard tendencies among some in the movement ran counter to the base of the principle: he noted that "some of us think umoja is getting all / afrikans to be an advocate of that which we believe in / we are so pure elitists in our small new fondness / just discovered the nguzo saba two years ago."[104] He went on to declare that

> the unity of our people means
> give and take, unity takes the conscious element
> of us bending
> to be with the unconscious, if we believe
> in unity, it is on us to be about it, others may

groove, bang and jive around but we
got to keep on reappearing day after day tirelessly yet
softly as in the eternal morning sun rising
always with patient understanding on our breath
ready to effect operational unity and
knowing that one lifetime of struggle ain't really long
others may give it up but if we sincerely believe
then we must stick, and welcome our people forever like
   nkrumah in ghana
struggling to propagate a pan-afrik reality.[105]

In the same poem, ya Salaam's views about Imani contemplate the problem of the cult of personality, which had direct implications for the US Organization and for CAP's structured reverence for the Maulana and Imamu.

"Some of us," ya Salaam stated, "were misled in the understanding of faith's sources and substance by believing that the principle meant that our leaders were infallible and our ideology / the only correct ideas happening."[106] The movement's survival throughout politically unfavorable circumstances rested with a more critical internalization of cultural nationalist ideals and constant reassessment. "Faith after all," he concluded, "is just daily practice guided by principles / the faithful are steady rollers who believe and do beyond belief."[107]

Ya Salaam's interest in gender roles inspired his departure from a patriarchal view of women and family, toward a feminist position in the late 1970s and 1980s.[108] Karenga and ya Salaam openly disagreed about how Black men should respond to women's criticisms of their sexism. Ya Salaam felt that many African American male critics had reacted defensively and needed to learn from voices such as those of Michele Wallace, author of *Black Macho and the Myth of the Superwoman*. Karenga, on the other hand, felt that certain feminist criticism, particularly Wallace's *Black Macho*, were polemical at best, filled with personal attacks, and gave an incorrect treatment of the Black Power movement and Black male and female relationships.[109] Nevertheless, Karenga was influenced positively by the expanded feminist discourse of the 1970s and went on to reject his own patriarchal formulations of the previous decade. In 1980 Ahidiana published Karenga's book *Beyond Connections: Liberation in Love and Struggle,* an analysis of sexism and unequal male and female relationships.[110]

Both Madhubuti and ya Salaam were key figures in Karenga's post-1975 Black nationalist activism. Both published his writings and sought his participation in various national and international forums and conferences. These opportunities gave Karenga a wider audience for the updated version of his philosophy and its relevance to the new political circumstances of the late 1970s and 1980s.

The Art of Nationalism

The marriage of art and politics was indeed a hallmark of twentieth-century Black nationalism. Minister Louis Farrakhan, the present leader of the Nation of Islam, known in the early 1960s as Minister Louis X, was a well-trained singer-musician and recorded a song promoting the NOI's views, "A White Man's Heaven Is a Black Man's Hell."[111] Even the use of jazz as a creative outlet for radical politics was not a historical novelty during the Black Power years. By 1929, two years after Marcus Garvey was forcibly exiled to Kingston, Jamaica, the UNIA chapter boasted of performances given by its own Universal Jazz Hounds.[112] Even the US Organization's political rival, the Black Panther Party, had its own band called "The Lumpen," and Elaine Brown, who would eventually ascend to a party leadership position in the late 1970s, had already spouted her organization's doctrine melodically in an album she recorded for Motown.

Many of the artists discussed in this section were not members of US but supported the organization's distinctive cultural-nationalist philosophy, as it spoke to a need for a new interpretive framework and provided an inspirational base for their works. Contemplating the relationship between artists and nationalism in general, theorist Anthony Smith queried "[W]ho, more than poets, musicians, painters and sculptors, could bring the national ideal to life and disseminate it among the people?"[113] The artists who accepted the task of giving public meaning to US's doctrine were assisted by the contours of a period that saw a rise in popular fascination with African culture. The arts provided the US Organization and its heirs with a platform for models of African American cultural revolution.

The violently turbulent upheavals in the US Organization and in the Black nationalist movement at large, from 1969 through the late 1970s, painted the blood-stained landscape in which US members and affiliated supporters of Kawaida persistently struggled to create a radical vision in the arts. Funk music, with its thick, steady, sometimes chaotic, and heavily improvisational rhythmic structure could very well serve as the soundtrack and trope for the unrelenting African American creative resistance in the midst of the state's assault on the Black Power movement. Among the multiple definitions and scenarios used to describe the genre and its philosophical underpinnings was theorist and historian Rickey Vincent's declaration that "funk is that nitty-gritty *thang* that affects people when things get heavy."[114] The weight of repression was ultimately too "heavy" for most US members to bear as the 1970s decade opened midway through the first term of a presidential administration dedicated to the politics of repression in the name of "law and order." In the face of this funk, however, the US and Kawaida-inspired activist work in the creative arts spoke concurrently to the turbulence of the times and the futuristic vision of a Black cultural-nationalist world.

7. Kwanzaa and Afrocentricity

Internal strife and repression from various law enforcement agencies ultimately led to a series of crises in the US Organization, whose sum total effectively ended US's flourishing as a powerfully influential vanguard force in the era of Black Power, from 1965 until 1971. US's influence, as expressed through other cultural nationalist organizations and sympathizers, persisted well into the late 1970s and received a major boost in the 1980s and 1990s through the Afrocentric movement and the Kwanzaa holiday.

US's participation in the Black Power movement coincided with an expanded popular interest in Africa that was due, in part, to a sense of optimism fostered by the numerous anticolonial struggles throughout the latter half of the twentieth century. When Karenga was released from prison in 1975, his interest in Africa had not waned. Just two years afterwards, he traveled to the continent for the first time to attend the Second Black and African Festival of Arts (FESTAC) in Lagos, Nigeria, and served as spokesperson for the American delegation to a colloquium on Black civilization and education. His speech added a diasporic perspective to the question of "What is Africa?," emphasizing its global reach: Africa is wherever African people are. "The speech," theorist Molefi Asante recounted, "drew the loudest and most prolonged applause."[1]

Radical times had changed by the 1980s, yet Karenga's revitalized US Organization continued to promote its leader's blueprint for reconnections to African culture. Toward that end, the
organization shifted away from violent resistance and some of its
older organizational methods. This transition was personified by
Karenga's return to the academy: he received a doctorate in political science in 1976 and even went on to complete a second
Ph.D. in social ethics in 1992.[2] US of the 1980s and 1990s but-
tressed Karenga's status as a leading scholar in the Afrocentric
movement of the 1980s and 1990s—an apex of activist scholarship, study groups, Black bookstores, independent Black schools,
and organizations focused on situating African philosophies and
culture at the center of social theory, pedagogy, cultural praxis,
and institutional arrangements. Certain Afrocentric ideas are indebted to earlier US Organization positions. Indeed, Karenga's
emphasis on "redefinition" during the Black Power years is a
forerunner to the focus on cultural authenticity and "centered-
ness" in Molefi Asante's theory of Afrocentricity.[3] In a speech
given in 1968, for instance, Karenga expressed a concern for developing an alternative "frame of reference" for teaching African
and African American history:

> In terms of frame of reference, let's take history as an example.
> If I am going to refer to someone as great as Marcus Garvey as
> a "Black Moses," what am I saying? I'm saying that Garvey was
> tough but Moses is really what's happening and Garvey at best
> is second. And if I want to call King Shaka a "Black Napoleon,"
> I'm saying that Napoleon is really what's happening and
> Shaka, well, he's Black.[4]

"Now," he went on to conclude, "I'm saying that without a change
of frame of reference we need not even teach Black subjects."[5]
Karenga continues to figure preeminently in African American

nationalist discourse. In the early 1980s he authored one of the most widely used textbooks for Black Studies, *Introduction to Black Studies*,[6] and by the 1990s Karenga had become a foremost scholar of classical African philosophy.[7] He also authored the mission statement for the 1995 Million Man March.[8] This post–Black Power activist scholarship also reflected a consistent tenacity on the part of the small but highly dedicated current US Organization (now called "Us"). In 1984 it planned and hosted the First Annual Ancient Egyptian Studies Conference, initiating the establishment of the Association for the Study of Classical African Civilizations. In fact, Us publishes most of Karenga's works through its own University of Sankore Press.[9]

The outpouring of Afrocentric scholarship, study groups, and cultural expression occurred in conjunction with massive public participation in the annual Kwanzaa holiday. During the 1970s Kwanzaa grew far beyond its Southern California roots as member organizations and affiliates of the Congress of African People brought the celebration to cities across the United States.[10] By the 1980s Kwanzaa had become widely celebrated by African Americans of diverse religious and political persuasions.

Karenga's 1998 commemorative edition of *Kwanzaa: A Celebration of Family, Community and Culture* appeared simultaneously with the U.S. Postal Service's issuance of the Kwanzaa stamp. That year, Us estimated that the holiday was embraced by "over 20 million celebrants" in the United States, the Caribbean, Europe, Latin America, and even continental Africa.[11] The US Organization's activism in the Black Power era and recent Afrocentric movement is part of a continuous, but nonetheless fluid and stormy, quest for radical alternatives extracted from its own interpretation of African culture.

The politics of collective identity stand at the fore of the African American freedom struggle vis-à-vis the history of enslavement and the systematic assault on diasporic connections to an African cultural identity. While US advanced its program of cultural reconstruction in the late 1960s, a paradigm shift in African American historiography was under way, overturning the assumptions that enslavement had completely shattered the continental African cultural foundations of its captives. Characterizations of African Americans as a people suffering from a debilitating cultural void helped inspire the US Organization's dynamic counterresponse: alternative life-cycle ceremonies, holidays, and united-front political formations. Ironically, these assumptions about African American culture evoked various expressions of an anti-folk sentiment and a measure of contempt for "everyday" Black cultural life.

Historians have shown that "Exodus," the motif of mass departure drawn from Old Testament narratives, remained an overriding theme in antebellum and post–Civil War African American resistance.[12] Radical organizations of the Black Power era were not exceptions to this pattern. The US Organization, though not in search of territory per se, positioned the Promised Land in a state of mind or consciousness. The group sought to commandeer a voyage out of the bondage of "Negro" identity to a Black one—shaped in the image of its own construction of Africa and Afroamerica. The pursuit of Black cultural revolution speaks directly to the politics of twentieth-century American institutional racism and the persistent defamation of African history and culture in the mass media and in popular culture. US, among others with cultural-nationalist leanings, produced aesthetic conceptions, philosophical paradigms, ritual representations, and political institutions that continue to defy the anti-African mandate of Western cultural hegemony in the post–Civil Rights/ Black Power era.

Glossary of Kiswahili and Zulu Terms

Hekalu: US's headquarters and temple.

Kanuni: rules.

Kawaida: that which is customary, the name of US's cultural nationalist philosophy and ideology. During the era of Black Power it had a quasi-religious as well as political dimension. However, during the 1970s, US discarded Kawaida's religious aspects, placing more emphasis on its function as a revolutionary ideology of social change.

Kiapo: oath.

Nguzo Saba (Seven Principles): *Umoja* (unity), *Kujichagulia* (self-determination), *Ujima* (collective work and responsibility), *Ujamaa* (cooperative economics), *Nia* (purpose), *Kuumba* (creativity), and *Imani* (faith).

Shahada: diploma.

US Titles and Units

Amiri: Simba commander.

Imamu: High priest.

Isihlangu (Zulu): US's executive committee within its governing Circle of Administrators.

Kaimu: Simba deputy commander.

Makamu: assistant chief of Simba unit.

Maulana (Master Teacher): During the Black Power period when Kawaida had a quasi-religious dimension, it also meant highest of high priests in the Kawaida faith.

Muminina: women of US.

Mwalimu: those studying to be priest-teachers of Kawaida.

Mwanafunzi: student-teacher, US member studying to be a Mwalimu.

Mzee: elder.

Ngao: shield, security chairman.

Saidi (Lords): unit of US consisting of men, usually over age twenty.

Shahidi: martyr, or Protector of the Faith.

Simba Wachanga (Young Lions): youth and paramilitary wing of US.

Simba Wadogo (Little Lions): drill team for boys.

Sultani: chief or leader of a Simba unit.

US Holidays and Rituals

Akika: US's nationalization ceremony for children.

Arusi: US's wedding ceremony.

Dhabihu: commemoration of Malcolm X's martyrdom and sacrifice.

Kuanzisha: Founders Day, September 7.

Kuzaliwa: Malcolm X's birthday, May 19.

Kwanzaa: seven-day holiday from December 26 until January 1, established by Maulana Karenga and US in 1966.

Maziko: US's funeral ceremony.

Uhuru Day: commemoration of the 1965 Watts Revolt, August 11.

Notes

NOTES TO CHAPTER 1

1. Clayborne Carson, "Revolt and Repression (1967–1970)," in Clayborne Carson, David Garrow, Vincent Harding, and Darlene Clark Hine (eds.), *A Reader and Guide, Eyes on the Prize: America's Civil Rights Years* (New York: Penguin Books, 1987), 218; Kathleen Rout, *Eldridge Cleaver* (Boston: Twayne Publishers, 1991), 102; Ronald Walters, *Pan Africanism in the African Diaspora: An Analysis of Modern Afrocentric Political Movements* (Detroit: Wayne State University Press, 1993), 66; Hugh Pearson, *The Shadow of the Panther: Huey Newton and the Price of Black Power in America* (New York: Addison-Wesley, 1994), 151, 181n, 236; Jim Haskins, *Power to the People: The Rise and Fall of the Black Panther Party* (New York: Simon and Schuster Books for Young Readers, 1997), 2; Jack Olsen, *Last Man Standing: The Tragedy and Triumph of Geronimo Pratt* (New York: Doubleday, 2000), 44–45; Kathleen Cleaver and George Katsiaficas (eds.), *Liberation, Imagination, and the Black Panther Party: A New Look at the Panthers and Their Legacy* (New York: Routledge, 2001), 81, 93–95, 200.

2. C. Batuta, "US—Black Nationalism on the Move," *Black Dialogue* 2:7 (Autumn 1966): 7.

3. Haskins, *Power to the People;* Nagueyalti Warren, "Pan-African Cultural Movements: From Baraka to Karenga," *Journal of Negro History* 75:1–2 (Winter/Spring 1990): 24–26; Ward Churchill and Jim Vander Wall, *Agents of Repression: The Secret Wars against the Black Panther Party and the American Indian Movement* (Boston: South End Press, 1988); Bruce Tyler, "Black Radicalism in Southern California, 1950–1982" (Unpublished Ph.D. dissertation, UCLA, 1983); Scot Ngozi-Brown, "The Us Organization, Maulana Karenga, and Conflict with the Black Panther Party: A Critique of Sectarian Influences on Historical Discourse," *Journal of Black Studies* 28:2 (November 1997): 157–170.

4. For an in-depth discussion of the emerging historiography on Black Power, see Peniel Joseph, "Black Liberation without Apology: Reconceptualizing the Black Power Movement," *Black Scholar* 31:3–4 (Fall/Winter 2001): 3–20.

NOTES TO CHAPTER 2

1. William Van Deburg, *New Day in Babylon: The Black Power Movement and American Culture, 1965–1975* (Chicago: University of Chicago Press, 1992), and *Modern Black Nationalism: From Marcus Garvey to Louis Farrakhan* (New York: New York University Press, 1997); John Bracey, August Meier, and Elliot Rudwick (eds.), *Black Nationalism in America* (Indianapolis and New York: Bobbs-Merrill, 1970); August Meier, *Negro Thought in America, 1880–1915* (Ann Arbor:

University of Michigan Press, 1966); Alphonso Pinkney, *Red, Black and Green: Black Nationalism in the United States* (New York: Cambridge University Press, 1976); E. U. Essien-Udom, *Black Nationalism: A Search for Identity in America* (New York: Dell, 1964); Howard Brotz (ed.), *Negro Social and Political Thought, 1850–1920: Representative Texts* (New York: Basic Books, 1966).

2. Meier, *Negro Thought in America*, 51; Brotz, *Negro Social and Political Thought*, 19–24; Essien-Udom, *Black Nationalism*, 39–44. For a comparative discussion of cultural and political nationalisms, see Avishai Margalit, "The Moral Psychology of Nationalism," in Robert McKim and Jeff McMahan (eds.), *The Morality of Nationalism* (New York: Oxford University Press, 1997), 77.

3. "Pre-Kwanzaa Celebration" (video recording, Grassroots Bookstore Archives, Salisbury, Maryland, December 6, 1998).

4. Scot Brown, "Interview with Maulana Karenga" (audio recording, July 11, 1998), side 1.

5. Ibid.

6. Ibid.

7. "First Book of Chronicles," 2:15, 12:11, 26:3, in *The Holy Bible* (King James Version) (Nashville: Thomas Nelson, 1977).

8. Scot Brown, "Interview with Arnetta Church Atkins," April 15, 2002, 1.

9. Scot Brown, "Interview with Maulana Karenga" (audio recording, July 11, 1998), side 1; idem, "Interview with Jean Morris" (notes, April 15, 2002); *The Beacon 1954* [Salisbury High School Yearbook], Charles H. Chipman Cultural Center Archives, n.p.; ibid., 1958, n.p.; ibid., 1959, 22; ibid., 1960, 20.

10. Scot Brown, "Interview with Jean Morris" (notes, April 15, 2002).

11. "New Name Is Tribute to Chipman," *Daily Times*, October 1, 1986, 11; Brown, "Interview with Jean Morris"; "Prof. Charles Chipman; Dedicated to Community," *Daily Times*, February 18, 1978, 5.

12. Brown, "Interview with Maulana Karenga" (audio recording, July 11, 1998), side 1.

13. Scot Brown, "Interview with Maulana Karenga" (transcript, October 11, 1994), 1–5.

14. "25 'Orators' Reach Speech Semi-Finals," *Los Angeles Collegian*, May 13, 1960, 1; "Bein, Everett Unopposed for Top Posts," *Los Angeles Collegian*, May 24, 1966, 1; "Everett Wins: VP Defeats AS Treasurer," *Los Angeles Collegian*, January 13, 1961, 1; Brown, "Interview with Maulana Karenga" (transcript, October 11, 1994), 3.

15. Brown, "Interview with Maulana Karenga" (transcript, October 11, 1994), 3; "AS Prexy Candidate Explains Platform," *Los Angeles Collegian*, January 10, 1961, 2.

16. "African History Course Offered Next Semester," *Los Angeles Collegian*, December 16, 1960, 1.

17. Brown, "Interview with Maulana Karenga" (transcript, October 11, 1994), 12.

18. Clay Carson, "A Talk with Ron Karenga: Watts Black Nationalist," *Los Angeles Free Press,* September 2, 1966, 12.

19. "Class in Swahili Planned at Fremont Adult School," *Herald-Dispatch,* October 17, 1964, 1–3.

20. Rocha Chimerah, *Kiswahili: Past, Present and Future Horizons* (Nairobi: Nairobi University Press, 1998), 146–147; "African Scholars at Lagos: A Sense of Disillusion," *New York Times,* January 28, 1977, A2.

21. "Fordham Adds Swahili Study to Curriculum," *Herald-Dispatch,* January 7, 1971, 1; "Swahili and Black Americans," *Negro Digest* 18:9 (July 1969): 4–8.

22. Abdallah Khalid, *The Liberation of Swahili from European Appropriation* (Nairobi: East African Literature Bureau, 1977); James de Vere Allen, *Swahili Origins: Swahili Culture and the Shungawa Phenomenon* (Athens: Ohio University Press, 1993); Derek Nurse and Thomas Spear, *The Swahili: Reconstructing the History and Language of an African Society, 800–1500* (Philadelphia: University of Pennsylvania Press, 1985); see also Avishai Margalit, "The Moral Psychology of Nationalism," in Robert McKim and Jeff McMahan (eds.), *The Morality of Nationalism,* 77. Karenga's persistent drive to incorporate African languages into the nascent US doctrine invites further reflection on Avishai Margalit's assertion that cultural nationalism "considers the nation an organic entity whose supreme expression is the national culture—particularly the national language" (p. 77).

23. Eileen Krige, *The Social System of the Zulus,* 4th ed. (London: Longmans Green, 1962), xi–xii.

24. Jomo Kenyatta, *Facing Mount Kenya: The Tribal Life of the Gikuyu* (London: Secker and Warburg, 1961), xxiii.

25. Maulana Karenga, in Clyde Halisi and James Mtume (eds.), *The Quotable Karenga* (Los Angeles: US Organization, 1967), 7.

26. Ibid., 15.

27. Kenyatta, *Facing Mount Kenya,* 131.

28. Ibid., 321.

29. "GSA Colloquium: Panelists Ponder Integration," *UCLA Daily Bruin,* December 13, 1963, 1.

30. Lilyan Kesteloot, *Intellectual Origins of the African Revolution* (Washington, D.C.: Black Orpheus Press, 1972), 20–21.

31. Brown, "Interview with Maulana Karenga" (transcript, October 11, 1994), 9.

32. Elston Carr, *UCLA Center for African American Studies: Robert Singleton* (Los Angeles: UCLA Oral History Program, 1999), 165. Singleton would later become the founding director of the Center for Afro-American Studies at UCLA.

33. Ibid.

34. Leopold Senghor, *On African Socialism* (New York: Praeger, 1964), 33.

35. Ibid., 38.

36. "Karenga, Black Panthers Speak Out," *Los Angeles Sentinel,* March 6, 1969, D2.

37. Senghor, *On African Socialism,* 49.

38. Ibid., 69. Senghor, like the anthropologists whose works Karenga was reading, viewed culture in a holistic fashion. He quoted Nilakanta Sastri's definition of culture as "the sum of objects, symbols, beliefs, feelings, values, and social forms that are transmitted from one generation to another in a given society" (p. 49).

39. Keith Mayes, "Rituals of Race, Ceremonies of Culture: Kwanzaa and the Making of a Black Power Holiday in the United States, 1966–2000" (Ph.D. dissertation, Princeton University, 2002), 90–91; Ahmed Sekou Toure, *The Political Leader Considered as the Representative of a Culture* (Newark: Jihad Productions, n.d.).

40. Julius Nyerere, *Ujamaa: Essays on Socialism* (London: Oxford University Press, 1968), 4–5, 8–9. This essay was originally published as a TANU—the Tanzanian ruling party—pamphlet in 1962.

41. Ibid., 1.

42. "Money in America" [lesson], 1–2, "School of Afroamerican Culture, n.d., Papers of Maulana Karenga and the Organization Us, African American Cultural Center, Los Angeles.

43. Karenga, in Halisi and Mtume, *The Quotable Karenga,* 4; "Karenga, Black Panthers Speak Out," *Los Angeles Sentinel,* March 6, 1969, D2.

44. J. D. Legge, *Sukarno: A Political Biography* (New York: Praeger, 1972), 184.

45. Peter Britton, "The Relevance of Javanese Traditions to an Understanding of the Political Philosophy of Guided Democracy" (unpublished B.A. honors thesis, University of Sydney, 1968), 101–103; Christine Drake, *National Integration in Indonesia: Patterns and Policies* (Honolulu: University of Hawaii Press, 1989), 76–79.

46. Maulana Karenga, "Indonesia-Sukarno," n.d., Papers of Maulana Karenga and the Organization Us, African American Cultural Center, Los Angeles.

47. Imamu [Clyde] Halisi (ed.), *Kitabu: Beginning Concepts in Kawaida* (Los Angeles: US Organization, 1971), 8.

48. Ibid.

49. "Tanzanians Vote to Liquidate Western Cultural Influence," *Herald-Dispatch,* December 3, 1966, 1, 3; "Swahili the Official Language for Tanzania," *Herald-Dispatch,* February 4, 1967, 1, 3.

50. Richard Wright, *The Color Curtain: A Report on the Bandung Conference* (New York: World Publishing, 1956).

51. Malcolm X, "Message to the Grassroots," in George Breitman (ed.), *Malcolm X Speaks,* 4th printing (New York: Pathfinder Press, 1993), 5.

52. Ibid.

53. Ministry of Foreign Affairs, Republic of Indonesia, *Asia-Africa Speaks from Bandung* (Djakarta: Ministry of Foreign Affairs, Republic of Indonesia, 1955), 27–28; Carlos Romulo, *The Meaning of Bandung* (Chapel Hill: University of North Carolina Press, 1956); Roselan Abdulgani, *The Bandung Connection: The Asia-Africa Conference in Bandung in 1955* (Singapore: Gunung Agung, 1981).

54. Tiger Slavik, "Human Rights Interview: Ron Karenga" (audio recording) (Los Angeles: Pacifica Radio Archive, June 6, 1966), side 1.

55. Edward W. Blyden, "The Call of Providence to the Descendants of Africa in America," in Howard Brotz (ed.), *Negro Social and Political Thought, 1850–1920* (New York: Basic Books, 1966), 112–139; James T. Holley, "A Vindication of the Capacity of the Negro Race for Self-Government and Civilized Progress," in Brotz, *Negro Social and Political Thought,* 142; Essien-Udom, *Black Nationalism,* 45–48.

56. Marcus Garvey, "African Fundamentalism: Font of Inspiration," in Robert Hill and Barbara Blair (eds.), *Marcus Garvey: Life and Lessons, a Centennial Companion to the Marcus Garvey and Universal Negro Improvement Association Papers* (Berkeley: University of California Press, 1987), 7–8.

57. Ibid.

58. Malcolm X, "Twenty Million Black People in a Political, Economic and Mental Prison," in Bruce Perry (ed.), *Malcolm X: The Last Speeches* (New York: Pathfinder Press, 1989), 33.

59. Ibid., 14–20; "'Negro Monster Stripped of His Culture,'—Malcolm X," *UCLA Daily Bruin,* November 29, 1962, 1.

60. "'Negro Monster Stripped of His Culture,'—Malcolm X," 1.

61. Wilson Jeremiah Moses, *Classical Black Nationalism: From the American Revolution to Marcus Garvey* (New York: New York University Press, 1996), 1–4.

62. Scot Brown, "Interview with Maulana Karenga" (transcript, October 11, 1994), 16–17.

63. Ibid.

64. C. Eric Lincoln, *Black Muslims in America* (Boston: Beacon Press, 1961), 28, 78.

65. Bertrand Russell, "Why I Am Not a Christian," in Al Seckel (ed.), *Bertrand Russell on God and Religion* (Buffalo: Prometheus Books, 1986), 57–71. This essay was first published in 1927; Brown, "Interview with Maulana Karenga" (transcript, October 11, 1994), 6.

66. Sterling Stuckey, in *Slave Culture: Nationalist Theory and the Foundations of Black America* (New York: Oxford University Press, 1967), 193–244, explored pre-twentieth-century debates over the appropriate name for people of African descent in the United States.

67. Lincoln, *Black Muslims in America,* 69.

68. "Mama, mama" [song], School of Afroamerican Culture, n.d., Papers of Maulana Karenga and the Organization Us, African American Cultural Center, Los Angeles.

69. Clay Carson, "A Talk with Ron Karenga: Watts Black Nationalist," *Los Angeles Free Press,* September 2, 1966, 12.

70. Ibid.

71. Ron Karenga et al., "What Is Black Power," audio recording of panel discussion (Los Angeles: Pacifica Radio Archive, July 23, 1966), tape 2, side 1. Other panelists present were Benjamin Wyatt, Albert Burton, Clifford Vaughs, Benjamin Handy, and Arnett Hartsfield.

72. Ibid.

73. William Van Deburg, *New Day in Babylon: The Black Power Movement and American Culture, 1965–1975* (Chicago: University of Chicago Press, 1992), 3.

74. Karenga, in Halisi and Mtume, *The Quotable Karenga,* 11.

75. Malcolm X, "Statement of Basic Aims and Objectives of the Organization of Afro-American Unity," in Abraham Chapman (ed.), *New Black Voices: An Anthology of Contemporary New Black Literature* (New York: New American Library, 1972), 563.

76. Organization of Afro-American Unity, "Basic Unity Program," in Steve Clark (ed.), *February 1965: The Final Speeches, Malcolm X* (New York: Pathfinder Press, 1992), 258.

77. Malcolm X, "The Ballot or the Bullet," in Breitman, *Malcolm X Speaks,* 41.

78. "Ron Karenga Speaks on 'Unity without Uniformity,'" *Los Angeles Sentinel,* April 11, 1968, B5; Karenga, in Halisi and Mtume, *The Quotable Karenga,* 17; Booker Griffin, "Operational Unity: A Positive Concept," *Los Angeles Sentinel,* February 22, 1968, 10B; Alphonso Pinkney, *Red, Black and Green: Black Nationalism in the United States* (New York: Cambridge University Press, 1976), 141.

79. Komozi Woodard, "Interview with Ron Karenga" (transcript, December 27, 1985), 5. Personal Papers of Komozi Woodard.

80. Brown, "Interview with Maulana Karenga" (transcript, October 11, 1994), 1–4; "Students Rally for Abolishment of Death Penalty," *Los Angeles Collegian* [month and page unknown], 1960.

81. Brown, "Interview with Maulana Karenga" (transcript, October 11, 1994), 4.

82. Ibid.

83. Woodard, "Interview with Ron Karenga" (transcript, December 27, 1985), 2.

84. "African-American Association," *Afro-American Dignity News,* November 2, 1964, 10.

85. Khalid Abdullah Tariq Al Mansour [Donald Warden], *Black Americans at*

the Crossroads: Where Do We Go from Here? (San Francisco: First African Arabian Press, 1981); Donald Warden, "The Afro-American Association: The California Revolt," *The Liberator* 3 (March 1963): 14–15.

86. "African-American Association," *Afro-American Dignity News,* November 2, 1964, 10.

87. Brown, "Interview with Maulana Karenga" (transcript, October 11, 1994), 25.

88. John Floyd, "Marcus, Marx, Malcolm, and Militants," *Los Angeles Sentinel,* May 20, 1971, 5.

89. "'Clean Ghetto' Is Issue for Negro, Warden Asserts," *UCLA Daily Bruin,* December 10, 1962, 1.

90. "GSA Colloquium: Panelists Ponder Integration," *UCLA Daily Bruin,* December 13, 1963, 1.

91. Brown, "Interview with Maulana Karenga" (transcript, October 11, 1994), 26.

92. Donald Warden, *Burn Baby, Burn* [phonograph] (Berkeley: Dignity LP, 1965).

93. Ibid.

94. Karenga et al., "What Is Black Power," tape 1, side 1.

95. "African-American Association," *Afro-American Dignity News,* November 2, 1964, 4.

96. Floyd, "Marcus, Marx, Malcolm, and Militants," 5.

97. Karenga, in Halisi and Mtume, *The Quotable Karenga,* 12.

98. "Separatism Labeled as 'Reverse Hitler,'" *Los Angeles Sentinel,* July 7, 1966, 1; Benjamin Muse, *The American Negro Revolution* (Bloomington: Indiana University Press, 1968), 230; Gene Roberts, "The Story of Snick: From 'Freedom High' to Black Power," in August Meier, Elliot Rudwick, and John Bracey, Jr., (eds.), *Black Protest in the Sixties: Articles from the New York Times* (New York: Markus Wiener, 1991), 139–153. This article was originally published in the *New York Times Magazine,* September 25, 1966.

99. Clay Carson, "A Talk with Ron Karenga: Watts Black Nationalist," *Los Angeles Free Press,* September 2, 1966, 12.

100. Abram Kardiner and Lionel Ovesey, *The Mark of Oppression: Explorations in the Personality of the American Negro* (Cleveland: World, 1962); Van Deburg, *New Day in Babylon,* 55–58.

101. Governor's Commission on the Los Angeles Riots, "Violence in the City: An End or Beginning?" December 2, 1965, 2–3, Kenneth Hahn Papers, Huntington Library, Pasadena, Calif.

102. Ibid.

103. Ibid., 7.

104. Ron Everett-Karenga et al., "A Black Power View of the McCone

Commission Report," December 1966, in *Records of the National Advisory Commission on Civil Disorders in Civil Rights during the Johnson Administration [microform]: A Collection from the Holdings of the Lyndon Baines Johnson Library, Austin, Texas*, Reel 9.

105. Daryl Scott, *Contempt and Pity: Social Policy and the Image of the Damaged Black Psyche, 1880–1996* (Chapel Hill: University of North Carolina Press, 1997), 164–167.

106. Ron Everett-Karenga et al., "A Black Power View," Reel 9, intro.

107. Ibid., 2.

108. Ibid.

109. Ibid., 1.

110. Van Deburg, *New Day in Babylon*, 58; Renate Zahar, *Frantz Fanon: Colonialism and Alienation* (New York: Monthly Review Press, 1974), 74–92.

111. Office of Policy Planning and Research, United States Department of Labor, *The Negro Family: The Case for National Action* (Washington, D.C.: Official Report, 1965), 30–35.

112. Ibid., 15–17.

113. Ibid., 29.

114. bell hooks, *Ain't I a Woman: Black Women and Feminism* (Boston: South End Press, 1982), 98–99.

115. Tracye Matthews, "'No One Ever Asks, What a Man's Role in the Revolution Is': Gender and the Politics of the Black Panther Party, 1966–1971," in Charles Jones (ed.), *The Black Panther Party Reconsidered* (Baltimore: Black Classic Press, 1998), 271–273.

116. Karenga, in Halisi and Mtume, *The Quotable Karenga*, 21.

117. Ibid.

118. Clay Carson, "A Talk with Ron Karenga: Watts Black Nationalist," *Los Angeles Free Press*, September 2, 1966, 12.

119. Ibid.

120. Maulana Ron Karenga, "Interview: KTLA News, January 8, 1971," video recording (Los Angeles: UCLA Film and Television Archives).

121. Krige, *The Social System of the Zulus*, 280.

122. Maulana Ron Karenga, "The Myth of a Beginning without a Beginning," n.d., 4, Personal Papers of Wesely Kabaila. The US Organization used the variant spelling "Nkulunkulu."

123. [US Organization Doctrine Booklet], n.d., 8.

124. Karenga, "Interview: KTLA News, January 8, 1971."

125. Imamu [Clyde] Halisi (ed.), *Kitabu: Beginning Concepts in Kawaida* (Los Angeles: US Organization, 1971), 7.

126. Ron Karenga, "Black Panthers Speak Out," *Los Angeles Sentinel*, March 6, 1969, D2.

127. Scot Brown,"Interview with Bobette Azizi Glover" (transcript, May 19, 2001), 25.

128. The southern roots of the US Organization's brand of cultural nationalism may be far more deeply burrowed in the ground than his oratorical preferences suggested. Randy Abunuwas-Stripling, a former US member, compared the teaching style of Maulana Karenga at the Soul Sessions to the approach of Black teachers in segregated schools of the South.

NOTES TO CHAPTER 3

1. C. Batuta, "US—Black Nationalism on the Move," *Black Dialogue* 2:7 (Autumn 1966): 7; Scot Brown, "Interview with Maulana Karenga" (transcript, October 11, 1994), 44; idem, "Interview with Karl Key-Hekima" (transcript, November 11, 1996), 4–5.

2. "An Interview with Hakim Jamal," *Long Beach Free Press,* September 17– October 1, 1969, 12.

3. *Message to the Grassroots,* May 21, 1966, 1, 5. This newspaper was short lived and may have folded just after the first issue went into print. It had certainly been discontinued by the time that Jamal left US in the late spring or summer of 1966. In August 1966 US introduced a new official newspaper called *Harambee;* its first edition commemorated the anniversary of the Watts Revolt. This author was able to locate one edition of the paper in the personal papers of Terry Carr-Damu.

4. By 1968 Jamal had founded the Malcolm X Foundation, based in Compton, which he argued was the true heir to Malcolm X's revolutionary legacy. Jamal also became a critic of US's cultural nationalism, contending that its emphasis on African culture diverted its members from participating in revolutionary action. See "'Operational Unity' Leaves Jamal Cold," *Los Angeles Sentinel,* April 18, 1968, A11; "An Interview with Hakim Jamal," 6, 12, 14.

5. Brown, "Interview with Karl Key-Hekima," 11.

6. "'Operational Unity' Leaves Jamal Cold," A11; "An Interview with Hakim Jamal," 6, 12, 14.

7. Scot Brown, "Interview with Oliver Massengale-Heshimu and Charles Massengale-Sigidi" (transcript, November 11, 1997), 5.

8. Scot Brown, "Interview with Tommy Jacquette" (audio recording, October 10, 1994), tape 1, side 1.

9. Brown, "Interview with Oliver Massengale-Heshimu and Charles Massengale-Sigidi," 7.

10. Scot Brown, "Interview with James Doss-Tayari," (November 12, 1996), 18.

11. Ibid., 18–19.

12. Scot Brown, "Interview with Ngoma Ali" (transcript, November 10,

1996), 5; Brown, "Interview with Karl Key-Hekima," 42; Amiri Baraka, *The Autobiography of LeRoi Jones* (Chicago: Lawrence Hill Books, 1997), 356.

13. Brown, "Interview with James Doss-Tayari," (November 12, 1996), 1–2.

14. "Natural Beauty of the Week," *Harambee,* August 11, 1966, 6.

15. Brown, "Interview with Oliver Massengale-Heshimu and Charles Massengale-Sigidi," 1–4.

16. Ibid., 3.

17. Ibid.

18. Scot Brown, "Interview with James Mtume" (transcript, January 16, 1997), 30.

19. Scot Brown, "Interview with C. R. D. Halisi" (transcript, November 11, 1996), 3; "Masters of Trickology," *Herald-Dispatch,* July 30, 1966, 1; Brown, "Interview with Oliver Massengale-Heshimu and Charles Massengale-Sigidi," 2.

20. Brown, "Interview with C. R. D. Halisi," 4.

21. Scot Brown, "Interview with Joann Richardson-Kicheko" (transcript, April 22, 1997), 1.

22. Scot Brown, "Interview with Maulana Karenga" (transcript, October 11, 1994), 53.

23. Maulana Ron Karenga to LeRoi Jones, December 19, 1967, Personal Papers of Komozi Woodard. The names and titles of members of both groups are listed on the letterhead.

24. Brown, "Interview with Maulana Karenga" (October 11, 1994), 53.

25. Maulana Ron Karenga to LeRoi Jones, December 19, 1967, Personal Papers of Komozi Woodard.

26. US Organization, "List of Titles" [1967?], Personal Papers of Ramon Tyson-Imara.

27. Ibid.

28. Imamu [Clyde] Halisi (ed.), *Kitabu: Beginning Concepts in Kawaida* (Los Angeles: US Organization, 1971), 4n. 8.

29. US Organization, "List of Titles."

30. School of Afroamerican Culture, "A Job for Everyone," 2, n.d., Papers of Maulana Karenga and the Organization US, African American Cultural Center, Los Angeles.

31. US Organization, "Seven Aspects of US" (US Doctrine Booklet), 31–32, n.d.; Halisi, *Kitabu,* 2.

32. Scot Brown, "Interview with Vernon Sukumu" (May 21, 2001), tape 1, side 1.

33. US Organization, "US Definitions" [1967?], Personal Papers of Ramon Tyson-Imara.

34. Scot Brown, "Interview with Wesely Kabaila" (transcript, October 11, 1994), 4.

35. Ibid.

36. Maulana Ron Karenga, "Kiapo: Oath" [1967?], Personal Papers of Ramon Tyson-Imara.

37. "US Cultural Organization Kanuni (Rules)," Personal Papers of Oliver Massengale-Heshimu.

38. Brown, "Interview with Karl Key-Hekima," 7.

39. Ibid.

40. Ibid.

41. Elijah Muhammad, *Our Saviour Has Arrived* (Atlanta: Messenger Muhammad Propagation Society, 199?), 111; idem, *Message to the Blackman in America* (Atlanta: Messenger Muhammad Propagation Society, 1997), 293; E. U. Essien-Udom, *Black Nationalism: A Search for Identity in America* (New York: Dell, 1964), 145.

42. "Doctrine List," n.d., Personal Papers of Wesely Kabaila; "Advocacy Class" (notes), May 8, 1968, Personal Papers of Wesely Kabaila.

43. "7 Basic Concepts in Brother Malcolm's Message," n.d., Personal Papers of Wesely Kabaila.

44. Brown, "Interview with Karl Key-Hekima," 9.

45. Ibid., 9–10.

46. Ibid., 10.

47. "Mwalimu Imara to Maulana Ron Karenga, 'Functions of the Kawaida Committee,'" August 23, 1967, 1, Personal Papers of Ramon Tyson-Imara.

48. "Shahada," July 14, 1967, Personal Papers of Oliver Massengale-Heshimu. The diploma's Kiswahili text reads: "Duara Ya Viogozi Ya US, Inc., UTEUZI WA CHAMA CHA UKAWAIDA CHA HEKALU IMEMTOLEA OLIVER MASSEN-GALE-HESHIMU CHEO CHA MWALIMU WA UKAWAIDA PAMOJA NA ZOTE ZA HAKI NA HESHIMA ZILOZOHUSIANA NACHO."

49. Ibid.

50. "Concept of Mwalimu," February 12, 1967, 1, Personal Papers of Oliver Massengale-Heshimu.

51. "Things to Be Done to Be an Mwalimu," March 3, 1967, 1, Personal Papers of Oliver Massengale-Heshimu. Over time, other Saidi also began shaving their heads and, among Black nationalists, the look became somewhat of an organizational trademark.

52. "Administrative Circle Report, Kawaida Committee," July 10, 1967, 2, Personal Papers of Ramon Tyson-Imara.

53. Ibid. Some former US members felt, due to their leader's tendency to micromanage the organization, that the *Walimu* (teachers) never received the opportunities to travel and set up new chapters as anticipated.

54. Brown, "Interview with Wesely Kabaila," 6, 8.

55. Ibid.

56. "Simba Wachanga Weekly Schedule," July 22, 1968–July 28, 1968, Papers of Maulana Karenga and the Organization Us, African American Cultural Center, Los Angeles.

57. Brown, "Interview with Oliver Massengale-Heshimu and Charles Massengale-Sigidi," 7.

58. Ibid., 22.

59. Ibid., 22–23.

60. Ibid., 23.

61. Ibid.

62. Ibid., 21.

63. Scot Brown, "Interview with Charles Johnson-Sitawisha" (transcript, September 9, 1995), 46.

64. Scot Brown, "Interview with Daryl Tukufu" (audio recording, August 2, 1997), side 1.

65. Ibid.

66. Ibid.

67. Maulana Ron Karenga, in Clyde Halisi and James Mtume (eds.), *The Quotable Karenga* (Los Angeles: US Organization, 1967), 9; Scot Brown, "Interview with Ngoma Ali" (transcript, November 10, 1996), 9–10; idem, "Interview with Daryl Tukufu" (audio recording, August 2, 1997), side 1.

68. Brown, "Interview with Daryl Tukufu," side 1.

69. Brown, "Interview with Ngoma Ali," 1, 2.

70. Ibid., 1.

71. Ibid., 9.

72. Karenga, in Halisi and Mtume, *The Quotable Karenga*, 20.

73. Ibid., 20.

74. Scot Brown, "Interview with Kamili Mtume" (audio recording, June 22, 1997), side 1.

75. Scot Brown, "Interview with Staajabu Heshimu" (audio recording, December 6, 1997), side 1.

76. Scot Brown, "Interview with Amina Thomas" (transcript, November 10, 1996), 5.

77. Brown, "Interview with Joann Richardson-Kicheko," 6.

78. Ibid., 7.

79. Scot Brown, "Interview with Letta Mbulu" (transcript, April 22, 1997), 9.

80. Brown, "Interview with James Doss-Tayari," 13.

81. Ibid.

82. Ibid.

83. Brown, "Interview with Joann Richardson-Kicheko," 3–4.

84. Ibid., 4.

85. Ibid.

86. Brown, "Interview with James Mtume," 4.

87. Ibid.

88. Brown, "Interview with Ngoma Ali," 13.

89. Ibid.

90. Ibid.

91. Brown, "Interview with Amina Thomas," 13.

92. Brown, "Interview with Oliver Massengale-Heshimu and Charles Massengale-Sigidi," 1–4.

93. Brown "Interview with Amina Thomas," 13.

94. Brown, "Interview with Kamili Mtume," side 1; idem, "Interview with Amina Thomas," 11–13.

95. Ingrid Banks, *Hair Matters: Beauty, Power and Black Women's Consciousness* (New York: New York University Press, 2000), 7–18.

96. Scot Brown, "Interview with Bobette Azizi Glover" (transcript, May 19, 2001), 4.

97. Robin D. G. Kelley, "Nap Time: Historicizing the Afro," *Fashion Theory: The Journal of Dress, Body and Culture* 1:4 (December 1997): 348, as quoted in Banks, *Hair Matters,* 9.

98. Brown, "Interview with Bobette Azizi Glover," 4.

99. Ibid.

100. Brown, "Interview with Ngoma Ali," 14.

101. Brown, "Interview with Charles Johnson-Sitawisha," 17.

102. Brown, "Interview with Oliver Massengale-Heshimu and Charles Massengale-Sigidi," 18–19.

103. Brown, "Interview with Kamili Mtume," side 1.

104. Brown, "Interview with James Mtume," 5

105. Ibid.

106. Karenga, in Halisi and Mtume, *The Quotable Karenga,* 20.

107. Brown, "Interview with Amina Thomas," 11; Tisho Moja to Amiri Jomo, "Doctrine Class Report," October 31, 1969, Papers of Maulana Karenga and the Organization Us, African American Cultural Center, Los Angeles.

108. Brown, "Interview with Karl Key-Hekima," 14.

109. The proportion of US families with multiple wives is not known. Calculating such a quotient is often complicated by the short-lived duration of such households.

110. Scot Brown, "Interview with Staajabu Heshimu" (audio recording, December 6, 1997), side 1.

111. Brown, "Interview with Amina Thomas" (transcript, November, 10, 1996), 9–10.

112. Ibid.

113. Brown, "Interview with James Doss-Tayari," 21.

114. Ibid.

115. Sandra Flowers, *African-American Nationalist Literature of the 1960's: Pens of Fire* (New York: Garland Publishers, 1996), xv.

116. Brown, "Interview with Joann Richardson-Kicheko," 12.

117. Brown, "Interview with Karl Key-Hekima," 14.

118. Ibid., 21. One axiom in the *Quotable Karenga* states, "We say male Supremacy is based on three things: tradition, acceptance and reason"; Tracye Matthews, "'No One Ever Asks, What a Man's Place in the Revolution Is': Gender and Politics of the Black Panther Party, 1966–1971," in Charles Jones (ed.), *Black Panther Party Reconsidered* (Baltimore: Black Classic Press, 1998), 272; Paula Giddings, *When and Where I Enter: The Impact of Race and Sex in America* (New York: Bantam Books, 1984), 64; James Cone, *Martin and Malcolm: A Dream or Nightmare* (Maryknoll, N.Y.: Orbis Books, 1991), 273–280; Mumininas of Committee for Unified NewArk, *Mwanamke Mwananchi (The Nationalist Woman)* (Newark: Mumininas of CFUN, 1971); bell hooks, *Ain't I a Woman: Black Women and Feminism* (Boston: South End Press, 1982), 95.

119. Benita Roth, "The Making of the Vanguard Center: Black Feminist Emergence in the 1960s and 1070s," in Kimberly Springer (ed.), *Still Lifting, Still Climbing: African-American Women's Contemporary Activism* (New York: New York University Press, 1999), 70–90.

120. John Bracey, August Meier, and Elliot Rudwick (eds.), *Black Nationalism in America* (Indianapolis and New York: Bobbs-Merrill, 1970), 72–74; Wilson Jeremiah Moses, *Classical Black Nationalism: From the American Revolution to Marcus Garvey* (New York: New York University Press, 1996), 2–5; Martha Lee, *The Nation of Islam: An American Millenarian Movement* (Lewiston, N.Y.: Edwin Mellon Press, 1988); Malcolm X, "God's Judgement of White America," in Benjamin Karim (ed.), *The End of White World Supremacy: Four Speeches by Malcolm X* (New York: Arcade Publishing, 1971), 124.

121. "Introduction to Maulana Karenga—by one of his followers," in Halisi and Mtume, *The Quotable Karenga,* 1; Brown, "Interview with Oliver Massengale-Heshimu and Charles Massengale-Sigidi," 17; Brown, "Interview with Wesely Kabaila," 2; Kabaila relates in his interview that upon hearing Karenga speak for the first time at a lecture in 1967, "[t]he only thing I can relate it to is what some Christians feel when they've had the calling of God" (p. 2).

122. "Introduction of Maulana," n.d., Personal Papers of Oliver Massengale-Heshimu.

123. Ibid.

124. Kwame Nkrumah, *Axioms of Kwame Nkrumah* (London: Nelson, 1967); Julius Nyerere, *Freedom and Unity: Uhuru na Umoja; A Selection from Writings and Speeches, 1952–65* (Dar es Salaam, Tanzania: Oxford University Press, 1966); Mao Zedong, *On the Correct Handling of Contradictions among the People* (7th ed.) (Peking [Beijing]: Foreign Language Press, 1966).

125. Brown, "Interview with James Mtume" (transcript, January 16, 1997), 20; Mu'ammar al-Qadhafi's *The Green Book* (London: Martin, Brian and O'Keeffe, 1976) appeared in English after the publication of *The Quotable Karenga*.

126. "Takwimu na Jedwali," n.d., Personal Papers of Oliver Massengale-Heshimu.

127. Prior to the popularity of the Black Panther Party for Self-Defense, the term "Black Panther" was seen by many northern radicals—inspired by the Black independent politics in Lowndes County, Alabama—as a descriptor for a broader thrust toward independent Black politics. In some measure, this accounts for the many different "Panther" political formations that emerged in the mid-1960s.

128. Thomas McCormick, *America's Half-Century: United States Foreign Policy in the Cold War and After* (Baltimore: Johns Hopkins University Press, 1995), 119.

129. "Militant Negro Leader: Ron Ndabezitha Karenga," *New York Times*, September 2, 1968, 13.

130. This view approximated the dominant perspectives of early Nation of Islam members in relation to Elijah Muhammad's prophesies. See Martha Lee, *The Nation of Islam: An American Millenarian Movement* (Lewiston, N.Y.: Edwin Mellon Press, 1988), 49–75; Brown, "Interview with James Mtume" (January 16, 1997), 8; Scot Brown, "Interview with George Subira" (audio recording, February 16, 1998), side 1.

131. Brown, "Interview with George Subira," side 1.

132. Ibid.

133. Maulana Ron Karenga in Imamu Halisi (ed.), *Kitabu: Beginning Concepts in Kawaida* (Los Angeles: US Organization, 1971), 14.

134. Ibid.

135. James W. Johnson, F. Frances Johnson, and Ronald Slaughter, *The Nguzo Saba and the Festival of the First Fruits: A Guide for Promoting Family, Community Values and the Celebration of Kwanzaa* (New York: Gumbs and Thomas, 1995).

136. Maulana Karenga, *Kwanzaa: A Celebration of Family, Community and Culture*, Commemorative Edition (Los Angeles: University of Sankore Press, 1998), 121.

137. Karenga in Halisi, *Kitabu*, 7; Earl Anthony, *The Time of Furnaces: A Case Study of Black Student Revolt* (New York: Dial Press, 1971), 24.

138. Stanley Crouch, "Christmas Equals Separation," *Harambee*, December 28, 1967, 2. Crouch, an active supporter of radical and Black nationalist organizations in Los Angeles during the late 1960s, was sympathetic to the US-styled rejection of Christmas and published a harsh condemnation of the holiday in the article cited above.

139. "In Perspective: Karenga's Mission Is for Posterity," *The Hilltop*, January 5, 1968, 3; Max Gluckmann, "Social Aspects of First Fruits Ceremonies among the South-Eastern Bantu," *Africa: Journal of the International Institute of*

African Languages and Cultures 11:1 (January 1938): 25–41; Karenga, *Kwanzaa,* 17–20.

140. Claude Clegg III, *An Original Man: Life and Times of Elijah Muhammad* (New York: St. Martin's Press, 1997), 255.

141. Karenga, *Kwanzaa,* 17n.5, 29.

142. Brown, "Interview with Karl Key-Hekima," 24; Keith Mayes, "Rituals of Race, Ceremonies of Culture: Kwanzaa and the Making of a Black Power Holiday in the United States, 1966–2000" (Ph.D. dissertation, Princeton University, 2002), 103.

143. Ibid., 24.

144. Ibid.

145. Elizabeth Softky, "A Kwanzaa Memory: Growing Up with Dr. Karenga," *Washington Post,* December 20, 1995, E1.

146. Ibid.

147. Brown, "Interview with Letta Mbulu," 13.

148. Ibid.

149. Ibid.

150. E. Frances White, "Africa on My Mind: Gender, Counter Discourse and African-American Nationalism," *Journal of Women's History* 2:1 (Spring 1990): 77.

151. Brown, "Interview with Staajabu Heshimu," side 1.

NOTES TO CHAPTER 4

1. Gerald Horne, *Fire This Time: The Watts Uprising and the 1960s* (Charlottesville: University Press of Virginia, 1995), 187, 202–203; Bruce Tyler, "The Rise and Decline of the Watts Summer Festival, 1965–1986," *American Studies* 31:2 (1990): 63; Herbert Haines, *Black Radicals and the Civil Rights Mainstream, 1954–1970* (Knoxville: University of Tennessee Press, 1988), 64; Jennifer Jordan, "Cultural Nationalism in the 1960s: Politics and Poetry," in Adolph Reed (ed.), *Race, Politics and Culture: Critical Essays on the Radicalism of the 1960s* (Westport, Conn.: Greenwood Press, 1986), 35–38. Jordan's essay makes the rather curious assertion that US and other cultural nationalists were only rhetorically critical of the Vietnam War and did not actively participate in the antiwar movement.

2. Clay Carson, "A Talk with Ron Karenga," *Los Angeles Free Press,* September 2, 1966, 12.

3. "First Annual Memorial Staged for Malcolm X," *Los Angeles Sentinel,* March 3, 1966, A11.

4. Ibid.

5. "Riots Disrupt Malcolm X Meeting," *Los Angeles Sentinel,* May 25, 1967, A3.

6. Ibid.

7. Ibid.

8. Scot Brown, "Interview with Kamili Mtume" (audio recording, June 22, 1997), side 1.

9. Scot Brown, "Interview with Charles Johnson-Sitawisha" (transcript, September 9, 1995), 4.

10. Ibid., 5–6. The US flyer for Malcolm X's birthday in 1968 urges the Los Angeles community: "'PEOPLE GET READY' for a BLACK HOLIDAY, No School, No Work to celebrate KUZALIWA (The Birth Of Malcolm X)" in "[Flyer for Kuzaliwa, May 17, 1968]," Personal Papers of Charles Johnson-Sitawisha.

11. "From the Office of Kenneth Hahn [re: demonstrations in Los Angeles Area High Schools and Colleges]," Kenneth Hahn Papers, Box 273, Folder 2a, Huntington Library, Pasadena, Calif.

12. Ibid.

13. "Parents Demand Changes," *Los Angeles Sentinel,* September 14, 1967, A1, A8.

14. Ibid., A8.

15. "Another View of Manual," *Harambee,* November 17, 1967, 1.

16. John Dunne, "The Ugly Mood of Watts," *Saturday Evening Post,* July 16, 1966, 86.

17. "Festival Welcomes Uhuru Militants," *Los Angeles Free Press,* August 18–24, 1967, 3.

18. Clayborne Carson, *In Struggle: SNCC and the Black Awakening of the 1960s* (Cambridge, Mass.: Harvard University Press, 1981), 255–257.

19. "Exclusive: Rap Brown Raps with Free Press," *Los Angeles Free Press,* August 18–24, 1967, 1.

20. William Van Deburg, *New Day in Babylon: The Black Power Movement and American Culture, 1965–1975* (Chicago: University of Chicago Press, 1992), 3.

21. "Will Watts Secede?" *The Movement,* July 1966, in Clayborne Carson (ed.), *The Movement 1964–1970* (Westport, Conn.: Greenwood Press, 1993), 132.

22. "Opposition Shown to Freedom City," *Los Angeles Sentinel,* July 28, 1966, 1A.

23. Raphael Sonenshein, *Politics in Black and White: Race and Power in Los Angeles* (Princeton, N.J.: Princeton University Press, 1993), 27.

24. John Dunne, "The Ugly Mood of Watts," *Saturday Evening Post,* July 16, 1966, 83–87; "Watts Waiting for D-Day," *New Republic,* June 11, 1966, 15–17; "Watts Today," *Life,* July 15, 1966, 62.

25. Dunne, "The Ugly Mood of Watts," 83.

26. "Watts Today," *Life,* July 15, 1966, 62; Dunne, "The Ugly Mood of Watts," 86.

27. Carson, *In Struggle,* 233; also, Carson notes that the SNCC national

leadership regarded the demise of the Freedom City campaign as an indication of Clifford Vaughs's lack of effectiveness and asked for his resignation and closed the Los Angeles office (p. 233). Another Los Angeles chapter of SNCC would be revived later in 1968.

28. Scot Brown, "Interview with Ken Msemaji" (May 20, 2001), 7.

29. "There Is a Movement Starting in Watts," *The Movement*, August 1966, in Clayborne Carson (ed.), *The Movement 1964–1970*, 142.

30. Carson, "A Talk with Ron Karenga," 12.

31. "Dr. King's Death Unifies LA Black Community," *Los Angeles Free Press*, April 12, 1968, 3.

32. "Partial List of Black Congress," *Harambee*, November 17, 1967, 8.

33. "Black Congress Aircheck" (audio recording) (Los Angeles: Pacifica Radio Archive, 1968), tape 2, side 2; "Soul Brothers Air Grievances," *Los Angeles Sentinel*, January 1, 1969, A1, B10.

34. "Black Congress Programs," n.d., 3, Personal Papers of Alfred Moore.

35. Mwalimu Ken Msemaji to Mwalimu Oliver Heshimu, September 3, 1968, Papers of Maulana Karenga and the Organization Us, African American Cultural Center, Los Angeles.

36. *Harambee*, August 11, 1966, 3; *Harambee*, September 15, 1966, 3; *Harambee*, October 13, 1966, 3; *Harambee*, November 17, 1967, 2; *Harambee*, December 28, 1967, 2.

37. "Introduction to Treaty," *Harambee*, November 17, 1967, 6.

38. "San Diego Rally Seeks to End Vietnam War," *Harambee*, December 28, 1967, 8. It should be noted that SNCC's early antiwar stance had a strong influence on US and other organizations that adopted it during the late 1960s.

39. "US Statement on the Viet Nam War, 1967," Personal Papers of Wesely Kabaila.

40. Scot Brown, "Interview with Thomas Belton" (audio recording, November, 27, 1998), side 1; idem, "Interview with Randolph Abunuwas-Stripling" (audio recording, May 16, 2002), side 1.

41. "Randolph Stripling to Amiri Jomo and Kaimu Weusi [1969]," Personal Papers of Randolph Stripling; Brown, "Interview with Thomas Belton" (audio recording, November 27, 1998), side 1; idem, "Interview with Randy Abunuwas-Stripling" (audio recording, May 16, 2002), side 1.

42. Wallace Terry, *Guess Who's Coming Home: Black Fighting Men Recorded Live* [Phonograph] (Detroit: Motown Record Corporation, 1972), side 2; Scot Brown, "Interview with Thomas Belton" (audio recording, November 27, 1998), side 1; idem, "Interview with Randy Abunuwas-Stripling" (audio recording, May 16, 2002), side 1.

43. Wallace Terry, "Bringing the War Home," *Black Scholar*, November 1970, 8.

44. Gary Solis, *Marines and Military Law in Vietnam: Trial by Fire* (Washington, D.C.: History and Museums Division Headquarters, U.S. Marine Corps, 1989), 129.

45. Wallace Terry, *Guess Who's Coming Home: Black Fighting Men Recorded Live* (phonograph) (Detroit: Motown Record Corporation, 1972), side 2.

46. Robert Mullen, *Blacks in America's Wars: The Shift in Attitudes from the Revolutionary War to Vietnam* (New York: Pathfinder Press, 1973), 80–81.

47. Solis, *Marines and Military Law in Vietnam*, 130.

48. Brown, "Interview with Thomas Belton," side 1.

49. "Black Power, 'Every Negro Is a Potential Blackman,'" *Herald-Dispatch*, February 22, 1968, 3, 8; Angela Davis, *Angela Davis: An Autobiography* (New York: Bantam Books, 1974), 165–166.

50. Carson, *In Struggle*, 282–283.

51. Ibid., 286.

52. Alphonso Pinkney, *Red, Black and Green: Black Nationalism in the United States* (New York: Cambridge University Press, 1976), 148.

53. Maulana Karenga, "Revolution Must Wait for the People," *Los Angeles Free Press*, May 16, 1969, 14.

54. "Black Power Rally" (audio recording) (Los Angeles: Pacifica Radio Archive, 1968), side 2; Scot Brown, "Interview with Ayuko Babu" (audio recording, November 9, 1996), tape 2, side 1. For sources and commentary on the Black Panther Party's public threats of violent reprisals against the government at the "Free Huey" rally, see Davis, *Angela Davis*, 165–166; "Black Power, 'Every Negro Is a Potential Blackman,'" 3, 8.

55. "Black Power Rally" (audio recording), side 2.

56. Scot Brown, "Interview with Ngoma Ali" (transcript, November 10, 1996), 16.

57. Ibid.

58. Ibid.

59. "Bank Robbery Nets US Member 25 Years," *Los Angeles Sentinel*, August 14, 1969, A3; "2 'US' Members Guilty of Crime," *Los Angeles Sentinel*, March 6, 1969, 1; Brown, "Interview with Ngoma Ali," 24–25.

60. "L.A.P.D. Raids US Headquarters; Arrests Two," *Los Angeles Sentinel*, January 15, 1970, A1, D2.

61. Federal Bureau of Investigation, "Everett Leroy Jones, FBI File #100-425307," December 24, 1967, 12, Amiri Baraka Papers, box 9, Moorland-Spingarn Research Center, Howard University, Washington D.C.

62. "Black Enigma," *Wall Street Journal*, July 26, 1968, 1, 15.

63. Ibid., 15.

64. Ibid., 1.

65. Ibid., 1.

66. "Karenga Speaks about Conflict with Panthers," *Los Angeles Free Press,* February 7, 1969, 1.

67. Earl Ofari and Ruth Hirshman, "Victim of Watergating, Ron Karenga: Interviewed by Earl Ofari and Ruth Hirshman" (audio recording) (Los Angeles: Pacifica Radio Archive, 1974), side 1.

68. Ibid.

69. Ibid.

70. "Black Enigma," *Wall Street Journal,* July 26, 1968, 1.

71. William Van Deburg, *New Day in Babylon: The Black Power Movement and American Culture, 1965–1975* (Chicago: University of Chicago Press, 1992), 85–86; Sonenshein, *Politics in Black and White,* 85; Gilbert Moore, *Rage* (New York: Carrol and Graf, 1993), 91; Kenneth O'Reilly, *"Racial Matters": The FBI's Secret File on Black America, 1960–1972* (New York: Free Press, 1989), 295, 336.

72. Ofari and Hirshman, "Victim of Watergating, Ron Karenga," side 1.

73. Ibid.

74. Ibid. While Karenga, in the interview with Ofari and Hirshman, conceded his tactical error in meeting with Reagan, he also pondered, "Why is it that Black people and White people in this country believe that if a Black man meets with a White man, that [the] White man automatically is more intelligent than he is, automatically more shrewd politically than he is, and automatically is going to make a fool of him and make him a patsy and a sellout for the people" (side 1).

75. "Militants Fight Blacks, White Men Settle Dispute," *Herald-Dispatch,* July 20, 1968, 1, 3. It should be noted that Pat Alexander, the editor of the *Herald-Dispatch,* had a general mistrust of militant organizations in the Black Power movement. In different instances she characterized both US and the Black Panther Party as fascistic. As a result, the paper's articles pertaining to local Black nationalist politics were often unapologetically polemical; "Members of US Blamed," *Los Angeles Sentinel,* July 11, 1968, A1, A8; Elaine Brown, *A Taste of Power: A Black Woman's Story* (New York: Pantheon Books, 1992), 115–116.

76. Davis, *Angela Davis,* 162; Brown, *A Taste of Power,* 124

77. James Forman, *The Making of Black Revolutionaries* (New York: Macmillan, 1972), 524, 528; Scot Brown, "Interview with Ayuko Babu" (audio recording, November 9, 1996), tape 1, side 2; Davis, *Angela Davis,* 163; Carson, *In Struggle,* 281; "Black Congress Chairman Quits," *Los Angeles Sentinel,* January 30, 1969, A1, A10.

78. Federal Bureau of Investigation, "SAC San Diego to Director," November 22, 1968, Black Nationalist Hate Groups File (100-448006, sec. 5), 1, in *COINTELPRO: The Counter Intelligence Program of the FBI.*

79. Federal Bureau of Investigation, "SAC Los Angeles to Director," September 25, 1968, Black Nationalist Hate Groups File (100-448006, sec. 3), 1, 3, in *COINTELPRO: The Counter Intelligence Program of the FBI.*

80. Ibid., 3.

81. Federal Bureau of Investigation, "SAC Los Angeles to Director," November 29, 1968, Black Nationalist Hate Groups File (100-448006, sec. 5), 1, in *COINTELPRO: The Counter Intelligence Program of the FBI.*

82. Ibid.

83. University of California, Los Angeles, Office of Public Information, "Release: Success of Minority High Potential Program Reported," February 12, 1969, 1, UCLA University Archives, RS 401, Chancellor's Office, Aministrative Subject Files of Frank Murphy, 1935–71, box 125, "High Potential Program" Folder; Floyd Hayes III and Francis Kiene III, "'All Power to the People': The Political Thought of Huey P. Newton and the Black Panther Party," in Charles Jones (ed.), *The Black Panther Party Reconsidered* (Baltimore: Black Classic Press, 1998), 168.

84. Hayes and Kiene, "'All Power to the People,'" 168–169.

85. Brown, *A Taste of Power,* 162–163; Gene Marine, *The Black Panthers* (New York: Signet Books, 1969), 209.

86. James Mtume, "Interview with George Ali-Stiner and Claude Hubert-Gaidi" (notes from audio recording, October 1998); Bobby Seale, *Seize the Time: The Story of the Black Panther Party and Huey P. Newton* (New York: Vintage Books, 1972), 273.

87. Gail Sheehy, *Panthermania: The Clash of Black against Black in One American City* (New York: Harper and Row, 1971), 16–18; Brown, *A Taste of Power,* 162–164; Hayes and Kiene, "'All Power to the People,'" 169.

88. "'US' Member Shot Panther in Back," *Herald-Dispatch,* August 21, 1969.

89. "Gun Battle before Murder?" *UCLA Bruin,* January 22, 1969, 1; "Campus Fracas Ends in Shooting," *Los Angeles Sentinel,* January 23, 1969, B5.

90. Mtume, "Interview with George Ali-Stiner and Claude Hubert-Gaidi."

91. Bakari Kitwana, "A Soldier's Story," *The Source,* February 1998, 132. For more details on Geronimo Pratt's reflections of the US/Panther conflict, see Jack Olsen, *Last Man Standing: The Tragedy and Triumph of Geronimo Pratt* (New York: Doubleday, 2000), 44–45, 59, 223–226.

92. Ibid.

93. "Karenga Denies Shooting of UCLA Black Panthers,*" Los Angeles Free Press,* January 31–February 7, 1969, 1; M. Ron Karenga, "A Response to Muhammad Ahmad," *Black Scholar* 9:10 (July/August 1978): 55–57; Scot Brown, "Interview with James Mtume"(transcript, January 16, 1997), 31–32; Mtume, "Interview with George Stiner-Ali and Claude Hubert-Gaidi."

94. "Cowardly Snakes Kill Panthers," *Black Panther,* February 2, 1969, 6; "Panthers Promise to Avenge Deaths," *Berkeley Barb,* January 24–30, 1969, 9; "Bobby Seale Talks to The Movement about L.A. Assassinations, Cultural Nationalism, Exausting All Political Means, Community Programs, Black Capitalism," *The Movement,* March 1969, in Clayborne Carson (ed.), *The Movement*

1964–1970 (Westport, Conn.: Greenwood Press, 1993), 562–564; "Los Angeles Panthers Await Justice for US Organization Pigs," *Black Panther,* February 2, 1969, 4.

95. Ward Churchill and Jim Vander Wall, *Agents of Repression: The Secret Wars against the Black Panther Party and the American Indian Movement* (Boston: South End Press, 1988), 42–43; Ekwueme Michael Thelwell, "Just to See What the End Will Be," Afterword in Gilbert Moore, *Rage* (New York: Carrol and Graf, 1993), 300–301; Bruce Tyler, "Black Radicalism in Southern California, 1950–1982," (unpublished Ph.D. dissertation, UCLA, 1983), 376. In separate published statements made by Louis Tackwood and a shadowy unidentifiable man calling himself "Othello," the men claimed that they had worked for the FBI or the local police, and that they funneled weapons to infiltrators and worked with them in US for the purpose of destabilizing the Black Panther Party. Othello's account, mysteriously told in an interview in *Penthouse* magazine, is cited in Huey Newton's Ph.D. dissertation, "War against the Panthers: A Study of Repression in America" (University of California, Santa Cruz, 1980), 104–110. Tackwood's story can be found in *The Glass House Tapes* (New York: Avon, 1973). His account added fuel to scholarly attempts at advancing similar allegations against US and Karenga. Somewhat troubling is the ease with which some historians have accepted the snitch-to-truth-teller conversion narratives offered by Tackwood or "Othello"; see Rod Bush, *We Are Not What We Seem: Black Nationalism and Class Struggle in the American Century* (New York: New York University Press, 1999), 217, for problematic use of Othello's story. Before the publication of *The Glass House Tapes,* Tackwood's credibility was shattered by constant changes in his story and his evasive and poor performance on a lie detector test for the *Los Angeles Times* and *Newsweek,* conducted by Chris Gugas, who at the time was the former president and current board chairman of the American Polygraph Association; see *Los Angeles Times,* October 17, 1971, 1, B1, B4, for details. While taking the test he specifically refused to answer questions relating to his claim that he supplied Karenga with guns and money to disrupt the Black Panther Party.

96. "US Members Lose Battle," *Los Angeles Sentinel,* September 11, 1969, A1, A12; "Tight Security at Panther's Trial," *Herald-Dispatch,* July 12, 1969, 2.

97. "Arguments Rage in Murder Trial," *Los Angeles Sentinel,* July 24, 1969, A1; "Stiner Brothers Get Life Sentence," *Los Angeles Sentinel,* November 30, 1969, A1, A9.

98. "20 Years Later, It's Still Prison," *San Francisco Chronicle,* August 4, 1994, sec. A, 15–16.

99. "FBI Looking for Fugitives among Guyana Survivors," *Los Angeles Times,* December 7, 1978, 22.

100. "20 Years Later, It's Still Prison," 15–16.

101. "Committee for Unified Newark Presents, 'An Evening of Soul and African Culture,'" *Black News* 1:4 (1970): 8.

102. Amiri Baraka, *The Autobiography of LeRoi Jones* (Chicago: Lawrence Hill Books, 1997), 390–391; Baraka recalls that the event took place at the Harlem Renaissance Ballroom.

103. Scot Brown, "Interview with Wesely Kabaila" (transcript, October 11, 1994), 15.

104. Scot Brown, "Interview with James Doss-Tayari" (November 12, 1996), 36–37; Brown, "Interview with James Mtume," January 16, 1997, 27.

105. Scot Brown, "Interview with Daryl Tukufu" (audio recording, August 2, 1997), side 2.

106. "Black Congress Chairman Quits," *Los Angeles Sentinel,* January 30, 1969, A1, A10.

107. "Black Power Thugs Warn Margaret Wright," *Herald-Dispatch,* January 18, 1969; "Soul Brothers Air Grievances," *Los Angeles Sentinel,* January 1, 1969, A1, 10B.

108. "Maulana Karenga Urges Conference on Community Unity," *Harambee,* April 25, 1969, 8. At the time of the publication of this edition of *Harambee,* the newspaper had returned to being an exclusive organ of the US Organization. Its entire editorial staff was composed of US members.

109. Alphonso Pinkney, *Red, Black and Green: Black Nationalism in the United States* (New York: Cambridge University Press, 1976), 142.

110. Ibid., 143.

111. Chuck Stone, "National Conference on Black Power," in Floyd Barbour (ed.), *The Black Power Revolt* (Boston: Extending Horizons Books, 1968), 190.

112. Ibid.

113. Ibid.

114. Komozi Woodard, *A Nation within a Nation: Amiri Baraka (LeRoi Jones) and Black Power Politics* (Chapel Hill: University of North Carolina Press, 1999), 84–85; idem, "The Making of the New Ark: Imamu Amiri Baraka (LeRoi Jones), and the Newark Congress of African People, and the Modern Black Convention Movement. A History of the Black Revolt and the New Nationalism, 1966–1976" (Ph.D. dissertation, University of Pennsylvania, 1991), 104–105; Stone, "National Conference on Black Power," 190.

115. "Black Power Conference 1967."

116. Nathan Wright Jr., *Let's Work Together* (New York: Hawthorne Books, 1968), 146.

117. Ibid.

118. Ibid., 163. Wright referred to this concept as "operational harmony."

119. Ibid.

120. Stone, "National Conference on Black Power," 196.

121. Baraka, *The Autobiography of LeRoi Jones,* 385.

122. Ibid., 383.

123. Ibid., 386.

124. "Black Convention: Prelude to Self-Government," *Black Newark* 1:2 (July 1968): 12.

125. Woodard, "The Making of the New Ark," 161.

126. "Black Power Rally" (audio recording) (Los Angeles: Pacifica Radio Archive, 1968), side 2; Baraka, *The Autobiography of LeRoi Jones,* 393.

127. Baraka, *The Autobiography of LeRoi Jones,* 385.

128. Imamu Amiri Baraka, "The Creation of the New Ark," unpublished manuscript, 91, Amiri Baraka Papers, Box 40, Moorland-Spingarn Research Center, Howard University, Washington, D.C.

129. Scot Brown, "Interview with Amina Thomas" (transcript, November 10, 1996), 7; idem, "Interview with Oliver Massengale-Heshimu and Charles Massengale-Sigidi" (transcript, November 11, 1996), 29. There was an apparent clash involving US's Simba and the Revolutionary Action Movement's Black Guards. This is briefly mentioned in an article by Nikki Giovanni, "Black Poems, Poseurs and Power," *Negro Digest* 18 (June 1969).

130. Brown, "Interview with Wesely Kabaila," 28.

131. Ibid., 29.

132. Woodard, *A Nation within a Nation,* 107, 281nn.68–69; idem, "The Making of the New Ark," 177.

133. Brown, "Interview with Amiri Baraka," 5.

134. Ibid.

135. "Maulana Ron Karenga to LeRoi Jones," December 19, 1967, Personal Papers of Komozi Woodard. The slogan "Anywhere we are, US is" is used as a logo at the top of the US organization's letterhead.

NOTES TO CHAPTER 5

1. Maulana Karenga, "Revolution Must Wait for the People," *Los Angeles Free Press,* May 16, 1969, 14.

2. Kathleen Cleaver, "A Panther Replies to Julius Lester," *The Guardian,* May 3, 1969, 7, 14.

3. October 1966, Black Panther Party Platform and Program, "What We Want/What We Believe," in Philip Foner (ed.), *Black Panthers Speak* (New York: J. B. Lippincott, 1970), 2–4.

4. Maulana Ron Karenga, "Maulana Ron Karenga: Statement by the Black Nationalist" (audio recording) (Los Angeles: Pacifica Radio Archive, 1969), side 1.

5. Ibid.

6. Ibid.

7. Ibid.

8. JoNina M. Abron, "'Serving the People': The Survival Programs of the Black Panther Party," in Charles Jones (ed.), *The Black Panther Party Reconsidered* (Baltimore: Black Classic Press, 1998), 177–192; "Bobby Seale Talks to The Movement about L.A. Assassinations, Cultural Nationalism, Exhausting All Political Means, Community Programs, Black Capitalism," in Clayborne Carson (ed.), *The Movement 1964–1970* (Westport, Conn.: Greenwood Press, 1993), 564; Fred Hampton, "You Can Murder a Liberator, but You Can't Murder Liberation," in Philip Foner (ed.), *Black Panthers Speak* (New York: J. B. Lippincott, 1970), 139.

9. Scot Brown, "Interview with C. R. D. Halisi" (transcript, November 11, 1996), 37.

10. Ibid.

11. Maulana Ron Karenga, "The Black Community and the University: A Community Organizer's Perspective," in Armstead Robinson, Craig Foster, and Donald Ogilvie (eds.), *Black Studies in the University: A Symposium* (New Haven: Yale University Press, 1969), 40–41; idem, "Kawaida and Its Critics," *Journal of Black Studies* 8:2 (December 1977): 125–148.

12. "Editorial: B.P.P. and P.F.P.," *Black Panther,* March 16, 1968, 3.

13. "Karenga Denies Shooting of UCLA Black Panthers," *Los Angeles Free Press,* January 31–February 7, 1969, 1.

14. Ibid.

15. Amiri Baraka, "Nationalism Vs PimpArt," in *Raise, Race, Rays, Raze: Essays since 1965* (New York: Random House, 1971), 129–130, originally published in the *New York Times,* November 1969.

16. Ibid., 129–130.

17. Karenga, "Maulana Ron Karenga," side 1; "Karenga Speaks about Conflict with Panthers," *Los Angeles Free Press,* February 1, 1969, 1.

18. "Karenga Denies Shooting of UCLA Black Panthers," *Los Angeles Free Press,* January 31–February 7, 1969, 1.

19. David Hilliard, "The Ideology of the Black Panther Party," in Philip Foner (ed.), *Black Panthers Speak* (New York: J. B. Lippincott, 1970), 122–123.

20. "Stokely Carmichael Denounces Panthers," *Los Angeles Sentinel,* July 10, 1969, A2; Eldridge Cleaver, "An Open Letter to Stokely Carmichael," in Philip Foner (ed.), *Black Panthers Speak* (New York: J. B. Lippincott, 1970), 104–108.

21. Cleaver, "An Open Letter to Stokely Carmichael," in Foner, *Black Panthers Speak,* 104–108.

22. Scot Brown, "Interview with Kwame Toure" (audio recording, April 19, 1997), side 1.

23. "Warning to So-called 'Paper Panthers,'" *Black Panther,* September 14,

1968, 10. This "Warning" appeared in several issues of the *Black Panther* during the late 1960s.

24. Ibid.

25. Ibid.

26. Maulana Ron Karenga, in Clyde Halisi and James Mtume (eds.), *The Quotable Karenga* (Los Angeles: US Organization, 1967), 1–8.

27. Baraka, "Nationalism Vs PimpArt," 129–130.

28. "Stokely's Jive," *Black Panther,* May 31, 1970, 20; Alprentice "Bunchy" Carter, "The Genius of Huey Newton," in Philip Foner (ed.), *Black Panthers Speak* (New York: J. B. Lippincott, 1970), 27–28; "Lumpenization: A Critical Error of the Black Panther Party," in Charles Jones (ed.), *The Black Panther Party Reconsidered* (Baltimore: Black Classic Press, 1998), 337–358.

29. "Stokely's Jive," 20.

30. "Los Angeles Panthers Await Justice for 'US' Organization," *Black Panther,* February 2, 1969, 4.

31. Ibid.

32. Elaine Brown, *A Taste of Power: A Black Woman's Story* (New York: Pantheon Books, 1992), 108.

33. Karenga, in Halisi and Mtume, *The Quotable Karenga,* 4.

34. Amiri Baraka, *The Autobiography of LeRoi Jones* (Chicago: Lawrence Hill Books, 1997), 391. From an official standpoint, the party also discouraged alchohol, drug abuse, theft, and mistreatment of "other party members or BLACK people at all." See Central Headquarters, "Rules of the Black Panther Party," in Philip Foner (ed.), *Black Panthers Speak* (New York: J. B. Lippincott, 1970), 4–6.

35. Linda Harrison, "On Cultural Nationalism," *Black Panther,* February 2, 1969, 6.

36. Huey Newton, "Huey Newton Talks to The Movement about the Black Panther Party, Cultural Nationalism, SNCC, Liberals and White Revolutionaries," in Philip Foner (ed.), *Black Panthers Speak* (New York: J. B. Lippincott, 1970), 50–51.

37. Bobby Seale, *Seize the Time: The Story of the Black Panther Party and Huey P. Newton* (New York: Vintage Books, 1970), 21–24, 113–121; Huey Newton, *Revolutionary Suicide* (New York: Harcourt Brace Jovanovich, 1973), 132.

38. Ibid.

39. Harrison, "On Cultural Nationalism," 6.

40. "The True Culture of Africans," *Black Panther,* February 17, 1969, 15–18.

41. Harrison, "On Cultural Nationalism," 6.

42. "SDS Resolution on the Black Panther Party," in Philip Foner (ed.), *Black Panthers Speak* (New York: J. B. Lippincott, 1970), 226.

43. Ibid., 227.

44. Julius Lester, "From the Other Side of the Tracks," *The Guardian*, April 19, 1969, 13.

45. Ibid., 13.

46. Kathleen Cleaver, "A Panther Replies to Julius Lester," *The Guardian*, May 3, 1969, 7, 14.

47. Ibid.

48. Ibid., 14.

49. Ibid.

50. Ibid.

51. "Stokely Carmichael Denounces Panthers," *Los Angeles Sentinel*, July 10, 1969, A2.

52. Brown, "Interview with Kwame Toure," side 1.

53. Mumia Abu-Jamal, "A Life in the Party: A Historical and Retrospective Examination of the Projections and Legacies of the Black Panther Party," in Kathleen Cleaver and George Katsiaficas (eds.), *Liberation, Imagination, and the Black Panther Party: A New Look at the Panthers and Their Legacy* (New York: Routledge, 2001), 48.

54. Ibid.

55. Brown, "Interview with Kwame Toure," side 1.

56. Harold Cruse, "Cultural Nationalism" (Los Angeles: Pacifica Radio Archive, 1970), side 1; Ernie Mkalimoto (now Ernie Allen Jr.), "Revolutionary Black Culture: The Cultural Arm of Revolutionary Nationalism," *Negro Digest* 19:2 (December 1969), was an effort to resolve the problematic terminology, resulting from the feud asserting that a people's national liberation struggle depends on revolutionary politics and culture. "It is impossible," he concluded, "to speak of Black nationalism without considering at the same time the question of black culture; culture and nationalism cannot be separated" (p. 13).

57. "Kawaida and Its Critics," *Journal of Black Studies* 8:2 (December 1977): 125–148; Brown, *A Taste of Power.*

58. Scot Brown, "Interview with Bobette Azizi Glover" (transcript, May 19, 2001), 9–10.

59. Scot Brown, "Interview with Charles Johnson-Sitawisha" (transcript, September 9, 1995), 34.

60. "Karenga, 2 Others Found Guilty of Torturing Woman," *Los Angeles Times*, May 30, 1971, B26; "Ron Karenga Convicted, Gets Ten Year Sentence," *Herald-Dispatch*, June 3, 1971, 1, 10; "US Leader Held in Asian-Type Torturing," *Los Angeles Sentinel*, A1, A8; Superior Court of the State of California for the County of Los Angeles, "A 264 545 Everett-Karenga, Ron N., et al.," Dept. 102, Arthur Alarcon, Judge.

61. "Karenga's Wife Tells All at Trial," *Los Angeles Sentinel*, May 20, 1971;

Superior Court of the State of California for the County of Los Angeles, "A 264 545 Everett-Karenga."

62. "Karenga's Wife Tells All at Trial"; "Karenga Feared Poisoning, Wife Testifies at Trial," *Jet,* June 3, 1971, 54; Superior Court of the State of California for the County of Los Angeles, "A 264 545 Everett-Karenga."

63. Superior Court of the State of California for the County of Los Angeles, "A 264 545 Everett-Karenga."

64. "Karenga, 2 Others Found Guilty of Torturing Woman," *Los Angeles Times,* May 30, 1971, 26; "Ron Karenga Convicted, Gets Ten Year Sentence," *Herald-Dispatch,* June 3, 1971, 1, 10.

65. Imamu Clyde Halisi, "Maulana Ron Karenga: Black Leader in Captivity," *Black Scholar* 3 (May 1972): 27–31. Also see Halisi (ed.), *Kitabu: Beginning Concepts in Kawaida* (Los Angeles: US Organization, 1971), 1n.1.

66. Scot Brown, "Interview with Gail Idili-Davis" (transcript, September 9, 2000), 7–10.

67. Ollie Johnson, "Explaining the Demise of the Black Panther Party: The Role of Internal Factors," in Charles Jones (ed.), *The Black Panther Party Reconsidered* (Baltimore: Black Classic Press, 1998), 406–407; Brown, *A Taste of Power,* 347–354.

68. Scot Brown, "Interview with Daryl Tukufu" (audio recording, August 2, 1997), side 2.

69. Ibid.

70. Scot Brown, "Interview with Oliver Massengale-Heshimu and Charles Massengale-Sigidi" (transcript, November 11, 1997), 27.

71. Scot Brown, "Interview with James Doss-Tayari" (November 12, 1996), 38.

72. "Black Power Feud Results in Shootings," *Los Angeles Sentinel,* March 20, 1969, A1, A10.

73. Zingha Uliza and Zingha Terema to Amiri Jomo, Matamba Tribe Meeting, November 19, 1969, Papers of Maulana Karenga and the Organization Us, African American Cultural Center, Los Angeles.

74. Amiri Jomo to "T" L/C Imamu Chache, *Matamba* Ororo Saba Program, [1969], Papers of Maulana Karenga and the Organization Us, African American Cultural Center, Los Angeles; Scot Brown, "Interview with Amina Thomas" (transcript, November 10, 1996), 21–23; idem, "Interview with Joann Richardson-Kicheko" (transcript, April 22, 1997), 18–19.

75. Haiba Karenga, "View from the Woman's Side of the Circle," *Harambee,* April 25, 1969, 4; Imamu Halisi, *Interview with Maulana Ron Karenga: July 14, 1973* (Los Angeles: Saidi Publications, 1973), 5; Maulana Ron Karenga, "In Love and Struggle: Toward a Greater Togetherness," *Black Scholar* 6:6 (March 1975): 16–28.

76. Scot Brown, "Interview with Ngoma Ali" (transcript, November 11, 1996), 23.

77. "Introduction of Maulana," n.d., Personal Papers of Oliver Massengale-Heshimu; Scot Brown, "Interview with George Subira" (audio recording, February 16, 1998), side 1; Maulana Ron Karenga, "Kiapo: Oath" [1967?], Personal Papers of Ramon Tyson-Imara.

78. Scot Brown, "Interview with Karl Key-Hekima" (transcript, November 11, 1996), 24–32; idem, "Interview with Staajabu Heshimu" (audio recording, December 6, 1997), side 2; idem, "Interview with Daryl Tukufu," side 2; idem, "Interview with Ngoma Ali," 33–36; idem, "Interview with Amina Thomas" (transcript, November 10, 1996), 32–39; idem, "Interview with James Mtume" (transcript, January 16, 1997), 35–32; idem, "Interview with Joann Richardson-Kicheko," 20–25; idem, "Interview with James Doss-Tayari," 44–45; Baraka, *The Autobiography of LeRoi Jones,* 392–393, 404; Komozi Woodard, *A Nation within a Nation: Amiri Baraka (LeRoi Jones) and Black Power Politics* (Chapel Hill: University of North Carolina Press, 1999), 165.

79. Brown, "Interview with Ngoma Ali," 33; idem, "Interview with James Doss-Tayari," 44–45.

80. Brown, "Interview with Karl Key-Hekima," 31–32; idem, "Interview with Staajabu Heshimu," side 2; idem, "Interview with Amina Thomas," 29–30; idem, "Interview with James Mtume" (transcript, January 16, 1997), 35–36; idem, "Interview with C. R. D. Halisi," 18–19.

81. "2 Former US Members Ambushed in View Park," *Los Angeles Sentinel,* August 27, 1970, A1, A8; "Ron Karenga Rebuffs Charges against US," September 30, 1970, A1, A8; Brown, "Interview with Joann Richardson-Kicheko," 21–25; idem, "Interview with Karl Key-Hekima," 30–31, 39–40; idem, "Interview with Staajabu Heshimu," side 2; idem, "Interview with James Mtume" (transcript, January 16, 1997), 38–41.

82. Brown, "Interview with Ngoma Ali," 33.

83. Brown, "Interview with James Doss-Tayari," 45.

84. Scot Brown, "Interview with Maulana Karenga" (audio recording, February 9, 1999), side 1.

85. Ibid.

86. Ibid.; Earl Ofari and Ruth Hirshman, "Victim of Watergating, Ron Karenga: Interviewed by Earl Ofari and Ruth Hirshman" (audio recording) (Los Angeles: Pacifica Radio Archive, 1974), side 2; M. Ron Karenga, "The Snitch, Trapping Truth and Other Obscenities," in *In Love and Struggle: Poems for Bold Hearts* (San Diego: Kawaida Publications, 1978), 22–23.

87. Woodard, *A Nation within a Nation,* 114–253.

88. Baraka, *The Autobiography of LeRoi Jones,* 403–405; Brown, "Interview with Daryl Tukufu," side 2; idem, "Interview with Ngoma Ali," 39–44; idem, "Interview with Wesely Kabaila" (transcript, October 11, 1994), 33–38.

89. Brown, "Interview with Daryl Tukufu," side 2.

90. Woodard, *A Nation within a Nation,* 180–181.

91. Cheo Hekima to Cadres, "Leo Baraka (7 Oktoba)," September 7, 1973, Amiri Baraka Papers, Box 19, Moorland-Spingarn Research Center, Howard University; Scot Brown, "Interview with James Mtume" (transcript, January 16, 1997), 43–46; idem, "Interview with Daryl Tukufu," side 2; "Leo Baraka . . . A Joyous Celebration," *Black Newark,* November 1972, 7.

92. Imamu Amiri Baraka, CFUN-CAP New Ark, Imamu Vernon Sukumu, Nia-CAP, San Diego, Balozi Zayd Muhammad, BCD-CAP, East Orange, "Vita!," n.d., Amiri Baraka Papers, Box 21, Moorland-Spingarn Research Center, Howard University.

93. Brown, "Interview with Ngoma Ali," 39–48; idem, "Interview with Daryl Tukufu," side 2. Ngoma Ali was among the group of Simba that was sent to both the 1970 CAP conference in Atlanta and to the 1972 conference in San Diego—whereas former US Simba Daryl Tukufu had joined CAP.

94. "The State: Parole Applications," *Los Angeles Times,* May 3, 1973, 2.

95. Muhammad Ahmad, "We Are All Prisoners of War," *Black Scholar,* October 1972, 3–5; "Maulana Karenga Benefit," *Black Newark,* September 1973, 2; Cheo Hekima for Imamu Amiri Baraka to EXCO, "Fundraiser for Maulana Karenga," June 22, 1973, Amiri Baraka Papers, Box 19, Moorland-Spingarn Research Center, Howard University; "CAP EXCO Meeting," June 2, 1973, Amiri Baraka Papers, Box 19, Moorland-Spingarn Research Center, Howard University; Irv Joyner, "Proclamation for the Law and Justice Council," Congress of African People, 2nd International Bi-annual Assembly, San Diego, California, August 31–September 4, 1972, Amiri Baraka Papers, Box 24, Moorland-Spingarn Research Center, Howard University.

96. Earl Ofari and Ruth Hirshman, "Victim of Watergating, Ron Karenga: Interviewed by Earl Ofari and Ruth Hirshman" (audio recording) (Los Angeles: Pacifica Radio Archive, 1974), sides 1–2.

97. Maulana Ron Karenga, "A Strategy for Struggle," *Black Scholar* 4:2 (November 1973): 8–21; idem, "Which Road: Nationalism, Pan-Africanism, Socialism?" *Black Scholar* 6:2 (October 1974): 21–31; idem, "In Love and Struggle: Toward a Greater Togetherness," *Black Scholar* 6:6 (March 1975): 16–28; idem, "In Defense of Sis. Joanne: For Ourselves and History," *Black Scholar* 6:10 (July/August 1975): 36–42.

98. Brown, "Interview with Amina Thomas," 39; idem, "Interview with C. R. D. Halisi," 38–39; idem, "Interview with Ngoma Ali," 48–49, 53.

99. "Whatever Happened to . . . Ron Karenga," *Ebony,* September 1975, 170; Woodard, *A Nation within a Nation,* 166.

100. "Dr. M. Ron Karenga: Back from Caveman's Captivity with Vigor," *Black News,* June/July 1977, 16–17; "Reaffirmation and Change: A Modest Contribution to the Council of Kawaida Elders," *Nkombo: A Quarterly Journal of Neo-Afrikan/American Culture* 5:2 (1977?): 17–18; "CAP: Going through Changes," *Unity and Struggle,* October 1974, 1, 10; "Haki Madhubuti and Jitu Weusi . . . Two

Reactionary Nationalists: Individualism Brings Two Resignations," *Unity and Struggle,* October 1974, 4.

101. Scot Brown, "Interview with Kalamu ya Salaam" (transcript, December 12, 1995), 24–25; Maulana Ron Karenga, *Kawaida Theory: An Introductory Outline* (Inglewood, Calif.: Kawaida Publications, 1980); "Nigeria Evoking a Long Past for U.S. Performers," *New York Times,* January 28, 1977, A2; Molefi Asante, "The 1977 FESTAC Situation," in *Malcolm X as Cultural Hero and Other Afrocentric Essays* (Trenton, N.J.: Africa World Press, 1993), 153–155.

102. "BBB Interviews Maulana Ron Karenga," *Black Books Bulletin* (Summer 1976): 32–39; Maulana Ron Karenga, "Corrective History," *First World* 1:3 (May/June 1977): 50–54; idem, *Beyond Connections: Liberation in Love and Struggle* (New Orleans: Ahidiana, 1978); idem, "Black Politics in 1980: The Problem of Structure and Strategy," *Black News* 4:1 (October 1978): 4–6.

103. Brown, "Interview with James Doss-Tayari," 53–54; idem, "Interview with Amina Thomas," 43–45.

104. Brown, "Interview with Oliver Massengale-Heshimu and Charles Massengale-Sigidi," 32.

105. Ibid.

NOTES TO CHAPTER 6

1. Hoyt Fuller, "Towards a Black Aesthetic," in Addison Gayle (ed.), *The Black Aesthetic* (New York: Doubleday, 1971), 9.

2. Maulana Ron Karenga, "Black Art: Mute Matter Given Force and Function," in Abraham Chapman (ed.), *New Black Voices: An Anthology of Contemporary New Black Literature* (New York: New American Library, 1972), 477–482. The essay was previously published in *Negro Digest,* January 1968.

3. Scot Brown, "Interview with Caiphus Semanya" (transcript, April 21, 1997), 5; Scot Brown, "Interview with Joann Richardson-Kicheko" (transcript, April 22, 1997), 4, 14.

4. Brown, "Interview with Caiphus Semanya," 5.

5. Scot Brown, "Interview with Letta Mbulu" (transcript, April 22, 1997), 15.

6. Brown, "Interview with Caiphus Semanya," 6.

7. Brown, "Interview with Joann Richardson-Kicheko," 17.

8. Ibid., 18.

9. "Taifa Dance Troupe Performance on the Rosey Grier Show, November 30, 1968" (video recording, UCLA Television and Film Archives).

10. Ibid.

11. Brown, "Interview with Joann Richardson-Kicheko," 17–18.

12. "Taifa Dance Troupe Performance."

13. Brown, "Interview with Caiphus Semanya," 11.

14. Ibid., 12.

15. "Black Culture Festival due Saturday at Art Museum," *Los Angeles Sentinel*, December 26, 1968, A4; "Black Power, 'Every Negro Is a Potential Blackman,'" *Herald-Dispatch*, February 22, 1968, 3.

16. Tiger Slavik, "Human Rights Interview: Ron Karenga, June 6, 1966" (audio recording) (Los Angeles: Pacifica Radio Archive), side 1.

17. "LAPD Raids US Headquarters, Arrests Two," *Los Angeles Sentinel*, January 15, 1970, A1, D2; Maulana Ron Karenga, "An Open Letter," *Herald-Dispatch*, September 17, 1970, 3. In the "Open Letter," Karenga admonishes the Black community in Los Angeles for isolating his organization during the crisis with the Black Panther Party. He contends here that the community has played a role in unjustly "immobilizing" US.

18. Scot Brown, "Interview with C. R. D. Halisi" (transcript, November 11, 1996).

19. Scot Brown, "Interview with James Mtume" (transcript, January 16, 1997), 1–2.

20. Ibid., 15.

21. Ibid., 14.

22. Scot Brown, "Interview with Albert Heath" (transcript, September 20, 1997, and November 10, 1997), 13.

23. Brown, "Interview with James Mtume" (transcript, January 16, 1997), 15; Kuumba (Albert Heath), *Kawaida,* phonograph (O'be Records, 1969), liner notes. The famous jazz trumpetor Don Cherry took on the name Msafari during the recording session of the album *Kawaida* in December 1969. This, however, was the first time that he had met Mtume.

24. Amiri Baraka, *The Autobiography of LeRoi Jones* (Chicago: Lawrence Hill Books, 1997), 388.

25. Ibid., 392.

26. Ibid., 392–403, 417; Brown, "Interview with James Mtume" (transcript, January 16, 1997), 36–40, 41–42; idem, "Interview with Daryl Tukufu" (audio recording, August 2, 1997); idem, "Interview with Ngoma Ali" (transcript, November 10, 1996), 37–38.

27. Kuumba (Albert Heath), *Kawaida* (phonograph).

28. Scot Brown, "Interview with James Mtume on Jazz Music" (transcript, February 4, 1998), 3.

29. LeRoi Jones, *Black Music* (New York: William Morrow, 1968).

30. Amiri Baraka, "Speech at San Francisco State College" [1967?], Amiri Baraka Papers, Box 8, Moorland-Spingarn Research Center, Howard University, Washington, D.C.

31. Imamu Halisi (ed.), *Kitabu: Beginning Concepts in Kawaida* (Los Angeles: US Organization, 1971), 4n.8.

32. Kuumba (Albert Heath), "Baraka," musical recording, *Kawaida* (phonograph). "All praise to the Black man" was also a favored US Organization rally-

ing cry. In some cases Karenga would open his speech by having the entire audience chant the phrase. It also had a spiritual significance to US advocates. Given Kawaida's humanistic spiritual orientation, the phrase was also used when giving thanks before eating meals.

33. Brown, "Interview with Albert Heath" (transcript, September 20, 1997, and November 10, 1997), 24.

34. Kuumba (Albert Heath), "Baraka," musical recording, *Kawaida* (phonograph).

35. Brown, "Interview with James Mtume on Jazz Music" (transcript, February 4, 1998), 9.

36. Ibid.

37. Brown, "Interview with Albert Heath" (transcript, September 20, 1997, and November 10, 1997), 30.

38. Kuumba (Albert Heath), "Kawaida," musical recording, *Kawaida* (phonograph).

39. Ibid.

40. Brown, "Interview with James Mtume on Jazz Music" (transcript, February 4, 1998), 10.

41. Ibid.

42. Ibid.

43. Brown, "Interview with Albert Heath" (transcript, September 20, 1997, and November 10, 1997), 36.

44. Brown, "Interview with James Mtume on Jazz Music" (transcript, February 4, 1998), 10.

45. Karenga, "Black Art," in Chapman, *New Black Voices*, 479.

46. Amiri Baraka, "For Maulana Karenga & Pharoah Sanders," in *Selected Poetry of Amiri Baraka/LeRoi Jones* (New York: William Morrow, 1979), 163.

47. Kuumba (Albert Heath), "Maulana," musical recording, *Kawaida* (phonograph).

48. Brown, "Interview with James Mtume" (transcript, January 16, 1997), 38–41; idem, "Interview with Karl Key-Hekima" (transcript, November 11, 1996), 38.

49. Kuumba (Albert Heath), "Maulana."

50. Brown, "Interview with James Mtume on Jazz Music" (transcript, February 4, 1998), 8.

51. Mtume Umoja Ensemble, "Invocation," in *Alkebulan: Land of the Blacks* (phonograph) (Brooklyn, N.Y.: The East, 1971).

52. Mtume Umoja Ensemble, *Alkebulan: Land of the Blacks* (phonograph, liner notes).

53. Brown, "Interview with James Mtume on Jazz Music" (transcript, February 4, 1998), 5.

54. Ibid.

55. Ibid.

56. Frank Kofsky, *Black Nationalism and the Revolution in Music* (New York: Pathfinder Press, 1970), 131–138; Ben Sidran, *Black Talk* (New York: Da Capo Press, 1971), 138–160.

57. During the late 1970s, Karenga published a collection of his own poems. See M. Ron Karenga, *In Love and Struggle: Poems for Bold Hearts* (San Diego: Kawaida Publications, 1978).

58. Maulana Karenga, in Clyde Halisi and James Mtume (eds.), *The Quotable Karenga* (Los Angeles: US Organization, 1967), 13.

59. Baraka, *The Autobiography of LeRoi Jones*, 350–351; "The Creation of the New Ark," unpublished manuscript, 48, Amiri Baraka Papers, Box 40, Moorland-Spingarn Research Center, Howard University, Washington D.C.

60. "The Creation of the New Ark," 48.

61. Ibid.

62. Ibid.

63. Ibid., 49.

64. Scot Brown, "Interview with James Doss-Tayari" (transcript, November 12, 1996), 24.

65. Amiri Baraka and Scot Brown, "Interview with Amiri Baraka" (transcript, January 5, 1996), 1–2.

66. Baraka, *The Autobiography of LeRoi Jones*, 350.

67. Karenga, "Black Art," 477–482. The essay was previously published in *Negro Digest*, January 1968.

68. Ibid. In *Introduction to Black Studies* (Los Angeles: University of Sankore Press, 1993), he stated, "In an earlier article on Black art, I criticized blues as being essentially focused on resignation, but as my critics have rightly observed, blues is much more multidimensional than that" (p. 407).

69. Sam Greenlee, *Blues for an African Princess* (Chicago: Third World Press, 1971); Kirk Hall, "blackgoldblueswoman," in Chapman, *New Black Voices*, 254; Larry Neal, "Early Mornin' Blues Riff," in *Hoodoo Hollerin' Bebop Ghosts* (Washington, D.C.: Howard University Press, 1974). This work was previously published in 1968.

70. Nikki Giovanni, in "Black Poems, Poseurs and Power," *Negro Digest* 18 (June 1969), stated that "the Maulana has pointed out rather accurately that 'The blues is counterrevolutionary'" (p. 30).

71. Sam Greenlee, "Soul Brothers," in *Blues for an African Princess* (Chicago: Third World Press, 1971), 27; also see Larry Neal's "The Ethos of the Blues," *Black Scholar* 3 (Summer 1972): 42–48.

72. James Cunningham, "Hemlock for the Black Artist: Karenga Style," in Chapman, *New Black Voices*, 483–490.

73. LeRoi Jones, "The Myth of a 'Negro Literature,'" in Raman Singh and Peter Fellowes (eds.), *Black Literature in America: A Casebook* (New York: Thomas

Crowell, 1970), 309. This essay was originally published in LeRoi Jones's *Home: Social Essays* in 1966.

74. Ibid.

75. Ron Everett-Karenga, "A Black Power View of the McCone Commission Report," December 1966, in *Records of the National Advisory Commission on Civil Disorders in Civil Rights during the Johnson Administration: A Collection of Holdings of the Lyndon Baines Johnson Library, Austin, Texas,* microfilm, Reel 9.

76. LeRoi Jones, "Speech at UCLA, April 5, 1967," UCLA University Archives, Audio Collection, Box 13.

77. Karenga, in Halisi and Mtume, *The Quotable Karenga,* 9, 30. In a speech at Rockland Palace in 1969, Baraka declared that "[t]he Negro artist who is not a nationalist at this late date is a white artist, even without knowing it"; see "Black Art, Nationalism, Organization, Black Institutions," in *Raise Race Rays Raze* (New York: Random House, 1971), 98.

78. Baraka, "Who will Survive America / Few Americans / very few Negroes / No crackers at all," in *Selected Poetry of Amiri Baraka/LeRoi Jones,* 156. During the 1960s, Kawaida had strong anti-Christian perspectives in its doctrine. Karenga stated that "Christianity is a white religion. It has a white God, and any 'Negro' who believes in it is a sick 'Negro.'" See *The Quotable Karenga,* 32.

79. Ibid.

80. Imamu Amiri Baraka and Fundi (Bill Abernathy), *In Our Terribleness: (Some elements and meaning in black style)* (New York: Bobbs-Merrill, 1970), 5; pages are not numbered.

81. Ibid., iii; pages are not numbered.

82. Imamu Amiri Baraka, "Come See about Me," in *Spirit Reach* (Newark: Jihad Productions, 1972), 8.

83. Ibid.

84. Imamu Amiri Baraka, "All in the Street," in *Spirit Reach* (Newark: Jihad Productions, 1972), 12.

85. Ibid.

86. "Takwimu na Jewali" [Seven Year Calendar], n.d., Personal Papers of Oliver Massengale-Heshimu.

87. Baraka, "In the Year," in *Selected Poetry of Amiri Baraka/LeRoi Jones,* 162.

88. Ibid.

89. Baraka, *The Autobiography of LeRoi Jones,* 435–436. For the original speech, see Imamu Amiri Baraka, "National Liberation and Politics," CAP Midwest Regional Conference, March 1974. Amiri Baraka Papers Collection, Syracuse University.

90. Baraka, *The Autobiography of LeRoi Jones,* 444.

91. Maulana Karenga, "Kawaida and Its Critics: A Sociohistorical Analysis," *Journal of Black Studies* 8 (December 1977): 142.

92. Haki Madhubuti, "The Latest Purge: The Attack on Black Nationalism

and Pan-Afrikanism by the New Left—the Sons and Daughters of the Old Left," in *Enemies: The Clash of the Races* (Chicago: Third World Press, 1978), 58. This essay was originally published in *Black Scholar* 6 (September 1974).

93. Haki Madhubuti, *From Plan to Planet, Life Studies: The Need for Afrikan Minds and Institutions* (Chicago: Broadside Press and Institute of Positive Education, 1970), 79. This book was originally published in 1973.

94. Ibid., 82.

95. Ibid., 50.

96. Ibid., 80.

97. Carolyn Rodgers, "Black Poetry—where it's at," in Thomas Kochman (ed.), *Rappin' and stylin' out: Communication in Urban Black America* (Chicago: University of Illinois Press, 1972), 338, originally published in *Negro Digest*, September 1969.

98. Haki Madhubuti, "THE REVOLUTIONARY SCREW (for my sisters)," in *Don't Cry, SCREAM* (Chicago: Third World Press, 1992), 57. Originally published in 1969.

99. Ibid., 33–34.

100. Kalamu ya Salaam, *Tearing the Roof of the Sucker: The Fall of South Africa* (New Orleans: Ahidiana, 1977); idem, *South African Divestment Showdown* (New Orleans: Ahidiana, 1978); idem, *Nuclear Power and the Black Liberation Struggle* (New Orleans: Ahidiana, 1977).

101. Arthenia Bates Millican, "Kalamu ya Salaam (Vallery Ferdinand III)," in Thadious Davis and Trudier Harris (eds.), *Dictionary of Literary Biography,* vol. 38, *Afro-American Writers after 1955: Dramatists and Prose Writers* (Detroit: Gale Research, 1985), 231–239; Scot Brown, "Interview with Kalamu ya Salaam" (transcript, December 12, 1995), 1–9.

102. Kalamu ya Salaam, *Hofi Ni Kwenu (My Fear Is for You)* (New Orleans: Ahidiana, 1973), 19–24; Karenga, in Halisi and Mtume, *The Quotable Karenga,* 20–21.

103. Kalamu ya Salaam, *Pamoja Tutashinda (Together We Will Win)* (New Orleans: Ahidiana, 1974), 10.

104. Ibid.

105. Ibid.

106. Ibid., 14.

107. Ibid., 14.

108. Arthenia Bates Millican, "Kalamu ya Salaam," 238–239; Kalamu ya Salaam, *Our Women Keep Our Skies from Falling* (New Orleans: Nkombo, 1980).

109. Kalamu ya Salaam, "Revolutionary Struggle/Revolutionary Love," *Black Scholar* 10:8,9 (May/June 1979): 20–24; M. Ron Karenga, "On Wallace's Myths: Wading thru Troubled Waters," *Black Scholar* 10:8,9 (May/June 1979): 36–38; Michele Wallace, *Black Macho and the Myth of the Superwoman* (New York: Dial Press, 1979).

110. M. Ron Karenga, *Beyond Connections: Liberation in Love and Struggle* (New Orleans: Ahidiana, 1978).

111. E. U. Essien-Udom, *Black Nationalism: A Search for an Identity in America* (Chicago: University of Chicago Press, 1962), 206.

112. Tony Martin, *Literary Garveyism: Garvey, Black Arts and the Harlem Renaissance* (Dover, Del.: Majority Press, 1983), 107.

113. Anthony Smith, *National Identity* (Las Vegas: University of Nevada Press, 1991), 92.

114. Rickey Vincent, *Funk: The Music, the People and the Rhythm of the One* (New York: St. Martin's Press, 1998), 3.

NOTES TO CHAPTER 7

1. Molefi Asante, *Malcolm X as Cultural Hero and Other Afrocentric Essays* (Trenton, N.J.: Africa World Press, 1993), 155.

2. Maulana Karenga, "Maat, the Moral Ideal in Ancient Egypt: A Study in Classical African Ethics" (Ph.D. dissertation, University of Southern California, 1994); idem, "Afro-American Nationalism: Social Strategy and Struggle for Community" (Ph.D. dissertation, United States International University, 1976).

3. Molefi Asante, *Afrocentricity* (Trenton, N.J.: African World Press, 1988), 19–21.

4. Maulana Ron Karenga, "The Black Community and the University: A Community Organizer's Perspective," in Armstead Robinson, Craig Foster, and Donald Ogilvie (eds.), *Black Studies in the University: A Symposium* (New Haven: Yale University Press, 1969), 43.

5. Ibid.

6. Maulana Karenga, *Introduction to Black Studies* (Los Angeles: University of Sankore Press, 1982).

7. Maulana Karenga, *Selections from the Husia: Sacred Wisdom of Ancient Egypt* (Los Angeles: University of Sankore Press, 1984); idem, "Black Studies and the Problematic of Paradigm: The Philosophical Dimension," *Journal of Black Studies* 18:1 (June 1988): 395–414; idem, "Afrocentricity and Multicultural Education: Concept, Challenge, and Contribution," in Benjamin P. Bowser, Terry Jones, and Gale Auletta Young (eds.), *Toward the Multicultural University* (Westport, Conn.: Praeger, 1995), 41–61; idem, *The Book of Coming Forth by Day: The Ethics of the Declarations of Innocence* (Los Angeles: University of Sankore Press, 1990); idem, "Maat, the Moral Ideal in Ancient Egypt: A Study in Classical African Ethics."

8. Haki R. Madhubuti and Maulana Karenga (eds.), *Million Man March, Day of Absence: A Commemorative Anthology* (Chicago: Third World Press, 1996).

9. The Organization Us, "The Organization Us: 30th Anniversary Celebration" [Program] (Los Angeles: African American Cultural Center, 1995).

10. For a thorough account of the process by which Kwanzaa became a holiday celebrated nationwide, see Keith Mayes, "Rituals of Race, Ceremonies of Culture: Kwanzaa and the Making of a Black Power Holiday in the United States, 1966–2000" (Ph.D. dissertation, Princeton University, 2002); also see Elizabeth Pleck, "Kwanzaa: The Making of a Black Nationalist, 1966–1990," *Journal of American Ethnic History* 20:4 (Summer 2001): 3–28.

11. Maulana Karenga, *Kwanzaa: A Celebration of Family, Community and Culture* (Los Angeles: University of Sankore Press, 1998), xiii–xvi.

12. Robin Kelley, *Freedom Dreams: The Black Radical Imagination* (Boston: Beacon Press, 2002), 16–17; Eddie Glaude Jr., *Exodus! Religion, Race and Nation in Early Nineteenth-Century Black America* (Chicago: University of Chicago Press, 2000), 1–18.

Bibliography

INTERVIEWS CONDUCTED BY SCOT BROWN

Randy Abunuwas-Stripling, May 16, 2002
Ngoma Ali, November 10, 1996
Aminifu, March 26, 1998
Arnetta Church Atkins, April 15, 2002
Ayuko Babu, November 9, 1996
Amiri Baraka, January 5, 1996
Thomas Belton, November, 27, 1998
James Doss-Tayari, November 12, 1996
Bobette Azizi Glover, May 19, 2001
C. R. D. Halisi, November 11, 1996
Albert Heath, September 20, 1997, November 10, 1997
Staajabu Heshimu, December 6, 1997
Gail Idili-Davis, September 9, 2000
Tommy Jacquette, October 10, 1994
Charles Johnson-Sitawisha, September 9, 1995
Wesely Kabaila, October 11, 1994
Maulana Karenga, October 11, 1994, July 11, 1998, February 9, 1999
Karl Key-Hekima, November 11, 1996
Oliver Massengale-Heshimu, November 11, 1996
Charles Massengale-Sigidi, November 11, 1996
Letta Mbulu, April 22, 1997
Jean Morris, April 15, 2002
Ken Msemaji May 20, 2001
James Mtume, January 16, 1997, February 4, 1998
Kamili Mtume, June 22, 1997
Joann Richardson-Kicheko, April 22, 1997
Caiphus Semanya, April 21, 1997
George Subira, February 16, 1998
Vernon Sukumu, May 21, 2001
Amina Thomas, November 11, 1996
Kwame Toure, April 19, 1997
Daryl Tukufu, August 2, 1997
Kalamu ya Salaam, December 19, 1995

AUDIO, TRANSCRIBED, AND TELEVISED SOURCES

Black Congress Aircheck. Audio recording. Los Angeles: Pacifica Radio Archive, 1968.

Black Power Rally. Audio recording. Los Angeles: Pacifica Radio Archive, 1968.

Karenga, Maulana Ron. "Interview: KTLA News." Video recording. Los Angeles: UCLA Film and Television Archives, January 8, 1971.

Karenga, Ron, et al. "What Is Black Power." Audio recording of Panel Discussion. Los Angeles: Pacifica Radio Archive, July 23, 1966.

Kuumba (Albert Heath). *Kawaida.* Phonograph. O'be Records, 1969.

"Maulana Ron Karenga: Statement by the Black Nationalist." Audio recording. Los Angeles: Pacifica Radio Archive, 1969.

Mtume, James. "Interview with George Stiner-Ali and Claude Hubert-Gaidi," October 1998. Audio recording.

Mtume Umoja Ensemble. *Alkebulan: Land of the Blacks.* Phonograph, 1971. The East, Brooklyn, N.Y.

Ofari, Earl, and Ruth Hirshman. "Victim of Watergating, Ron Karenga: Interviewed by Earl Ofari and Ruth Hirshman." Audio recording. Los Angeles: Pacifica Radio Archive, 1974.

"Pre-Kwanzaa Celebration." Video recording. Grassroots Bookstore Archives, Salisbury Maryland, December 6, 1998.

Slavik, Tiger. "Human Rights Interview: Ron Karenga." Audio recording. Los Angeles: Pacifica Radio Archive, June 6, 1966.

"Taifa Dance Troupe Performance on the Rosey Grier Show." Video recording. UCLA Film and Television Archives, November 30, 1968.

Wallace, Terry. *Guess Who's Coming Home: Black Fighting Men Recorded Live.* Phonograph. Detroit: Motown Record Corporation, 1972.

Warden, Donald. *Burn Baby, Burn.* Phonograph. Berkeley: Dignity LP, 1965.

Woodard, Komozi. "Interview with Ron Karenga." Transcript. December 27, 1985.

UNPUBLISHED DOCUMENTS

Superior Court of the State of California for the County of Los Angeles. "A 264 545 Everett-Karenga, Ron N., et al.," Dept. 102, Arthur Alarcon, Judge.

[US Organization Doctrine Booklet] (no date).

ARCHIVAL MATERIALS AND PERSONAL PAPER COLLECTIONS

Amiri Baraka Papers. Moorland-Spingarn Research Center, Howard University, Washington, D.C.

The Beacon [Salisbury High School Yearbook], 1954, 1958, 1959, 1960. Charles H. Chipman Cultural Center Archives, Salisbury, Maryland.

Civil Rights Movement in the United States. University of California at Los Angeles Special Collections.

Film and Television Archives. University of California at Los Angeles.

Kenneth Hahn Papers. Huntington Library, Pasadena, California.

Papers of Maulana Karenga and the Organization Us. African American Cultural Center, Los Angeles.

Personal Papers of Charles Johnson-Sitawisha, in the hand of Charles Johnson-Sitawisha.

Personal Papers of Wesely Kabaila, in the hand of Wesely Kabaila.

Personal Papers of Oliver Massengale-Heshimu, in the hand of Oliver Massengale-Heshimu.

Personal Papers of James Mtume, in the hand of James Mtume.

Personal Papers of Ramon Tyson-Imara, in the hand of Ramon Tyson-Imara.

Personal Papers of Komozi Woodard, in the hand of Komozi Woodard.

UCLA Center for African American Studies: Robert Singleton. Los Angeles: UCLA Oral History Program, 1999.

University of California at Los Angeles. University Archives.

GOVERNMENT PUBLICATIONS AND DOCUMENTS

Everett-Karenga, Ron, et al. "A Black Power View of the McCone Commission Report." December 1966. In *Records of the National Advisory Commission on Civil Disorders in Civil Rights during the Johnson Administration [Microform]: A Collection from the Holdings of the Lyndon Baines Johnson Library,* Austin, Texas. Reel 9.

Federal Bureau of Investigation. "Black Nationalist Hate Groups File, 100-448006." Sections 1–23. In *COINTELPRO: The Counter Intelligence Program of the FBI* [Microfilm]. Wilmington, Del.: Scholarly Resources, 1978.

Governor's Commission on the Los Angeles Riots. *Violence in the City: An End or Beginning?* December 2, 1965.

Office of Policy Planning and Research, United States Department of Labor. *The Negro Family: The Case for National Action.* Washington, D.C.: Official Report, 1965.

NEWSPAPERS AND MAGAZINES

Afro-American Dignity News
Berkeley Barb
Black Books Bulletin
Black Dialogue
Black Newark
Black News
Black Panther

Black Panther Party Intercommunal News Service
Cricket: Black Music in Evolution
Ebony
Essence
The Guardian
Harambee
Herald-Dispatch
Hilltop
Jet
L.A. Watts Times
Liberator
Life Magazine
Long Beach Free Press
Los Angeles Collegian
Los Angeles Free Press
Los Angeles Sentinel
Los Angeles Times
Message to the Grassroots
The Movement
Muhammad Speaks
Negro Digest
New Republic
New York Times
Nkombo
Salisbury Daily Times
San Francisco Chronicle
Saturday Evening Post
Soulbook
The Source
UCLA Daily Bruin
Unity and Struggle
Wall Street Journal
Washington Post

BOOKS, PAMPHLETS, ARTICLES, AND PUBLISHED PROCEEDINGS

Abdulgani, Roselan. *The Bandung Connection: The Asia-Africa Conference in Bandung in 1955.* Singapore: Gunung Agung, 1981.

Akoto, Kwame Ageyei. *Nationbuilding: Theory and Practice in Afrikan Centered Education.* Washington D.C.: Pan Afrikan World Institute, 1992.

Alcock, Anthony, Brian Taylor, and John Welton, eds. *The Future of Cultural Minorities.* New York: St. Martin's Press, 1979.

Allen, James de Vere. *Swahili Origins: Swahili Culture and the Shungawa Phenomenon.* Athens: Ohio University Press, 1993.

Al Mansour, Khalid Abdullah Tariq [formerly Donald Warden]. *Black Americans at the Crossroads: Where Do We Go from Here?* San Francisco: First African Arabian Press, 1981.

Anthony, Earl. *The Time of Furnaces: A Case Study of Black Student Revolt.* New York: Dial Press, 1971.

Asante, Molefi. *Afrocentricity.* Trenton: African World Press, 1988.

———. *Malcolm X as Cultural Hero and Other Afrocentric Essays.* Trenton: Africa World Press, 1993.

Bambara, Toni Cade. *The Black Woman: An Anthology.* New York: Signet, 1970.

Banks, Ingrid. *Hair Matters: Beauty, Power and Black Women's Consciousness.* New York: New York University Press, 2000.

Baraka, Amiri (Imamu, LeRoi Jones). *The Autobiography of LeRoi Jones.* Chicago: Lawrence Hill Books, 1997.

———. *Black Music.* New York: William Morrow, 1968.

———. "Black Revolutionary Poets Should Also Be Playwrights." *Black World* 21:6 (April 1972): 4–6.

———. "The Creation of the New Ark." Unpublished manuscript. Amiri Baraka Papers, Box 40, Moorland-Spingarn Research Center, Howard University.

———. *Raise Race Rays Raze.* New York: Random House, 1971.

———. *Selected Poetry of Amiri Baraka/LeRoi Jones.* New York: William Morrow, 1979.

———. *Spirit Reach.* Newark: Jihad Productions, 1972.

Baraka, Imamu Amiri, and Fundi (Bill Abernathy). *In Our Terribleness: (Some elements and meaning in black style).* New York: Bobbs-Merrill, 1970.

Barbour, Floyd, ed. *The Black Power Revolt.* Boston: Extending Horizons Books, 1968.

Batuta, C. "US—Black Nationalism on the Move." *Black Dialogue* 2:7 (Autumn 1966): 7.

Beale, Frances. "Slave of a Slave No More: Black Women in Struggle." *Black Scholar* 6:6 (March 1975): 2–10.

Berendt, Joachime, and Gunther Huesman. *The Jazz Book: From Ragtime to Fusion and Beyond.* Chicago: Lawrence Hill Books, 1992.

Bowser, Benjamin P., Terry Jones, and Gale Auletta Young, eds. *Toward the Multicultural University.* Westport, Conn.: Praeger, 1995.

Bracey, John, August Meier, and Elliot Rudwick, eds. *Black Nationalism in America.* Indianapolis and New York: Bobbs-Merrill, 1970.

———. *Black Protest in the Sixties: Articles from New York.* New York: Markus Wiener, 1991.

Breitman, George, ed. *Malcolm X Speaks.* New York: Pathfinder Press, 1993.

Britton, Peter. "The Relevance of Javanese Traditions to an Understanding of the Political Philosophy of Guided Democracy." Unpublished B.A. honors thesis, University of Sydney, 1968.

Brotz, Howard, ed. *Negro Social and Political Thought, 1850–1920: Representative Texts.* New York: Basic Books, 1966.

Brown, Elaine. *A Taste of Power: A Black Woman's Story.* New York: Pantheon Books, 1992.

Bush, Rod. *We Are Not What We Seem: Black Nationalism and Class Struggle in the American Century.* New York: New York University Press, 1999.

Carmichael, Stokely, and Charles Hamilton. *Black Power: The Politics of Liberation in America.* New York: Vintage Books, 1967.

Carson, Clayborne. *In Struggle: SNCC and the Black Awakening of the 1960s.* Cambridge, Mass.: Harvard University Press, 1981.

Carson, Clayborne, David Garrow, Vincent Harding, and Darlene Clark Hine, eds. *A Reader and Guide, Eyes on the Prize: America's Civil Rights Years.* New York: Penguin Books, 1987.

Chapman, Abraham, ed. *New Black Voices: An Anthology of Contemporary New Black Literature.* New York: New American Library, 1972.

Chimerah, Rocha. *Kiswahili: Past, Present and Future Horizons.* Nairobi: Nairobi University Press, 1998.

Churchill, Ward, and Jim Vander Wall. *Agents of Repression: The Secret Wars against the Black Panther Party and the American Indian Movement.* Boston: South End Press, 1988.

Citizens Research and Investigation Committee and Louis Tackwood. *The Glass House Tapes.* New York: Avon, 1973.

Clark, Steve, ed. *February 1965: The Final Speeches, Malcolm X.* New York: Pathfinder Press, 1992.

Cleaver, Kathleen, and George Katsiaficas, eds. *Liberation, Imagination, and the Black Panther Party: A New Look at the Panthers and Their Legacy.* New York: Routledge, 2001.

Clegg, Claude III. *An Original Man: Life and Times of Elijah Muhammad.* New York: St. Martin's Press, 1997.

Cone, James. *Martin and Malcolm: A Dream or Nightmare.* Maryknoll, N.Y.: Orbis Books, 1991.

Cruse, Harold. *The Crisis of the Negro Intellectual: A Historical Analysis of the Failure of Black Leadership.* New York: Quill, 1984.

Davis, Angela. *Angela Davis: An Autobiography.* New York: Random House, 1974.

Davis, Thadious, and Trudier Harris, eds. *Dictionary of Literary Biography,* vol. 38, *Afro-American Writers after 1955: Dramatists and Prose Writers.* Detroit: Gale Research, 1985.

Donaldson, Gary. *The History of African-Americans in the Military.* Malabar: Krieger, 1991.

Drake, Christine. *National Integration in Indonesia: Patterns and Policies.* Honolulu: University of Hawaii Press, 1989.

Essien-Udom, E. U. *Black Nationalism: A Search for Identity in America.* New York: Dell, 1964.

Flowers, Sandra. *African-American Nationalist Literature of the 1960's: Pens of Fire.* New York: Garland Publishers, 1996.

Foner, Philip, ed. *Black Panthers Speak.* New York: J. B. Lippincott, 1970.

Forman, James. *The Making of Black Revolutionaries.* New York: Macmillan, 1972.

Freed, Donald. *The Trial of Bobby Seale, Erika Huggins and the Black Panther Party.* New York: Simon and Schuster, 1973.

Gayle, Addison, ed. *The Black Aesthetic.* New York: Doubleday, 1971.

Giddings, Paula. *When and Where I Enter: The Impact of Race and Sex in America.* New York: Bantam Books, 1984.

Glaude, Eddie, Jr. *Exodus! Religion, Race, and Nation in Early Nineteenth-Century Black America.* Chicago: University of Chicago Press, 2000.

Gluckmann, Max. "Social Aspects of First Fruits Ceremonies among the South-Eastern Bantu." *Africa: Journal of the International Institute of African Languages and Cultures* 11:1 (January 1938): 25–41.

Greenlee, Sam. *Blues for an African Princess.* Chicago: Third World Press, 1971.

Haines, Herbert. *Black Radicals and the Civil Rights Mainstream, 1954–1970.* Knoxville: University of Tennessee Press, 1988.

Halisi, Clyde (Imamu Halisi). *Interview with Maulana Ron Karenga: July 14, 1973.* Los Angeles: Saidi Publications, 1973.

———. *Kitabu: Beginning Concepts in Kawaida.* Los Angeles: US Organization, 1971.

———. "Maulana Ron Karenga: Black Leader in Captivity." *Black Scholar* 3:9 (May 1972): 26–31.

Halisi, Clyde, and James Mtume, eds. *The Quotable Karenga.* Los Angeles: US Organization, 1967.

Harding, Vincent. *There Is a River: The Struggle for Freedom in America.* New York: Vintage Books, 1981.

Haskins, Jim. *Power to the People: The Rise and Fall of the Black Panther Party.* New York: Simon and Schuster Books for Young Readers, 1997.

Henderson, Errol. "The Lumpenproletariat as Vanguard? The Black Panther Party, Social Transformation, and Pearson's Analysis of Huey Newton." *Journal of Black Studies* 28:2 (November 1997): 171–199.

Hill, Robert, and Barbara Blair, eds. *Marcus Garvey: Life and Lessons, A Centennial Companion to the Marcus Garvey and Universal Negro Improvement Association Papers.* Berkeley: University of California Press, 1987.

Holy Bible (King James Version). Nashville: Thomas Nelson Publishers, 1977.

hooks, bell. *Ain't I a Woman: Black Women and Feminism.* Boston: South End Press, 1982.

Horne, Gerald. *Fire This Time: The Watts Uprising and the 1960s.* Charlottesville: University Press of Virginia, 1995.

Jamal, Hakim. *From the Dead Level: Malcolm X and Me.* New York: Random House, 1972.

Johnson, James W., F. Frances Johnson, and Ronald Slaughter. *The Nguzo Saba and the Festival of the First Fruits: A Guide for Promoting Family, Community Values and the Celebration of Kwanzaa.* New York: Gumbs and Thomas, 1995.

Jones, Charles, ed. *The Black Panther Party Reconsidered.* Baltimore: Black Classic Press, 1998.

Joseph, Peniel. "Black Liberation without Apology: Reconceptualizing the Black Power Movement." *Black Scholar* 31:3–4 (Fall/Winter 2001): 3–20.

Kardiner, Abram, and Lionel Ovesey. *The Mark of Oppression: Explorations in the Personality of the American Negro.* Cleveland: World, 1962.

Karenga, Maulana (Maulana Ron Karenga, M. Ron Karenga). "Afro-American Nationalism: Beyond Mystification and Misconception." *Black Books Bulletin* 6:1 (Spring 1978): 7–12.

———. *Beyond Connections: Liberation in Love and Struggle.* New Orleans: Ahidiana, 1978.

———. "Black Studies and the Problematic of Paradigm: The Philosophical Dimension." *Journal of Black Studies* 18:1 (June 1988): 395–414.

———. *Book of Coming Forth By Day: The Ethics of the Declarations of Innocence.* Los Angeles: University of Sankore Press, 1990.

———. "Ideology and Struggle: Some Preliminary Notes." *Black Scholar* 6:5 (January/February 1975): 23–30.

———. "In Defense of Sis. Joanne: For Ourselves and History." *Black Scholar* 6:10 (July/August 1975): 36–42.

———. *In Love and Struggle: Poems for Bold Hearts.* San Diego: Kawaida Publications, 1978.

———. "In Love and Struggle: Toward a Greater Togetherness" *Black Scholar* 6:6 (March 1975): 16–28.

———. *Introduction to Black Studies.* Los Angeles: University of Sankore Press, 1982 (1st ed.), 1993 (2d ed.).

———. "Kawaida and Its Critics: A Socio-Historical Analysis." *Journal of Black Studies* 8:2 (December 1977): 125–148.

———. *Kawaida Theory: An Introductory Outline.* Inglewood: Calif. Kawaida Publications, 1980.

———. *Kwanzaa: A Celebration of Family, Community and Culture.* Commemorative Edition. Los Angeles: University of Sankore Press, 1998.

———. *Kwanzaa: Origin, Concepts, Practice.* Los Angeles: Kawaida Publications, 1977.

―――. "Maat, the Moral Ideal in Ancient Egypt: A Study in Classical African Ethics." Unpublished dissertation, University of Southern California, 1994.

―――. "On Wallace's Myths: Wading Thru Troubled Waters," *Black Scholar* 8:9 (May/June 1979): 36–39.

―――. "The Oppositional Logic of Malcolm X: Differentiation, Engagement and Resistance." *Western Journal of Black Studies* 17:1 (Spring 1993): 6–16.

―――. "Overturning Ourselves: From Mystification to Meaningful Struggle." *Black Scholar* 4 (October 1972): 6–14.

―――. "A Response to Muhammad Ahmad on the Us/Panther Conflict." *Black Scholar* 9:10 (July/August 1978): 55–57.

―――. *Selections from the Husia: Sacred Wisdom of Ancient Egypt.* Los Angeles: University of Sankore Press, 1984.

―――. "A Strategy for Struggle." *Black Scholar* 4:2 (November 1973): 8–21.

―――. "Which Road to Revolution: Nationalism, Pan-Africanism or Socialism?" *Black Scholar* 6:2 (October 1974): 21–31.

Karim, Benjamin, ed. *The End of White World Supremacy: Four Speeches by Malcolm X.* New York: Arcade Publishing, 1971.

Kelley, Robin. *Freedom Dreams: The Black Radical Imagination.* Boston: Beacon Press, 2002.

Kenyatta, Jomo. *Facing Mount Kenya: The Tribal Life of the Gikuyu.* London: Secker and Warburg, 1961.

Kesteloot, Lilyan. *Intellectual Origins of the African Revolution.* Washington, D.C.: Black Orpheus Press, 1972.

Khalid, Abdallah. *The Liberation of Swahili from European Appropriation.* Nairobi: East African Literature Bureau, 1977.

Kijembe, Adhama. "Swahili and Black Americans." *Negro Digest* 18:9 (July 1969): 4–8.

Kochman, Thomas, ed. *Rappin' and Stylin' Out: Communication in Urban Black America.* Chicago: University of Illinois Press, 1972.

Kofsky, Frank. *Black Nationalism and the Revolution in Music.* New York: Pathfinder Press, 1970.

Krige, Eileen. *The Social System of the Zulus.* 4th ed. London: Longmans Green, 1962.

LaFeber, Walter. *The American Age: United States Foreign Policy at Home and Abroad.* Vol. 2, *Since 1896.* New York: W. W. Norton, 1994.

Lee, Martha. *The Nation of Islam: An American Millenarian Movement.* Lewiston, N.Y.: Edwin Mellon Press, 1988.

Legge, J. D. *Sukarno: A Political Biography.* New York: Praeger, 1972.

Lincoln, C. Eric. *Black Muslims in America.* Boston: Beacon Press, 1961.

Madhubuti, Haki (Don L. Lee). *Don't Cry, SCREAM.* Chicago: Third World Press, 1992. (Originally published 1969.)

―――. *Enemies: The Clash of the Races.* Chicago: Third World Press, 1978.

Madhubuti, Haki (Don L. Lee). *From Plan to Planet, Life-Studies: The Need for Afri-kan Minds and Institutions.* Chicago: Broadside Press and Institute of Positive Education, 1973.

———. *We Walk the Way of the New World.* Detroit: Broadside Press, 1970.

Major, Reginald. *A Panther Is a Cat.* New York: William Morrow, 1971.

Marine, Gene. *The Black Panthers.* New York: Signet, 1969.

Martin, Tony. *Literary Garveyism: Garvey, Black Arts and the Harlem Renaissance.* Dover, Del.: The Majority Press, 1983.

Mayes, Keith. "Rituals of Race, Ceremonies of Culture: Kwanzaa and the Making of a Black Power Holiday in the United States, 1966–2000." Ph.D. dissertation, Princeton University, 2002.

McCormick, Thomas. *America's Half-Century: United States Foreign Policy in the Cold War and After.* Baltimore: Johns Hopkins University Press, 1995.

McKim, Robert, and Jeff McMahan, eds. *The Morality of Nationalism.* New York: Oxford University Press, 1997.

Meier, August. *Negro Thought in America, 1880–1915.* Ann Arbor: University of Michigan Press, 1966.

Ministry of Foreign Affairs, Republic of Indonesia. *Asia-Africa Speaks from Bandung.* Djakarta: Ministry of Foreign Affairs, Republic of Indonesia, 1955.

Mkalimoto, Ernie. "Revolutionary Black Culture: The Cultural Arm of Revolutionary Nationalism." *Negro Digest* 19:2 (December 1969): 11–17.

Moore, Gilbert. *Rage.* New York: Carrol and Graf, 1993.

Moses, Wilson Jeremiah. *Classical Black Nationalism: From the American Revolution to Marcus Garvey.* New York: New York University Press, 1996.

Muhammad, Elijah. *Message to the Blackman in America.* Atlanta: Messenger Muhammad Propagation Society, 1997.

———. *Our Saviour Has Arrived.* Atlanta: Messenger Muhammad Propagation Society, n.d.

Mullen, Robert. *Blacks in America's Wars: The Shift in Attitudes from the Revolutionary War to Vietnam.* New York: Pathfinder Press, 1973.

Mumininas of Committee for Unified NewArk. *Mwanamke Mwananchi (The Nationalist Woman).* Newark: Mumininas of CFUN, 1971.

Muse, Benjamin. *The American Negro Revolution.* Bloomington: Indiana University Press, 1968.

Neal, Larry. "The Ethos of the Blues." *Black Scholar* 3 (Summer 1972): 42–48.

———. *Hoodoo Hollerin' Bebop Ghosts.* Washington, D.C.: Howard University Press, 1974.

Newton, Huey. *Revolutionary Suicide.* New York: Harcourt Brace Jovanovich, 1973.

———. "War against the Panthers: A Study of Repression in America." Unpublished dissertation, University of California, Santa Cruz, 1980.

Ngozi-Brown, Scot (Scot Brown). "The Us Organization, Maulana Karenga, and Conflict with the Black Panther Party: A Critique of Sectarian Influences on Historical Discourse." *Journal of Black Studies* 28:2 (November 1997): 157–170.

Nkrumah, Kwame. *Axioms of Kwame Nkrumah.* London: Nelson, 1967.

Nurse, Derek, and Thomas Spear. *The Swahili: Reconstructing the History and Language of an African Society, 800–1500.* Philadelphia: University of Pennsylvania Press, 1985.

Nyerere, Julius. *Ujamaa: Essays on Socialism.* London: Oxford University Press, 1968.

Olsen, Jack. *Last Man Standing: The Tragedy and Triumph of Geronimo Pratt.* New York: Doubleday, 2000.

O'Reilly, Kenneth. *"Racial Matters": The FBI's Secret File on Black America, 1960–1972.* New York: Free Press, 1989.

Organization Us. "The Organization Us: 30th Anniversary Celebration." [Program]. Los Angeles: African American Cultural Center, 1995.

Pearson, Hugh. *The Shadow of the Panther: Huey Newton and the Price of Black Power in America.* New York: Addison-Wesley, 1994.

Perry, Bruce, ed. *Malcolm X: The Last Speeches.* New York: Pathfinder Press, 1989.

Phillips, Frederick. "Ntu Psychotherapy: An Afrocentric Approach." *Journal of Black Psychology* 17 (Fall 1990): 55–74.

Pinkney, Alphonso. *Red, Black and Green: Black Nationalism in the United States.* New York: Cambridge University Press, 1976.

Pleck, Elizabeth. "Kwanzaa: The Making of a Black Nationalist, 1966–1990." *Journal of American Ethnic History* 20:4 (Summer 2001): 3–28.

Porter, Lewis, and Michael Ullman. *Jazz: From Its Origins to the Present.* Englewood Cliffs, N.J.: Prentice Hall, 1993.

Redding, Saunders. "The Black Arts Movement in Negro Poetry." *American Scholar* 42 (Spring 1973): 330–336.

Reed, Adolph, ed. *Race, Politics and Culture: Critical Essays on the Radicalism of the 1960s.* Westport, Conn.: Greenwood Press, 1986.

Robinson, Armstead, Craig Foster, and Donald Ogilvie, eds. *Black Studies in the University: A Symposium.* New Haven: Yale University Press, 1969.

Romulo, Carlos. *The Meaning of Bandung.* Chapel Hill: University of North Carolina Press, 1956.

Rout, Kathleen. *Eldridge Cleaver.* Boston: Twayne, 1991.

Schulberg, Budd, ed. *From the Ashes: Voices of Watts.* New York: New American Library, 1967.

Scott, Daryl. *Contempt and Pity: Social Policy and the Image of the Damaged Black Psyche, 1880–1996.* Chapel Hill: University of North Carolina Press, 1997.

Seale, Bobby. *Seize the Time: The Story of the Black Panther Party and Huey P. Newton.* New York: Vintage Books, 1970.

Seckel, Al, ed. *Bertrand Russell on God and Religion.* Buffalo, N.Y.: Prometheus Books, 1986.

Senghor, Leopold. *On African Socialism.* New York: Praeger, 1964.

Shakur, Assata. *Assata: An Autobiography.* Westport, Conn.: Lawrence Hill, 1987.

Shaw, Henry, Jr., and Ralph Donnelly. *Blacks in the Marine Corps.* Washington, D.C.: History and Museums Division Headquarters, U.S. Marine Corps, 1988.

Sheehy, Gail. *Panthermania: The Clash of Black against Black in One American City.* New York: Harper and Row, 1971.

Sidran, Ben. *Black Talk.* New York: Da Capo Press, 1971.

Singh, Raman, and Peter Fellowes, eds. *Black Literature in America: A Casebook.* New York: Thomas Crowell, 1970.

Smith, Anthony. *National Identity.* Las Vegas: University of Nevada Press, 1991.

Solis, Gary. *Marines and Military Law in Vietnam: Trial by Fire.* Washington, D.C.: History and Museums Division Headquarters, U.S. Marine Corps, 1989.

Sonenshein, Raphael. *Politics in Black and White: Race and Power in Los Angeles.* Princeton, N.J.: Princeton University Press, 1993.

Springer, Kimberly, ed. *Still Lifting, Still Climbing: African-American Women's Contemporary Activism.* New York: New York University Press, 1999.

Stuckey, Sterling. *Slave Culture: Nationalist Theory and the Foundations of Black America.* New York: Oxford University Press, 1987.

Terry, Wallace. "Bringing the War Home." *Black Scholar* 2 (November 1970).

Toure, Ahmed Sekou. *The Political Leader Considered as the Representative of a Culture.* Newark: Jihad Productions, n.d.

Turok, Ben, ed. *Revolutionary Thought in the 20th Century.* London: Zed Press, 1980.

Tyler, Bruce. "Black Radicalism in Southern California, 1950–1982." Unpublished dissertation, University of California at Los Angeles, 1983.

———. "The Rise and Decline of the Watts Summer Festival, 1965–1986," *American Studies* 31:2 (1990): 61–81.

Van Deburg, William. *New Day in Babylon: The Black Power Movement and American Culture, 1965–1975.* Chicago: University of Chicago Press, 1992.

———, ed. *Modern Black Nationalism: From Marcus Garvey to Louis Farrakhan.* New York: New York University Press, 1997.

Vincent, Rickey. *Funk: The Music, the People and Rhythm of the One.* New York: St. Martin's Press, 1998.

Wallace, Michele. *Black Macho and the Myth of the Superwoman.* New York: Dial Press, 1979.

Walters, Ronald. *Pan-Africanism in the African Diaspora: An Analysis of Modern Afrocentric Political Movements.* Detroit: Wayne State University Press, 1993.

Warfield-Coppock, Nsenga. *Afrocentric Theory and Applications.* Vol. 1, *Adolescent Rites of Passage.* Washington, D.C.: Baobab Associates, 1990.

Warren, Nagueyalti. "Pan-African Cultural Movements: From Baraka to Karenga." *Journal of Negro History* 75:1–2 (Winter/Spring 1990): 16–27.

Washington, Joseph. "Black Nationalism: Potentially Anti-Folk and Anti-Intellectual." *Black World* 22 (July 1973): 32–39.

White, E. Frances. "Africa on My Mind: Gender, Counter Discourse and African-American Nationalism." *Journal of Women's History* 2:1 (Spring 1990): 73–97.

Willis, Winston. "Leadership Issues of the Black Panther Party, 1966–1971." Unpublished Master's thesis, Cornell University, 1993.

Woodard, Komozi. "The Making of the New Ark: Imamu Amiri Baraka (LeRoi Jones), and the Newark Congress of African People, and the Modern Black Convention Movement. A History of the Black Revolt and the New Nationalism, 1966–1976." Ph.D. dissertation, University of Pennsylvania, 1991.

———. *A Nation within a Nation: Amiri Baraka (LeRoi Jones) and Black Power Politics.* Chapel Hill: University of North Carolina Press, 1999.

Wolfe, Tom. *Radical Chic and Mau-mauing the Flak Catchers.* New York: Farrar, Straus and Giroux, 1970.

Wright, Nathan, Jr. *Let's Work Together.* New York: Hawthorne Books, 1968.

Wright, Richard. *The Color Curtain: A Report on the Bandung Conference.* New York: World Publishing, 1956.

ya Salaam, Kalamu. *Hofi Ni Kwenu (My Fear Is for You).* New Orleans: Ahidiana, 1973.

———. *Nuclear Power and the Black Liberation Struggle.* New Orleans: Ahidiana, 1977.

———. *Our Women Keep Our Skies from Falling.* New Orleans: Nkombo, 1980.

———. *Pamoja Tutashinda (Together We Will Win).* New Orleans: Ahidiana, 1974.

———. "Revolutionary Struggle/Revolutionary Love." *Black Scholar* 10:8,9 (May/June 1979): 20–24.

———. *South African Divestment Showdown.* New Orleans: Ahidiana, 1978.

———. *Tearing the Roof off the Sucker: The Fall of South Africa.* New Orleans: Ahidiana, 1977.

Zahar, Renate. *Frantz Fanon: Colonialism and Alienation.* New York: Monthly Review Press, 1974.

Index

Italic numbers refer to pages in the photographic insert.

Hakim Jamal and, 38–39; "Message to the Grassroots," 16; and Organization of Afro-American Unity, 22–25, 105; united-front approach of, 24, 79, 81, 105

Malcolm X Foundation, 39, 173n. 4

male dominance: Karenga on, 33, 56, 157, 178n. 118; Moynihan report on, 32; polygamy and, 62–65; in US social organization, 56–58

"Mama, Mama" (song), 20–21

Manual Arts High School, 77–78

Margalit, Avishai, 167n. 22

marines, *12*, 86–87

Marx, Karl, 13–14, 150, 151, 152

Massengale-Heshimu, Oliver: and Black Congress, 84; in Circle of Administrators, 43; joins US, 41; as Mwalimu, 43, 52–53; as not returning to new US, 130; as Simba instructor, 54; in Swahili classes, 39; wedding ceremony of, *7*

Massengale-Sigidi, Charles, 39, 41, 43, 54, 60, 135

Matamba paramilitary wing, 123

"Maulana" (song), 141–42

"Maulana" (title), 43

"Maulana and Word Magic" (Halisi), 141

Maziko, 69, 164

Mazuri, Ali, 10

Mbulu, Letta, *12*, 57, 71–72, 132–33, 135

McCone Commission Report, 29–32

McKissick, Floyd, *9*

"Message to the Grassroots" (Malcolm X), 16

Message to the Grassroots, 39, 173n. 3

messianic leadership styles, 66–67

Mfikiri, Tommy. *See* Jacquette-Mfikiri, Tommy (Halifu)

Micheaux, Billy, 143

Million Man March, 161

Mkalimoto, Ernie (Ernie Allen, Jr.), 27, 29, 191n. 56

Modern Black Convention Movement, 3–4, 100, 105

Mohlomi, Ernest Thuso, *12*, 133

Moorish Science Temple, 35, 49, 67

Moses, Wilson, 18–19

Moynihan, Daniel, 32–33

Msemaji, Ahera, 43, 56

Msemaji, Ken. *See* Seaton-Msemaji, Ken

Mtume, James: African name for, 59; distributing literature, *5*; jazz background of, 136–37; joins CFUN in Newark, 138; and *Kawaida* album, 138, 139–40, 141, 142; leaves US, 138, 142; in Mtume Umoja Ensemble, 142–43; music for boot dance by, 135; parents' response to nationalism of, 62; in Pasadena group, 42, 136; popular music of, 144; *The Quotable Karenga* edited by, 67

Mtume, Kamili, 62, 76, 141

Mtume Umoja Ensemble, 142–43

Muhammad, Balozi Zayd, 127

Muhammad, Elijah, 18, 49

Mumia Abu-Jamal, 117–18

Muminina, 56–58; during The Crisis, 122; group at 1967 wedding, *8*; in US structure, 42, 43

music: blues, 145–46, 147, 198n. 68; funk, 147, 158; jazz, 136–44, 147, 157

Mwalimu, 52–53; during The Crisis, 122; in structure of US, 42, 43; student-teacher relationship with Karenga, 45

Mwanafunzi, 43, 52, 122

name changes, 58–60, 137

Nasser, Gamal Abdel, 17, 68

National Black Political Convention (1972), 3, 100, 126

National Conference on Black Power (1967), 100–102, 103–4

nationalism: Sukarno's five principles of, 15–16. *See also* Black nationalism

"National Liberation and Politics" (Baraka), 151

Nation of Islam (NOI): alternative lifestyle required by, 21; as bridge between prewar and Black Power nationalists, 18–19, 24; on enslavement's effects, 18; Farrakhan, 157; Karenga as generationally distinct from, 21–22; Kawaida religion influenced by, 34, 35; on Malcolm X as a traitor, 75–76; messianic leadership style in, 67; numerology in, 49; Ramadan celebrated in December by, 70; on terminology for African Americans, 19–20

Ndugu, 143

Negritude, 13
Negro/Black distinction, 20–21
Negro Family, The (Moynihan Report), 32–33
Nehru, Jawaharlal, 17, 68
New Afroamerican Movement, 129
Newark (New Jersey): Baraka's involvement in politics in, 102; Black Political Convention of 1968, 103; Black Power Conference of 1967, 99; Committee for Unified Newark, 3, 81, 102–5, 125, 126–28, 137–38; Gibson elected mayor, 104; National Congress on Black Power of 1967, 99, 100–102; rebellion of 1967, 101; Spirit House, 144
Newton, Huey: on African culture and cultural nationalism, 114; in Afro-American Association, 27, 29; "Free Huey" rally of February 1968, 88; at Uhuru Day celebration, 78–79; violent tactics of, 114, 122
Nguzo Saba (Seven Principles of Blackness): and "A Job for Everyone" lesson, 44; and Kawaida creation myth, 35; and Kwanzaa, 70; Madhubuti on, 152–53, 154; numerology in, 49; in Salaam, 155; socialism in, 15; in song "Kawaida," 140; and Sukarno's Gotong-rojong, 16; in US oath, 46
Nia Cultural Organization, 129
Njuku, Robaire, 41
Nkrumah, Kwame, 12, 66, 67
Nkulunkulu, 34–35
Nrefu-Belton, Thomas, 87
numerology, 49
Nyerere, Julius, 12, 14–15, 16, 66
Nyeusi, Sanamu, *4*, 38, 41

OAAU (Organization of Afro-American Unity), 22–25, 105
On African Socialism (Senghor), 13
"On Cultural Nationalism" (Harrison), 114–15
Organization of Afro-American Unity (OAAU), 22–25, 105

Pamoja Tutashinda (Together We Will Win) (ya Salaam), 155
pan-Africanism: of Ahidiana, 154; Baraka

alienating himself from, 150; and Kiswahili, 10; and Malcolm X's united-front approach, 79; Negritude, 13; Sixth Pan-African Congress, 105; Taifa Dance Troupe and, 133–34, 135, 136
"Panther" formations, 28–29
Pantja Sila, 15, 16
patriarchy. *See* male dominance
Peace and Freedom Party, 1, 109
Peace and Power campaign, 103, 104
personality cult, 65–67, 127, 156
Pinkney, Alphonso, 89, 100
Pinkney, Ted, 103
political power, aspects of, 103
polygamy, 62–65, 127
Powell, Adam Clayton, 101
Pratt, Geronimo, 96–97
Prince Hall Masons, 49
Project Sisterhood, 7

Quotable Karenga, The, 67, 140–41, 144, 155, 178n. 118

Ralph, Leon, 30
Reagan, Ronald, 93, 184n. 74
Reddin, Thomas, 92
Revolutionary Action Movement, 188n. 129
"REVOLUTIONARY SCREW (for my sisters), The" (Madhubuti), 154
Richardson-Kicheko, Joann, 42, 57, 59, 133, 134, 135
Rodgers, Carolyn, 153
Rose-Aminifu, Buddy, 42
Russell, Bertrand, 19, 33

Saidi: attempt to force Karenga to rest, 124; conflict with Simba, 125; during The Crisis, 122–23; underground activities of, 90, 91; in US hierarchy, 42, 43
Sales, Brian "Chambuzi," *16*
Salisbury High School, 9
Sanchez, Sonia, 153
Sanders, Pharoah, 142
San Diego chapter of US, 44
Sastri, Nilakanta, 168n. 38
Saturday Evening Post, 80
School of Afroamerican Culture, 20, 40, 41, 42, 56

About the Author

Scot Brown is Associate Professor of history at the University of California at Los Angeles. His writings on African American resistance, social movements, and cultural nationalism have appeared in the *Black Scholar, Journal of Black Studies, American National Biography, Journal of Negro History,* and *Contributions in Black Studies.*